This book

is sent to your library

without obligation, in response

to your recent request to

The National Book Foundation.

THE PUBLISHERS

A Christian View
of
Men and Things

A Christian View
of
Men and Things

The Payton Lectures
delivered in condensed form at the

FULLER THEOLOGICAL SEMINARY
Pasadena
1951

by

GORDON H. CLARK

Professor of Philosophy, Butler University

WM. B. EERDMANS PUBLISHING COMPANY
Grand Rapids **Michigan**

. . . now learn too late
How few sometimes may know, when thousands err.

PARADISE LOST VI 148.

Acknowledgments

First, acknowledgments and expressions of gratitude are hereby made to Butler University, its President, Maurice O. Ross, and its Board of Directors for a Faculty Fellowship that reduced my teaching load and gave opportunity for writing this volume.

Second, appreciation and thanks are due to my friends, Dr. Carl F. H. Henry and Dr. Edward John Carnell, of Fuller Theological Seminary, for reading and criticizing the manuscript in careful detail.

Then, cheerful acknowledgment and credit is given to the publishers and holders of copyrights for permission to quote. The precise details are in each case given in the footnote under the quotation. The firms and persons involved are the following: The Abingdon Cokesbury Press; The American Association for the Advancement of Science; The American Political Science Review; Appleton-Century-Crofts; The Bar Association Journal; Professor Edgar Sheffield Brightman; The University of Chicago Press; E. P. Dutton and Co.; Harper and Brothers; The Harvard University Press; Alfred A. Knopf, Inc.; Longmans Green and Co.; The Macmillan Co.; Methuen and Co.; W. W. Norton and Co.; Oxford University Press; Prentice-Hall, Inc.; Charles Scribner's Sons; John Wiley and Sons.

Table of Contents

I

INTRODUCTION

CHAPTER I

Introduction

A STABLE civilization, so it is plausibly argued, always rests on a substantial unanimity of thought. But when the ordinary differences of opinion multiply, widen, and deepen, when the educational systems have contradictory aims, when class consciousness divides the people, and when nations support irreconcilable ideals, the result is war, revolution, brutality, and chaos.

The Purpose and Limits of This Book

The comparatively peaceful nineteenth century reflected the substantial unanimity of opinion and educational aims of western civilization. Particularly in Great Britain and America the prevailing philosophy was broadly Christian. People rather consciously believed that God more or less directly governs the universe, and the curricula of American colleges usually culminated in a course in Theism. For over a century Bishop Butler's famous *Analogy of Religion* was a standard textbook, and toward the end of that era James Orr's *The Christian View of God and the World* became almost as popular.

Today all this is changed. Perhaps the majority of the population would still say that they believe in God, if they were required to answer a questionnaire, but if it is necessary to ask people pointed questions in order to elicit an acknowledgment of God, the response is not so much a serious conviction as it is the vestigial remains of their grandparents' religion. Clearly, the idea of God does not dominate contemporary thinking. The topics of the day are discussed both in private conversations and in the popular periodicals without any suggestion that theology might have a bearing on them. Even devoted Christians fail to see any close connection between their faith and other matters of interest. Similarly in the colleges, not only have the specific courses in theism been dropped, but the Christian presuppositions that previously pervaded the entire curriculum have been abandoned, and the philosophy that most influences the students in all departments is humanism or naturalism. At least humanism may be considered the most influential if the term is taken to include not only the evangelistic humanists who encourage themselves with the defection of the churches,[1] but also the less zealous advocates of theories which either ignore the existence of God or pay little more than lip service to some vague divine principle.

The attitude that even if God exists, he is not particularly important for the problems of society, is mirrored in several reviews of the American educational system. As a distinguished example, consider the Report of the Harvard Committee. This document admits that a stable society requires a common philosophy, the lack of which produces social disintegration and war. It then complains that after the common curriculum with its central theistic philosophy was discarded and replaced by an emphasis on vocationalism, the schools failed to provide their students and their subject matter with any unifying principle. Aside from the wider social and political effects, the immediate educational result has been confusion. The report says, "Sectarian, particularly Roman Catholic, colleges have of course their solution, which was generally shared by American colleges until less than a century ago: namely, the conviction that Christianity gives meaning and ultimate unity to all parts of the curriculum, indeed to the whole life of the college. Yet this solution is out of the question in publicly supported colleges and is practically, if not legally, impossible in most others. . . . But whatever one's views, religion is not now for most colleges a practicable source of intellectual

---

1. *Cf.* Corliss Lamont, *The Meaning of Humanism,* in The Humanist, Summer 1942, p. 45.

unity."[2]   Such estimates of American education may be interpreted as an admission that the present ills of society have
resulted from a general repudiation of the theistic philosophy
on which western civilization was originally erected; but they
are also a denial that that basis can again serve the same integrating purpose. To save society in its time of peril, these educators hope to replace the old ideas with a new synthesis that can
prove acceptable to the modern temper.

Possibly these men are right in suggesting that theism will
never again unify education or serve as a basis of social stability.
The opponents of Christianity are not the only persons who
consider this a plausible prediction. Even the Christian with
the strongest conviction of the coherence and truth of his
position may be tempted to suspect that the nations of the
world, as evidenced by their recent actions and plans for the
future, are too brutal, bloodthirsty, and insane to accept the
truth. Guessing the future, however, is hazardous without first
formulating a philosophy of history to indicate the regularity
with which civilizations grow, change, and decay. And to
show that secularism does not always give satisfaction, one
may mention that within the last few years, a small number
of philosophers have moved from the left to the right. C. E. M.
Joad tried humanism and found it disappointing. An agnostic
from his student days with a deep-seated suspicion of Christianity, he says, "In the course of time I came to be known as
a rationalist, and in this capacity was frequently in demand
for lectures and articles which adopted an attitude hostile to revealed religion and to the Christian Church in particular."[3] In
this volume Professor Joad now makes a sort of recantation.
The book jacket says, "England's great philosopher, formerly
an agnostic, tells how present world events have brought him to
a new belief in God." He even confesses to a sense of sin, and
in fact it was precisely the problem of evil that led him to adopt
a species of theistic philosophy. While it should not be supposed

---

2. *General Education in a Free Society* (Report of the Harvard Committee), p. 39, (Harvard University Press, 1945).

3. *God and Evil*, p. 10, (Harper & Brothers, 1943).

that Joad has become a champion of orthodox Christianity, his volume is witness to some change of mind that can fairly be described as a move from the left to the right. A second instance is that of A. E. Taylor. Taylor was never so antagonistic to Christianity as was Joad, but it may be said that between the publication of his *Elements of Metaphysics* and his last book,[4] he progressed to a more vital belief in God and to a much more distinctly Christian position. Most outstanding of these examples is the brilliant and humorous author of the *Screwtape Letters,* C. S. Lewis. In his several volumes he has completely repudiated his earlier naturalism to become the proponent of what many would call a very orthodox faith indeed.

These are, in different degrees, three instances of the repudiation of the prevailing humanistic philosophy and the acceptance of some form of theism. But while these men have moved to the right, they can hardly be said to have developed theism into a comprehensive system of philosophy. Rather they have been content or perhaps compelled to center their attention on the basic proposition that God exists. Philosophy, as the integration of all fields of study, is a wide subject, and if theism is to be more than imperfectly justified, it will be necessary to show its implications in many of these fields. A God, or a belief in God that had no repercussions either in sociology or epistemology would be of little philosophic import. What theism needs therefore is an application to all phases of learning. The three philosophers named are perfectly well aware of this, and each carries out such a program within the limits of his immediate purpose. Unfortunately, even if necessarily, these limits are restrictive; and unfortunately, even if not necessarily, there are too few authors. In comparison, the more numerous humanists have developed secular philosophy to a much greater degree. Naturalistic studies exist in every field of learning. Logic, ethics, psychology, politics, zoology, and history all have received detailed naturalistic

---

4. *Does God Exist?* (The Macmillan Company, 1947).

constructions. And this fact, no doubt, is one reason for the prevailing philosophic atmosphere.

Under these conditions the advocate of theism faces a task of great proportions with meager promise of results. It would take the brilliance of a Plato and the systematic thoroughness of an Aristotle to equal the studies of naturalism in all their detail. But there are more modest projects not entirely devoid of value. In the first place, although a theistic philosophy of systematic proportions has not been developed to meet contemporary needs, and in fact awaits a modern Augustine, some elements and implications of theism are available in several fields. These can be added to, and then arranged so as to give some prospect of what a theistic worldview would be. In the second place, from the mass of naturalistic literature a picture may be drawn that will clarify theism by contrast. The divergent implications of the two types of thought can be traced through the various subjects of academic interest. Such a clarification and comparison will be of use in understanding both points of view, and it might perhaps enable the reader to estimate how much of his intellectual capital is the result of reflective choice and how much is the result of imperceptible and desultory social absorption. In the third place, nothing will be lost if the whole can be phrased in the elementary form of an introduction to philosophy. To this end, as well as to the other two, an attempt has here been made to include sufficient detail from history, politics, and science with the hope that the result will not be too superficial a survey. The student will, however, more adequately realize this hope, if he will study the contexts from which the quotations and references have been taken.

Within limits, then, such is the threefold purpose of this book.

The Questions of Philosophy

When a person is first introduced to philosophy, when he first comes up against the perplexity of abstract problems, he is bewildered. Philosophy is a puzzle to him. It is a puzzle in somewhat the same sense that intertwined nails or spheres that come apart and may be put together again are puzzles to a curious boy.

These puzzles are not a bad illustration of philosophic perplexity because in both cases it is possible to push around the pieces without seeming to make much progress. And in both cases this is a large part of the fun. A puzzle too easily solved is not worth much. Of course a puzzle that is too complicated sometimes causes discouragement; but it whets the appetite of a keen mind. It arouses a determination that this little gadget shall not get the better of me! And the illustration points to another similarity also. While apparently little progress is made as a boy pushes the pieces here and there, suddenly the puzzle solves itself. This happens in philosophy, too; though not in the same degree of perfection. But nonetheless it is true that a student may work on a limited problem for some time with no obvious success; he may experience an acute sense of frustration; he may set it aside in despair; and then as he hurries to the Saturday football game, the solution will bowl him over like a two-hundred-pound tackle.

Whether we try our skill or not, every one of us has a great puzzle on our hands. It is the world of men and things. The world is a very intricate puzzle. One reason why the world is such an intricate puzzle is that I am a part of the world, and I am fearfully and wonderfully made. The great astronomical expanse with its stars, its nebulae, its mystery of space and time, is not more marvellous than its tiny inhabitant who tries to understand it. "Man is but a reed, the weakest thing in nature; but he is a thinking reed. It is not necessary that the entire universe arm itself to crush him. A vapor, a drop of water suffices to kill him. But though the universe should kill him, man would still be nobler than what kills him, because he knows that he dies; and the advantage that the universe has over him, the universe knows nothing of. Thus all our dignity consists in thought."[5] We shall never, certainly in this life we shall never fathom these mysteries as a boy solves

_____
5. Pascal, *Pensées*.

his ten-cent puzzle. But the attempt to solve the riddle is the more enjoyable as philosophy is superior to the toy. And it is correspondingly more profitable.

That there are difficulties is not to be denied. But there is one consolation: when a boy tries to solve his puzzle by one method and fails, he may turn the puzzle upside down and begin from a different angle. So too in philosophy, if one phase of the universal problem generates no enthusiasm, if one chapter seems to discuss uninteresting material, it is always possible to turn to another phase. An ancient philosopher with a mathematical mind asserted that the circle was the most beautiful of all figures. At any rate the beauty of philosophy is its circularity, for one may begin at any point and by constantly making progress return to the same point again. In the meantime he will have made the circuit of things seen and things unseen, and he will have discovered some of the beauty of both. The universe, with its vast astronomy, with its thinking reed, with the history and politics of nations, is God's handiwork and has been excellently well made. At least, so the Christian believes. But how can one know that it is beautiful unless thought is expended, unless time is taken to examine it, unless the purpose of its darker hues and the lines of its actors are understood? After an artist produces his piece, the public gains appreciation only by seeing how each stroke of the brush, or each line of the poem, fits the whole. A work of art is an integrated whole; it is not a disjointed aggregation of unrelated things; and knowledge and appreciation depend on an understanding of the plan according to which it was formed. No doubt the public fails fully to appreciate and fully to understand the genius of the artist; but it seems irrational, tragic, inconceivable that an omnipotent artist should let his fairest flower be born to blush unseen and waste its sweetness on the desert air. In other words, philosophizing is an act of worship.

Not only is philosophy difficult because of its great complexity, but it also has the reputation of being dull, academic, and impractical. When an uninitiated reader attempts to go through a chance volume of philosophy, he is likely to be im-

pressed with its irrelevance to important human affairs. Or, if he suspects that something important is buried beneath the professional verbiage, he may fail to disinter the mummy from its abstract sarcophagus. One of the best ways, in fact the only way of avoiding such failure is to clarify the matters that are being discussed. A system of philosophy purports to answer certain questions. To understand the answers, it is essential to know the questions. When the questions are clearly put, there is less likelihood that the answers will seem irrelevant to important issues. The problems with which the world confronts us are many, and many of them are as pressing as they are philosophic. In the last few years, for example, the perplexities of history and the paradoxes of politics have been lifted from the halls of academic learning and from the legislative chambers, and have been deposited in the nurseries and on the dinner tables of every home. The price of potatoes and eggs depends on the November ballot. Should the party favoring the strictest regulation be elected? Which party would give the best government? Which is the best kind of government? Which can actually work under the present conditions? Or can none work? Where is history taking us? Does history repeat itself? Is civilization on the verge of collapse? What causes, if any, control history? Is history a haphazard and unintelligible sequence of events, or does history have a meaning? Has God revealed any answer, or any partial answer to these questions? Is it necessary to believe in God in order to answer these questions? Or is atheistic communism the true solution?

Such questions as these are not irrelevant. They are among the most pressing questions of the present century. The most hard-headed of practical men cannot set them aside as the unreal abstractions of a slightly demented professor. And yet, practical as they are, they are not for that reason less difficult, less abstract, less philosophic, than what might serve to caricature a thinker whose head is in the clouds.

One who has not spent much time studying these questions may be tempted to give quick and easy answers. But each quick answer raises other questions. And the further the investigation is pursued, the more difficult it is seen to be. This does not mean that there are no solutions, but it assuredly means that the puzzle has more aspects than one suspected at the start. An extraordinary genius, an intellectual giant greater than the world has ever seen, might at once grasp the subject matter in magnificent outline; but no one below the rank of Plato, Augustine, or Hegel, can start from scratch and expect to go very far unaided. These three philosophers, and others, have studied these matters with great attention and ability. It would be foolish to disregard their work, for even if and when they are mistaken, their views are instructive. It is just as necessary, and sometimes it is even more important to see the unsatisfactory conclusion of a plausible suggestion, than it is to be given an absolutely true hint without a knowledge of its implications. If one wishes to arrive at a philosophy of history, therefore, some attention must be paid to the history of philosophy.

In studying the philosophy of history, and very obviously in the study of politics, it soon becomes evident that deeper problems are involved. Indisputable is the presence of ethical considerations. A declaration of war by Congress, a war launched without a formal declaration, the system of communism based on the theory of the economic determination of history, Stalin's view of murder as a political instrument, are not only matters of politics: they are matters of morality as well. The totalitarian theory that the individual person exists only for the welfare of the state; the opinion that society is an organism in which man is an expendable corpuscle of its blood stream; the denial of minority rights—or the assertion of minority rights; all these involve decisions concerning morality. They involve a theory of the value of life. Is life of so little value that an individual must be sacrificed for a group? If a high value is placed on life, is capital punishment wrong, or is it for this very reason justified and necessitated? What is the purpose of life? Indeed, has life any purpose at all? Or, doesn't anything make any difference? Is there any distinction at all between right and wrong? If there is, is this distinction the same in all countries

and all ages, or does each society make its own ethical code?
Are the answers to these questions in any way dependent on
theology? Can human values be justified only on the basis of
God's existence, or can a godless humanism succeed in making
life desirable?

Once again these questions cannot safely be neglected. A
skepticism or a despair that would hold them unanswerable,
and a devout other-worldly religiosity that might consider them
unimportant, are alike too dangerous to adopt. At least we
hope that they can be answered, and we feel sure that they are
practical, important, and relevant. Yet it will take little reflection to conclude that these questions demand hard thinking.
Here are puzzles far more intricate than those a boy can solve.
Small wonder therefore if the language sometimes matches the
subject in its difficulty.

But if questions of ethics are to be asked, one must go still
further. Ethical distinctions can be maintained for man only
if he is an inhabitant of a world in which morality is possible.
If the world with man in it is nothing but a machine whose
inviolable mechanism grinds out an unintelligible destiny, it
would seem difficult to believe in the possibility of morality.
Suppose life is only a physico-chemical reaction. Suppose what
we call thinking is but the electrical energy of nervous excita-
tion. Then could a reasonable case be made out for morality?
Or if man is the evolutionary product of a chance collocation
of inanimate particles, can any sacredness be assigned to life?
If the world is such, why should not Lenin and Stalin murder
their opponents? Or, again, if there is a God, and if God has
made this world, and if in particular he has performed miracles
at certain times in its history, one must ask what sort of world
it is, what can be meant by natural law, and what is the function of science? These are not frivolous questions.

But they are difficult, they are very difficult questions. We
puzzle over them; we turn the puzzle upside down; we become
entangled in our own devices. Then it is natural to feel discouraged, we give up hope, and we are tempted to say that there
is no answer. The subject matter is so complex, and the the-

ories advanced are still more so; and who knows, anyhow? One man thinks one thing and another thinks another. And of all people the philosophers, who have paid the most attention to these enigmas, are in the greatest disagreement. It is not that two competing answers are proposed for each question —in that case we could toss a coin and be right half the time— but there are innumerable opinions on each question, and it is doubtful that even one of them is right. The sources of error, of deception, of distortion are so manifold that perhaps a source of truth does not even exist. At least no one knows where it is. No one's opinion is superior to any other. Nobody really knows anything. Oh, perhaps God knows, if there is a God; but how can man know? What is knowledge? Is knowledge just belief? Is knowledge the same thing as faith? And does faith have reasonable grounds that can be known as reasonable, or is faith without solid foundation? Do we just believe that we believe? And is it worthwhile trying to solve such abstract, speculative, philosophic riddles?

The Unity of Truth

Discouraged though one may be by this time and paralyzed at the immensity of the task, yet even the asking of these questions results in a gain. Throughout the pages ahead this point will be illustrated constantly so as to develop a detailed understanding of the matter, but the reflective reader must already see, what had previously escaped his attention, that these questions are all interrelated. An answer to any one of them affects the answer to every other. And this is an extremely important conclusion. Perhaps at this early stage one should not call it a conclusion but only a suspicion or hypothesis, for not everyone who is known as a philosopher has agreed. William James, in his *A Pluralistic Universe*[6] stresses the disconnectedness of things. Wholes are to be explained by parts and not parts by wholes, he says; one group of events, though interrelated among themselves, may be unrelated to another group; there is no dominating unity — however much may be reported as present

6. Pp. 7ff, 124, 321-322, *et passim.*

at any effective center of consciousness, something else is self-governed, absent, and unreduced to unity. In one place James denies the need of answering a question which many others have thought as important as it is difficult: "Not why evil should exist at all, but how we can lessen the actual amount of it, is the sole question we need there to consider." Of course, if a question is literally meaningless (such as, why is music oblong?) it is really not a question at all and does not need to be answered. But if a question is not senseless, by what right can a philosophy rule it out of court? Even if it were quite trivial, it should find its place and its answer in some minor subdivision of the truth. Then, too, one might ask how James discovered that some groups of events are unrelated to other groups? Or, more exactly, since he allows "external" relations and denies only "internal" relations, one might ask how James could discover that something is absent from and unreduced to unity by every effective center of consciousness? In other words, does James have a valid argument for the conclusion that there is no Omniscient Mind whose thought is systematic truth? He may then be caught on the horns of the dilemma he tried to escape. Irrational chaos and Hegelian monism were equally repellent to him. He wanted to find a middle ground. But perhaps there is no escape from irrational chaos except, not exactly Hegelian monism, but a logical completeness of some sort. It would be surprising, would it not, if social stability could be based on incoherence, or even large scale disconnectedness? At any rate, the suspicion that the introductory questions are all related and that an answer to any one of them affects the answer to every other would accord with the theistic belief in divine omniscience. The discouragement, the reflection, the suspicion of the previous pages do not prove or demonstrate the existence of an omniscient God; but if there is such a God, we may infer that all problems and all solutions fit one another like pieces of a marvelous mosaic. The macrocosmic world with its microcosmic but thoughtful inhabitant will not be a fortuitous aggregation of unrelated elements. Instead of a series of disconnected propositions, truth will be a rational system, a logically ordered series, somewhat like geometry with its theorems and axioms, its implications and presuppositions. And each part will derive its significance from the whole. Christianity therefore has, or, one may even say, Christianity *is* a comprehensive view of all things: it takes the world, both material and spiritual, to be an ordered system. Consequently, if Christianity is to be defended against the objections of other philosophies, the only adequate method will be comprehensive. While it is of great importance to defend particular points of special interest, these specific defenses will be insufficient. In addition to these details, there is also needed a picture of the whole into which they fit. This comprehensive apologia is seen all the more clearly to be necessary as the contrasting theories are more carefully considered. The naturalistic philosophy that engulfs the modern mind is not a repudiation of one or two items of the Christian faith leaving the remainder untouched; it is not a philosophy that is satisfied to deny miracles while approving or at least not disapproving of Christian moral standards; on the contrary both Christianity and naturalism demand all or nothing: compromise is impossible. At least this will be true if the answer of any one question is integral with the answers of every other. Each system proposes to interpret all the facts; each system subscribes to the principle that this is one world. A *universe*, even James' pluralistic universe, cannot exist half theistic and half atheistic. Politics, science, and epistemology must all be one or the other.

The hypothesis of divine omniscience, the emphasis on the systematic unity of all truths, and the supposition that a particular truth derives its meaning or significance from the system as a whole does not imply that a man must know everything in order to know anything. It might at first seem to; and Plato, who faced the same difficulty, tried to provide for two kinds of knowing so that in one sense a man might know everything and in another sense not know and learn a particular truth. At the moment, let an illustration suffice. To appreciate an intricate and beautiful mosaic, we must see it as a whole; and the parts are properly explained only in terms of the whole; but it does not follow that a perception of the pieces and some fragmentary information is impossible without full appreciation. Or to pass from illustration to reality: a child in first grade learns that two plus two is four. This arithmetical proposition is true and the greatest mathematician cannot disprove it. But the mathematician sees this truth in relation to a science of numbers; he understands how this sum contributes to phases of mathematics that the child does not dream of and may never learn; he recognizes that the significance of the proposition depends on its place in the system. But the child in school knows that two and two are four, and this that the child knows is true. Omniscience, even higher mathematics, is not a prerequisite for first grade.[7]

Method: The Law of Contradiction

The difficulties inherent in philosophy and exemplified in the series of questions set forth above are matched by the difficulties of selecting a starting point and a method of procedure. To one who has just begun to philosophize and who wishes to defend theism, it might seem most natural to prove the existence of God right at the first. This would dispose of naturalism, and in the time remaining one could proceed to elaborate some metaphysics, epistemology, psychology. and other parts of a well-rounded system. As a matter of fact this has been the traditional approach; and if the arguments for the existence of God are valid, the method is sound. But are the arguments valid? Some people maintain that they are; but even if they are, the more they are studied, the harder it becomes to state them in an unobjectionable form. The ontological argument[8] has provoked volumes of discussion. Students, when they meet

7. Descartes, who, though not the greatest was an eminent mathematician, in his *Discours de la Méthode* (near the end of Part II) wrote: "As the truth on any particular point is one, whoever finds it knows all that there is to be known; . . . for example, a child who, instructed in arithmetic, has made an addition according to the rules, can be assured of having found, with reference to that sum, all that the human mind is capable of knowing."

8. St. Anselm, *Proslogium,* chapters 2 and 3.

it for the first time, react with intense suspicion but find themselves unable to discover any flaw in it. And scholars have regarded it as the perfection of profundity or as the veriest nonsense. If there is any obligation to discuss it here, the obligation must be shirked. The cosmological argument has not met with such extreme reactions; it seems to be more sober, and lists among its defenders the distinguished names of Plato, Aristotle, Thomas Aquinas, and John Locke.[9] Although a short statement of the argument fails to do it justice, Kant's summary may be used to indicate the common core of ideas found in all its forms: "If something exists, an absolutely necessary being must likewise exist; now I, at least, exist; consequently there exists an absolutely necessary being." Kant then continues: "In this cosmological argument are assembled so many sophistical propositions, that speculative reason seems to have exerted in it all her dialectical skill to produce a transcendental illusion of the most extreme character."[10] Kant's analysis of the argument is technical, and it would be better to consider Hume's[11] more popular refutation of the combined cosmological and teleological arguments. The argument for the existence of God depends, says Hume, on the inference that the marks of intelligence and design visible in the universe require intelligent forethought and cannot be the result of chance. Then Hume notes, as an essential principle of logic, that the conclusion of an argument cannot go beyond the evidence in the premises. "A body of ten ounces raised in any scale may serve as a proof that the counterbalancing weight exceeds ten ounces; but can never afford a reason that it exceeds a hundred." The cause, if its existence and nature are to be based on the observation of its effects, can never be assumed to be greater than sufficient to produce the observed effects. And once a cause is proved in

9. Plato, *The Laws* Book X; Thomas Aquinas, *Summa Theologica,* I, Q.2, Art. 3; John Locke, *An Essay Concerning Human Understanding,* Book IV, Chapter 10; perhaps the most complete statement of the cosmological argument is found in Aristotle's *Physics,* Book VIII.

10. *Critique of Pure Reason,* The Ideal of Pure Reason, Section Fifth, B634.

11. *An Enquiry Concerning Human Understanding,* Section XI, Of a Particular Providence and of a Future State.

this way, it is impossible "to return back from the cause and infer other effects from it, beyond those by which alone it is known to us. No one, merely from the sight of one of Zeuxis' pictures, could know that he was also a statuary or architect." Similarly, if there is a valid inference from the world to God, the God so proved can be assigned only those qualities sufficient to produce the observed effects. Such an argument might prove the existence of a very powerful God, but it could not prove the existence of an omnipotent God. Nor could it prove that God was more just and blessed than the proportion of observable happiness to misery in the world allows; and therefore there would be no reason to suppose that in the future God will make some adjustment for the sufferings of the innocent. To these considerations, someone is sure to reply that a half-finished building, surrounded with heaps of stone, mortar, and planks, is sufficient reason to infer, not only the existence of a contractor or architect, but also his return to complete the job. Similarly, when the injustice of the world shows its incompleteness so plainly, can it not be logically inferred that God will return to make a more impartial distribution of his favors? The answer is, No. There is reason to expect a contractor to complete a half-finished building; but this reason is based on our many previous experiences with contractors and half-finished buildings. Sometimes there are delays, but contractors usually finish the job. In the case of God and the world, however, no such reason exists. God is not one of a group that we have seen usually acting in a certain way, and this world is not one of a number of worlds that we have seen in various stages of their construction. This is the only world we have ever seen, and the mere fact that parts of it do not please us, as a contractor's kitchen plan may not please a good housewife, does not prove that the world is unfinished. If in addition to this popular analysis of Hume's, criticism is also directed against the validity of any inference from effect to cause — a matter that was granted for the sake of argument — it will be even less easy to place confidence in the proofs of God's existence. The more the arguments are studied, the less valid they seem. Because of this the argument for a theistic world view cannot begin with the traditional proofs of God's existence. These proofs are seen to raise many questions; and if they should be valid, they could not be shown to be valid without a great amount of prior discussion on metaphysics, epistemology, and other elements of a well-rounded system.

Of course, the proofs of God's existence are not the only arguments which upon examination disclose suspicious intricacies. All philosophy is intricate. Behaviorism in psychology, utilitarianism in ethics, the Newtonian law of gravitation, and the Marxian interpretation of history are all defended by elaborate and plausible arguments. When first read, they seem unanswerable. But minds as keen as Hume's have attacked these positions very effectively. Theism is not the only philosophy that faces difficulties. All arguments seem doubtful. And what is worse, as the student makes his way through the mazes of speculation, he begins to see that even though some sequences of thought are logically valid, they all depend on original assumptions. Just as the theorems of geometry are deduced from the axioms, so the conclusions of behaviorism are deduced from the assumption that mind is a physiological process, utilitarianism from the assumption that pleasure is the good, and gravitation from a theory of space and time. But what about these assumptions or axioms? Can they be proved? It would seem that they cannot, for they are the starting points of an argument, and if the argument starts with them, there is no preceding argumentation. Accordingly, after the humanist or theist has worked out a consistent system by arranging all his propositions as theorems in a series of valid demonstrations, how is either of them to persuade the other to accept his unproved axioms? And the question is all the more perplexing when it is suspected that the axioms were chosen for the express purpose of deducing precisely these conclusions.

At this point even those who have advanced beyond the first lesson in philosophy may quit in despair. Previously we were discouraged because the task seemed difficult; but now it seems impossible. Nothing can be proved; nothing can be known; why keep on trying? The attitude evokes some sympathy; for if no method of procedure can be found, the flesh may be willing, but the spirit will be weak. The remedy is to lay aside the study that cramps the mind and go out for a game of tennis. After this refreshment one will be more ready to face the possibility of skepticism.

There is a great deal of comfort in skepticism. If truth is impossible of attainment, then one need not suffer the pains of searching for it. No more will come the disappointment of discovering a flaw in a hard wrought and hitherto trusted argument. No more will it be necessary to lay another heavy foundation among the ruins of a magnificent edifice. Skepticism dispenses with all effort. It may be despair, but it is such a comfortable despair. Unfortunately, most unfortunately, even the comfort of despair is not permitted the weary thinker, for, even if nothing else can be demonstrated, the falsity of skepticism can. Skepticism is the position that nothing can be demonstrated. And how, we ask, can you demonstrate that nothing can be demonstrated? The skeptic asserts that nothing can be known. In his haste he said that truth was impossible. And is it true that truth is impossible? For, if no proposition is true, then at least one proposition is true — the proposition, namely, that no proposition is true. If truth is impossible, therefore, it follows that we have already attained it.

From this fact can be derived a method of procedure for discussing humanism and theism. If it can be shown that a proposed system of philosophy, Aristotelianism or Spinozism for example — or if it can be shown that a particular proposition, whether it be a first principle or a subsidiary side issue — implies that knowledge is impossible, then that proposition or system may be eliminated from further consideration. Skepticism refutes itself because it is internally self-contradictory. If skepticism is true, it is false. And when a more elaborate complex of ideas is internally inconsistent, the complex must be rejected.

This is similar to the method called *reductio ad absurdum* in geometry. A thesis has been proposed for examination, for example, that the interior angles of a triangle are greater than 180 degrees. From this assumption a series of deductions is made, until finally it is demonstrated that this thesis implies that a right angle is equal to an obtuse angle. This conclusion is absurd or self-contradictory; the logic by which it was deduced from the thesis is valid; therefore the thesis is false. By this method the argument for a theistic worldview would be obliged to examine the absolute idealism of Hegel, the dialectical materialism of Marx, the systems of Berkeley and Bergson, and show them to be incoherent. The method of procedure stresses coherence or self-consistency, and the implications of each position must be traced out to the end. A *reductio ad absurdum* would be the test.

The legitimacy of such a procedure will cause little dissent, but objections will soon be raised as to its sufficiency. It is widely admitted that skepticism is self-contradictory and must therefore be false. Other views, especially subsidiary contentions, can also be eliminated. But suppose, what now seems likely, that after all these eliminations, three or even two imposing systems remain, each coherent within itself, neither leading to skepticism, but mutually contradictory. What then? Now, there is a theory that the ultimate test of truth is coherence, and on this theory it would be impossible to have two self-consistent, mutually contradictory philosophies. A false statement, so it is said, will always, if pursued far enough, imply its own falsity. If this coherence theory of truth should be established, then we could rely with confidence on this application of the law of contradiction. Its sufficiency would be inherent in the nature of truth. The mere fact that the coherence theory of truth would eliminate a final impasse might even be reason enough for adopting it. One might hold that all other theories of truth lead to skepticism, and that therefore the coherence theory alone is coherent and true. Possibly all this is so, but surely it needs some more talking about. And in talking about it, there can be no logical objection to using the law of contradiction as far as it will go. Perhaps it will go further than is now expected.

Method: Choice

But suppose there still remain two or more fairly self-consistent but mutually incompatible systems of thought. This is likely to be the case even if the coherence theory of truth is correct, for the coherence theory cannot be applied with final satisfaction unless one is omniscient. Since life is short and since the implications of various propositions have not been exhausted, there may remain false positions whose absurd conclusions have not yet been deduced. We may therefore be left with large but incomplete worldviews. Instead of being thoroughly integrated, the opposing systems will lack some parts and connections. Nonetheless they will be worldviews on a large scale. Each one will have its first principles, the outlines will be plainly drawn, the main figures will have been painted in, and considerable detail will have been finished. Even though the artists have had neither time nor genius to finish their pictures, the contrast between them is unmistakable. What must be done?

Must anything be done? Can we not simply look at both pictures and go our way without expressing any preference? Most people, with their interest in the comics, do not even look at these great works of art; and since the coherence theory of truth and dialectical materialism mean nothing to them, they are incapable of having a preference. And cannot students of philosophy, and even advanced scholars, consider carefully and make no choice?

But suspension of judgment is more difficult than it would at first seem. It is difficult because the situation goes beyond the esoteric futility of the proverbial arm chair and ivory tower and involves the most intense issues of personal and social stability. To use William James' language, it is a forced and vital option. Suspension of judgment may seem possible and even necessary in relatively trivial matters. One need not give immediate assent to the claims of a new toothpaste or to a new planetesimal theory. But even in these cases the refusal to accept the claims is not so much the absence or suspension of judgment as it is the acceptance of a different judgment. The belief that toothpaste advertisements are fraudulent is itself a belief. Instead of suspending judgment, one has judged unfavorably. Or one may use the toothpaste because of the judgment that it can do no harm and may possibly do some good. Even in these trivial matters suspension of judgment is not easy to achieve. In fact it is impossible. Whether it is toothpaste or theism, one must either accept it or go without. Presumably the blessing of God rests only on those who believe in Him. As Christ said, "he that is not with me is against me," and "he that is not against us is on our part." One must therefore be either for or against; there is no neutral or intermediate position. Suspension of judgment seems possible only when the practical business of living is excluded from consideration. If this unreal abstraction is repudiated, it will be seen that everyone lives either with the fear of God before his eyes or not. Our preferences, our standards of morality, our purpose in life accord with a theistic worldview or they do not. And if they do not, we are acting on the assumption, whether we admit it or not, that there is no God to hold us responsible. Suspension of judgment, so-called, is but a disguised, if dignified, form of unbelief. A choice therefore cannot be avoided.

The philosophically minded may be repelled by the notion of choice because it seems to smack of unphilosophical arbitrariness. The theory of vital options dimmed the lustre even of William James in some quarters. But it is easier to be repelled by the notion of choice than it is to show that choice is not necessary. Yet also it must be admitted that choice is sometimes arbitrary and whimsical. The majority of the population choose religious, political, and philosophical beliefs that form the weirdest patterns. Still the choice of an ultimate principle or of a system of philosophy is not necessarily or ordinarily a personal whim or an arbitrary decision. Such a choice is the result of a long course of study to organize one's universe. It is made with a fairly clear consciousness of the implications in many fields of inquiry. A whim, on the other hand, is the choice of some special factor without regard to the rest of life or to one's other beliefs. Choice, however, is unavoidable because first principles cannot be demonstrated, and though some choices are arbitrary, the philosophical choice has regard to the widest possible consistency. Choice therefore is as legitimate as it is inevitable.

Admittedly the theistic view of the world faces difficulties. There are questions to which Christianity seems to give an inadequate answer or none at all. But does anyone claim that pragmatism or realism or idealism gives adequate answers to all questions? Is humanism or naturalism free of difficulty? There has been an immense amount, not merely of inadequacy but of inconsistency in some of the greatest philosophers. In fact a student might be tempted to suggest that the greatness of a philosopher is directly proportional to the number of his contradictions. Kant, for example, the source of all contemporary philosophies, or at least the funnel through which all modern ideas have passed, is unbearably self-contradictory. Not only are there the gigantic contradictions which Jacobi and the post-Kantians saw at first — we may forgive or at least sympathize with big blunders — but there are the innumerable detailed inconsistencies from paragraph to paragraph almost all the way through.[12] No philosopher is perfect and no system can give man omniscience. But if one system can provide plausible solutions to many problems while another leaves too many questions unanswered, if one system tends less to skepticism and gives more meaning to life, if one worldview is consistent while others are self-contradictory, who can deny us, since we must choose, the right to choose the more promising first principle?

---

12. *Cf.* Norman Kemp Smith, *A Commentary on Kant's Critique of Pure Reason*; the notes of Erich Adickes: In diesem Abschnitt herrscht die grösste Unklarheit ... Das dunkelste Stück der Kritik, von manchen deshalb für das tiefsinnigste gehalten ... Systematische Spielerei ohne wissenshaftlichen Wert; also other comments and commentators.

II

THE PHILOSOPHY OF HISTORY

CHAPTER II

The Philosophy of History

ONE of the most inviting gateways to philosophic thinking is the study of history. And for this reason, rather
than for any strictly logical principle of arrangement, history
is here made the first subject of discussion. Some divisions of
philosophy concern fine points not readily appreciated, the discussion of which may become discouragingly technical; and
therefore most people ignore them. But history in all its extent, the philosophy of history rather than the history of any
single nation, presents problems so large, and, in this age, it
presents points so blunt, that it is next to impossible to overlook them.

Most obvious are those problems that come with pressing,
practical urgency. The devastation of World War II and its
chaotic aftermath call for reconstruction. But the plans of
procedure differ. For example, the United States in spite of a
drastic plan early proposed by Morgenthau decided that a
prosperous Germany is essential to the well-being of Europe;
and the lessons of history were adduced as evidence. On the
other hand, France appealed to the lessons of history to show
that a vigorous Germany is a menace to peace and particularly to France; and accordingly she went further in disman-
tling the industries in her zone. Both countries believe that it
is possible to learn from history, but what it is that can be
learned, what it is that history teaches, is a matter of no small
disagreement.

Disagreement occurs not merely over plans of reconstruction
in Europe; it is even questioned whether reconstruction is possible. And again history is called upon to furnish the evidence.
Some people believe that European civilization is shattered

beyond repair, and that even the United States will be dragged down to oblivion. Of course, patriotic Americans are likely to think that the United States will last forever. Or it is probably more accurate to say that they *don't think* it will perish. This thoughtless confidence in our land has some basis in fact. Before the late war both Germany and Russia underestimated our ability to produce. Perhaps we ourselves underestimated it, for the building of a Navy after the inexcusable disaster at Pearl Harbor and the enormous production of all the goods of war needed by Britain and Russia, were nothing less than phenomenal. Could not this miracle of management be repeated in another time of danger? Does not the executive ability of our country's industrial leaders guarantee America's perpetuity?

There are deeper reasons for confidence in our land. Underlying managerial ability is the individual freedom protected by our Constitution. In no other land have private citizens enjoyed such freedom. The absence of a venal, tax-consuming bureaucracy with its arbitrary and inelastic regulations has encouraged individual initiative. People with ideas were free to experiment; and the result has been not just the invention, but the actual production and distribution of mechanical devices to an extent almost undreamed of in other countries of the twentieth century. French and British scientists are as brilliant as American scientists; inventive genius is not restricted to the United States; and yet Europe never has enjoyed electric refrigerators, washing machines, automobiles, and bath tubs in American abundance. Will not the freedom of business initiative that has produced our comforts continue to guarantee us a permanently high standard of living?

In some ancient Eastern lands it was customary, when approaching the monarch, to say, "O King, live forever." Nonetheless those kings died and their kingdoms also died. Babylonia and Assyria, Egypt and Rome, were once great nations. Today they are but areas for archaeological excavation. Can America escape their fate? Is there anything inherent in our culture and civilization that protects this nation from decay?

Throughout the past, cultures have arisen and have crumbled to ruins. If this is the lesson of history, it becomes a real question whether or not our world, our western civilization, has already come to its inglorious end.

The general problem of history, of which such matters as the reconstruction of Europe and the decay of western civilization are subsidiary parts, is the formulation of a law which will enable us to understand the course of events and to make a probable guess about the future. The idea of law is familiar in science. In physics the scientists have formulated the law of the pendulum. There are many pendulums: some are long, some are short; some have heavy weights and some have light weights; some swing on thin strings, some on thick; some are black and others are green or blue. The aim of science is to state a point of similarity among all pendulums and thereby come to an understanding of that phenomenon. After experimentation the physicists announced that the period of the swing is proportional to the square root of the length. This is true of all pendulums. Now, then, can there be similarly a science or law of all history? Is there anything true of all civilizations? Do they parallel each other in their development? Does history repeat itself? Or, do the vicissitudes of men arrange themselves in a continuous linear progression, each nation and epoch surpassing its predecessor in an invincible advance from barbarism to perfection? Or is history perhaps haphazard, without any law at all?

Karl Marx

These arresting problems which today make the philosophy of history an inescapable subject of widespread interest have not always attracted the attention of the best minds. The ancient Greeks, great philosophers, scientists, and artists though they were, had virtually no interest in history as such. In more recent centuries also some philosophers seem to have considered history as relatively unimportant. Either they regarded it as completely devoid of significance, or if they granted it some slight value, still in comparison with the physics, mathematics, and cosmology that reveal the inner secrets of the universe, history seemed too trivial to waste time upon. But with Hegel at the beginning of the nineteenth century history became a matter of serious consideration, and since that time its appeal has steadily increased.

Although Hegel was the first in modern times to look at history in all its scope, his views are too complex, too greatly dependent on a grandiose system of philosophy, and even insufficiently rewarding at this early stage of the discussion, to be reviewed now. After he died, his students divided into right and left wings. Karl Marx and Friedrich Engels, the leaders of the left wing, published the Communist Manifesto in 1847, and worked out a system of dialectical materialism that was put into effect in Russia by Lenin and that continues to force itself on the world. Dialectical materialism is also a theory of the universe. It predicts the extinction of life and a time when only the aimless atoms shall continue to move through space. Because this phase of the theory transcends history, it will be omitted here. There are also ethical considerations that must be postponed to the appropriate place, and attention must be centered on its philosophy of history.

According to Marx, history is not a haphazard series of events; but, rather, one event follows another, one nation supplants another, or, more accurately, one type of civilization replaces another by the operation of a fixed and definite cause. That cause is economic pressure. Ever since the invention of private property, society has been divided into two classes: the *haves* and the *have-nots*. History is a struggle for wealth, and if one man is rich, another must be poor. This class struggle explains the course of history. The fundamental proposition that forms the nucleus of Marxism was stated by Engels in his Preface to the *Communist Manifesto*: "In every historical epoch the prevailing mode of economic production and exchange, and the social organization necessarily following from it, form the basis upon which is built up, and from which alone can be explained the political and intellectual history of that epoch." This principle would be misunderstood if it were restricted to the political history of nations. The social philosophy that preceded Marx, including Hegel's philosophy of history, considered the nation as the most important unit of social study, and Hegel went so far as to imply that history culminated in the Prussian state. Marx, however, not only ridiculed Hegel on this point, but he ceased to look on nations as isolated units. A number of contiguous nations possess the same general culture, and hence the unit of study may be called a civilization or culture: in this case European civilization. Thus Marx does not merely mean that nations rise and fall by economic pressure. The principle of the *Communist Manifesto* is that the whole intellectual tone of an age is completely explained by contemporary methods of production and exchange. For example, medieval philosophy and politics were what they were as a result of the peasants' methods of labor; and the different, modern outlook on life was caused by bourgeois industrialism. Or, Marx would have to argue, the religion of the Hebrews differed from the religions of Egypt and Assyria because their farming and commerce were different. And the dogmatic metaphysics of Aristotle and the Stoics in the fourth and third centuries succumbed to the general skepticism of the second and first centuries before Christ because of some change in the methods of production and exchange.

Now, it is perfectly obvious that economic factors have a deep and widespread influence on the character of a civilization. Not only the details of proposed legislation, but also the morals, the worldview, and even the art and religion of large bodies of people are affected by economic considerations. But to grant that economic motives have a widespread effect on the form and development of civilization is far from granting that everything can be so explained. It is far from granting that economics is the only principle by which the political and intellectual history of an epoch can be understood. Of course Marx does not deny that non-economic factors produce social results. Undoubtedly religious ideas had something to do with the Protestant Reformation. But while such non-economic factors exist and play their role, they in turn are the results of the contemporary methods of labor. Economics is not the only factor, but it is the sole basic factor. This admission of the existence of other factors, though they are made secondary to the methods of production and exchange, preserves more plausibility for the theory than it would otherwise have had. But reflection may bring to mind some such examples as the following. The mode of production by serfs in Czarist Russia and that by the slaves in our antebellum South must have been substantially the same. If they differed somewhat, the difference could hardly have been so great as to explain and cause the tremendous difference between the Protestantism and Jeffersonian democracy of the South and Russia's autocracy and Greek Catholicism. In fact, until the recent past all countries have been mainly agricultural, and the methods have been basically the same; yet the intellectual histories of China, Persia, Russia, and France show much greater difference than the Marxist theory would lead one to expect. Again, the communistic industrialization of Russia is technologically comparable with American industry, but obviously the social, political, intellectual and religious ideas of the two countries are wide of each other. Of course these and other examples do not amount to a formal disproof of Marx's principle. Perhaps Marx could defend his position by showing that the method of welding in Russia differs from the American method, and that Russian welding causes atheism, while American welding allows the churches considerable freedom. But if the examples do not formally disprove Marxism, they may perhaps reduce its plausibility. They may make it appear as an oversimplification of the problem, and thus lead to a desire to examine other philosophies of history. However, even if Marx failed, at least he saw history as a problem and made a determined attempt to solve it.

The Philosophy of Progress

Before Marx and Hegel recognized the need of a general philosophy of history, partial and desultory reflections had been accumulating for two hundred years. In seventeenth century France the literary world, with little consciousness of the implications, began a debate, the echoes of which were still reverberating in 1827 when Victor Hugo published the *Préface de Cromwell.* The dispute concerned the relative merits of ancient and modern authors. One side maintained that the golden age was long past and that now the world could expect only literary senility. The other side believed in progress.[1]

Perrault, the author of *Mother Goose Stories* and *Fairy Tales,* argued that the powers of nature have always been the same; oak trees are no less sturdy today than they were centuries ago; and consequently human ability to produce literature has not deteriorated. Not only is there no deterioration; there is progress. The purpose of literature is to please the human heart; a knowledge of the human heart therefore is necessary if an author is to succeed; and since knowledge increases by accumulation, it follows that Corneille, even if his powers of imagination were no greater than those of Homer or Sophocles, understood vengeance and jealousy better than the ancients, and so was able to construct superior plays.

This restricted literary controversy initiated a broad examination of political and social history in general, with the result that a radically new worldview came to supplant the older ways of looking at things. Indeed, Marx himself was but one of the contributors to this development.

Through the Middle Ages the prevailing philosophy had been a mixture of Christianity, Platonism, and Aristotelianism. Christianity contributed the notion of redemption from sin, with a final judgment and an eternal destiny. Plato and Aristotle furnished the idea that knowledge, meditation, and contemplation were inherently valuable. Together the two sources, even if both were misunderstood, produced an otherworldliness that disparaged the immediate interests of the present. Whatever significance was attributed to the human

---

1. This discussion, particularly the enumeration of the elements that compose the concept of progress, depends largely on the excellent volume by J. B. Bury, *The Idea of Progress,* (Macmillan and Co. Ltd., 1920).

race, whatever value could be found in man's activities, whatever meaning an individual life might have, all depended on a final destiny. Since the day of judgment, when God would terminate history, might arrive at any time, there was not much sense in speculating about the possible politics and wars of A. D. 6000. Even the politics of the day were not particularly important. This common outlook was to pass away. In the following centuries there would still be talk of God, and some people would continue to believe in a life beyond the grave; but these religious notions were no longer to be the generally accepted criterion by which social values should be measured. Civilization was to become secular.

The change made its advance through the participation of many authors. Opposition to Aristotle and to the inherent value of knowledge was popularized by Francis Bacon, who taught a willing audience that the purpose of knowledge is the control of nature for the increase of man's happiness here on earth. Gone is the Christian motif. Happiness has been substituted for heaven. Then Descartes by his scientific work and Spinoza by his logic developed the concept of inviolable mechanical law. This concept both undermined belief in providence and also promised assurance that nothing could prevent indefinite scientific progress. Since Descartes and his associates made as brilliant a record of scientific discovery as Racine and Corneille made in literature, it was natural to ask whether there could not be progress in social conditions also. To this phase of the problem, the eighteenth century devoted its best energies. Optimism now ran high, as can be seen in a book by Mercier, entitled *The Year* 2440. He pictures a happy state of affairs in which France and England are no longer enemies. The population of France has increased by half, and Paris is a sanitary, well-lighted city. Education is governed by the ideas of Rousseau, and while modern languages are taught in the schools, Latin and Greek are not, for the ancient literature was useless and pernicious and has been deliberately destroyed by fire. Economic prosperity is main-

tained because government officials estimate the capacities of
each adult and assign employment on that basis.

Mercier's eighteenth century imagination was no more
optimistic than the general temper of the times.   Even if there
was to be a revolution, the political planners were sure that
it would inaugurate permanent felicity.

When the French Revolution brought The Terror instead of
felicity, Condorcet, hiding from Robespierre and the guillotine,
still maintained his belief in progress.   It would be slower than
they had thought, but there could never be a relapse into barbarism because the knowledge of physics must always increase.

Whereas the eighteenth century had centered its attention
narrowly on politics, the nineteenth saw the rapid growth of
wider social speculation.   This gave a broader base to the
concept of progress, and reinforced the optimistic temper that
had been only temporarily shaken by the Revolution.   Comte,
following the ideas of Saint Simon, believed that society should
be and would be organized by its superior members.   Popular
sovereignty and human equality are slogans necessary to produce a needed revolution, but they are nonetheless anarchical
and vicious.   In the Middle Ages priests dominated the scene.
Now scientists will dominate.   The golden age is upon us,
for Catholicism is in ruins, militarism is on the decline, and
the epoch has arrived when large scale warfare will cease.

In England the concept of progress developed less turbulently.
Adam Smith expected the indefinite increase of wealth. Gibbon
studied the decline and fall of Rome and concluded that civilization would never again collapse. Darwin's theory of evolution, closing on the optimistic note of progress toward perfection, enabled Spencer to construct a happy sociology.   Good
social habits, acquired in the course of history, are an aid to
survival, and these acquired characteristics will be inherited
and increased as time goes on.   Progress cannot be blocked.

In his *Social Statics* Spencer writes:[2]   "The inference that
as advancement has been hitherto the rule, it will be the rule
henceforth, may be called a plausible speculation.   But when

2. Chapter Two, *The Evanescence of Evil.*

it is shown that this advancement is due to the working of a universal law; and in virtue of that law it must continue until the state we call perfection is reached, then the advent of such a state is removed out of the region of probability into that of certainty. . . . Progress therefore is not an accident but a necessity. As surely as a blacksmith's arm grows large and the skin of a laborer's hand becomes thick; . . . as surely must the things we call evil and immorality disappear; so surely must man become perfect."

With Spencer the theory of progress is virtually completed. To bring it into sharper focus, it may be wise to turn from the historical sketch to an enumeration of the elements that compose the complete concept.

Negatively, progress is the denial of divine providence; or, positively, progress is a natural process. It was thought that if God exercised control over the affairs of men, if therefore he could cause mankind to retrogress, or, if as is plainly taught in the Bible, he might bring the world to an end, there could be no guarantee of indefinite amelioration. Accordingly, progress must be a natural process. Whatever factors in nature it may depend upon, it cannot depend on the will of a Supreme Being.

Since progress is a natural process, it must always have been in operation. Pendulums did not first begin to swing as indicated the year the law of the pendulum was discovered. Similarly, as long as human beings have existed, they must have been improving. There was therefore no ancient golden age, but on the contrary every succeeding generation advances beyond the preceding. And it likewise follows from the concept of a natural process that it must extend into the indefinite future. Neither a supernatural day of judgment, nor any accident of history can be admitted as setting a limit or fixed boundary to progress. If the world were to come to an end in A. D. 2000, the concept of progress would be useless. Admittedly the second law of thermodynamics predicts a time when the amount of available energy in the universe will be insufficient to support life. But this condition is far in the future and is not supposed to invalidate the theory. It is not necessary to insist that mankind will exist forever; but, as J. B. Bury estimated it, we must be prepared to suppose that the human race will continue for 60,000 years. This would be sufficient time to make the concept of progress meaningful.

Then, too, progress must occur in all spheres of human interest. Accumulation of scientific information is not sufficient; there must be social and moral improvement as well. And philosophical improvement. Just as the concepts that dominated antiquity made way for the medieval synthesis, and as the medieval worldview faded before the illumination of modern times, so we must expect that the philosophy of today will be replaced by a better viewpoint in centuries to come.

And finally, if progress is a natural law, it must be conceived as necessary and inevitable. The same argument that puts history beyond divine control also removes it from the fickleness of human whims. Man no doubt is the important factor in history, and his will accomplishes results, but it is as much the nature of the human will to choose the direction of progress as it is the nature of the pendulum to swing in regular periods. Like the other laws of nature, continuous improvement must be taken as a part of the order of things.

Such in outline is the meaning of the concept. The question now is whether or not progress is in fact the law of history. The most promising method of answering this question is to search nature for causes that would produce and insure progress. If these causes can be found, the theory may be considered established. In general it may be said that three types of cause have been invoked: scientific knowledge, political or social planning, and biological evolution.

The appeal to the increase of scientific knowledge is perhaps the least satisfactory, because in one form the alleged cause is of dubious efficacy and in another form it is only a partial manifestation of more general cause. Scientific knowledge is a dubious cause of progress if it is assumed, as was sometimes the case, that all improvement depends basically on knowledge alone. It is clear today as it has never been before that the increase of scientific knowledge in nuclear fission can produce an atomic bomb, but it cannot prevent war. Similarly a great advance in medical knowledge may benefit the sick, but it also may result in a biological warfare that could extinguish the human race. Since therefore scientific knowledge is instrumental, since it can as easily produce evil as good, it cannot guarantee progress. On the other hand, if it were granted for the sake of argument that the accumulation of scientific information inevitably produces moral improvement, if it could be proved that the Japanese in assimilating western science became less brutal than otherwise they would have been, still it would be necessary to seek a cause to guarantee scientific advance. The Middle Ages, following upon the work of men such as Aristarchus, Archimedes, Ptolemy, and Galen, should suffice to show that scientific advance is not automatic. Unless an underlying cause can be found, in biology perhaps, this explanation of progress begs the question.

Historically, however, the next appeal was not to biology but to political and social planning. It was assumed that human nature is malleable in the hands of a legislator. And this idea is found not only in 18th century France, but it is also an essential element in present day communistic theory. By enacting and enforcing a given set of laws, the advocates of this theory expect to produce a new type of human nature. The more idealistic proponents of this view look forward to a race of human beings free from jealousy and anger, who, content with an equal distribution of wealth, never suspect that dishonesty, burglarly, or war might produce a profit. Now, this metamorphosis may or may not be possible; but if it is, it is still no guarantee of progress, for on these conditions a worse type of human nature can be produced as easily as a better type. If rulers in the past have debased their people, enslaved them, reduced them to the status of animals, what is to prevent present and future political planners from following the same procedure?

To avoid the criticism that political planning is too narrow a basis for progress, exponents of this form of the theory enlarged their view to take in man's entire social environment. Thus the development of the better human nature will result not from legislation alone, but from custom and social pressure as well. While this is undoubtedly a broader basis, it is open to exactly the same objections. If it should be true that human nature is malleable, the society can produce bad results as well as good, and is therefore no guarantee of progress.

The third cause sought to guarantee progress was biological evolution; but it was an evolution extended to moral as well as physical qualities. On the theory that good moral and social qualities have a survival value, it is not the good but the bad who die young; and since the evil type is dying out, every succeeding generation has a larger proportion of good people. Such is the import of the significant paragraph from Spencer quoted above. This attempt to guarantee indefinite progress depends on one or two assumptions: first, that morality has a survival value; and, second, that acquired moral characteristics are inherited. Though this second assumption is an integral part of communistic theory, it may not be necessary to other forms of the theory. But in any case both of these assumptions are doubtful. Biologists, aside from Marxist biologists, usually deny that acquired physical characteristics are inherited; and if this is true, it would seem that acquired moral characteristics have even less of a chance of being transmitted to succeeding generations. It is also doubtful that moral qualities uniformly contribute to survival. Certain types of immorality are physically debilitating and the contrary virtues produce health and prolong life. But as for other virtues equally necessary to inaugurate Utopia, there is surely as much evidence that the ruthless survive and propagate their kind as that the mild and peace loving animals survive. For example, Tennyson, in the fervor of evolutionary faith, described nature as red with tooth and claw. And is man unnatural? But when present political realities and unpleasant evidences of civilized savagery are used as objections to evolutionary optimism, the reply is usually made that a century or several centuries are inconsiderable in the vast extent of evolutionary time : in a thousand years, or a hundred thousand, the present downward wiggle in the generally upward line of progress will be invisible. This is a most disconcerting reply. When the evidence from the past turns out to be inadequate, appeal is made to a far distant and unknown future. Logicians classify such a reply as a *petitio principii*. Two formal points may be made. First, the observable material of biology does not prove that mankind is the goal of evolution or is "better" than any other species of animal. The bare fact that the human brain is considerably larger than the brain of any other species is no indication that blind evolutionary forces aimed at man as a climax. As well might a rhinoceros argue that since he has the thickest of all skins (if this be true), he is the crowning glory of biology. The only way to arrive at an evaluative conclusion is to smuggle into the premises some evaluative principle never seen under a microscope. Empirical observation can easily determine which brain is largest and which skin is thickest, but it is impotent to conclude that one is better than the other or that one is the purpose of all past biological phenomena. In the second place, this reply fails to consider the possibility that the human race, like other species, may become extinct before the far distant future arrives. Empirical observation, no matter how much information it accumulates from the past, cannot guarantee the existence of any species. Relatively complex types have disappeared and very simple organisms continue to exist. Why may not the human race also disappear? Can man's vaunted rationality be trusted to save him? On the contrary, man's genius seems bent on a suicidal war in which those who are not burned to death will suffer the sterilizing effects of radiation or the slow degeneration of disease. Besides this, the erosion of the land, with whatever help Malthus may provide, threatens us with the evil arrows of famine. And perhaps most dangerous to the continuation of the race is the possibility that the tsetse fly and his brother insects will inherit the earth. It follows from this that the theory of evolution cannot well be accepted as a bonded guarantee of progress.

In addition to these criticisms of special forms of the theory of progress, there are more general considerations that apply to all forms.

Most basic of all constituents of any theory of progress is the idea of a goal. In colloquial language, when anyone is said to be making progress, it means that he has a goal in view and is getting nearer to it. If there is no goal, it seems difficult to talk of progress. Proponents of progress have taken three different positions on this matter. Some have asserted the existence of a known goal, such as human happiness. Others have asserted a goal but have disclaimed any knowledge of what it is. Ernest Renan, for example, consoled himself with the certainty that we must arrive *somewhere*. Still others deny that there is any goal. At least such would seem to be the view of J. B. Bury[3] when he warns against the illusion of finality.

If the last of these three, *viz.,* the view that there is no purpose or final cause in nature, were to be adequately argued, it would require interminable metaphysical discussion; but apart from the metaphysics of the question, it is still pertinent to emphasize that the denial of a goal empties the word progress of all meaning. Change, aimless change, that does not proceed in a determinate direction, cannot be called progress; and a determinate direction exists only in virtue of the end or goal that sets the direction.

The second view, that there is a goal toward which humanity is moving but that the nature of the goal is unknown, is scarcely more satisfactory. History may be moving in a set direction, but unless we know the nature of the end, we cannot decide whether the result will be good or bad. One must be very optimistic indeed if he is satisfied to arrive only *somewhere*.

The first view, that there is a known goal, is free from the logical difficulties of the other two views. It reduces to a question of fact or perhaps two questions. One question would

---

3. *Op. cit.,* p. 351.

be whether or not happiness on earth, irrespective of a future life, is desirable in itself. Hamlet said,

> ... *To die, to sleep;*
> *To sleep: Perchance to dream; aye, there's the rub;*
> *For in that sleep of death what dreams may come,*
> *When we have shuffled off this mortal coil,*
> *Must give us pause....*

Or, if it be assumed that earthly happiness is the goal, the second question is whether or not humanity is really moving in that direction. Are men today happier than they were ages ago, but less happy than they will be centuries hence? Is the empirical evidence sufficient to remove doubt as to the past and skepticism as to the future?

There is one final and far-reaching objection to the theory of progress. Bury mentions it at the end of his book, but shies away from it. The objection lies in the fact that the theory of progress requires the idea of progress to progress. Consider the following statement.[4]

"The distinctive feature of this tradition is emphasis upon liberty as both a requisite and a measure of progress. Its liberty or freedom, of course, comprises or implies justice, equality, and any other aspectual qualities of the 'good society.' Its society, however, is no mere aggregate of reified aspects, but a living, functioning organization or 'organism'; and its good society is no static conception, but is essentially social process whose goodness is progress[5] and progress not only in terms of prevailing criteria, but also in the criteria themselves."

This means that liberty and, of course, justice and equality, have been the requisite and measure of progress until now.

---

4. Henry C. Simons, *Economic Policy for a Free Society,* pp. 1, 2. (University of Chicago Press, 1948).

5. Confusion is abundant in the debate as to whether centralized government or individual liberty is the more efficient means to progress. In these arguments progress has ceased to be a change toward an end and has become itself the end. Instead of asking whether liberty or totalitarianism is the goal of progress, both opponents welcome change for the sake of change. Such writers are justifiably optimistic, for their endeavors are certain to be rewarded.

But since there must be progress in the criteria themselves, the criteria of liberty and justice must be transcended. The better society of tomorrow will no longer count liberty and justice good. The goodness of a society is no such static ideal, but rather, goodness consists in progress itself. The good society is not moving in a definite direction toward a fixed goal; it is merely moving. But more than this: if the goodness of society consists in its "progress" toward no static goal; if, that is, progress itself is the criterion of progress, and if, as the author said, the criteria must change; then tomorrow the ideal of progress itself, as well as the ideal of justice, must be abandoned. In other words, if progress is the law of history, if our moral and intellectual baggage is superior to that of antiquity; and if our society and our ideas are to grow into something better and vastly different; if our imagination is to evolve to a degree not now imaginable; if all the old concepts which served their time well are to be replaced by new and better concepts, does it not follow that the theory of progress will be discarded as an 18th and 19th century notion, which no doubt served its age well, but which will then be antiquated and untrue?

Could it be that the best contemporary evidence of progress is a growing disbelief in "progress"?

Spengler and Toynbee

The superficial optimism that dominated the thought of the nineteenth century was suddenly shattered by World War I. And at the same time the study of history became much more thorough and detailed. Oswald Spengler's two great volumes on *The Decline of the West* impress the reader with extensive erudition in defiant disarray.

Spengler censures the restricted outlook of his predecessors. They had chosen Europe as the all important center of history for the poor reason that they happened to live there. And the Napoleonic period, a period of twenty-five years at the most, received more emphasis than twenty-five centuries of Egyptian history. Of course, the history of Greece and Rome was also studied, but China, India, and Africa went unnoticed. This attempt to write a European history, a method which effectively obscures the real problem, prevents the discovery of any parallelism between China and the Aztecs. Without a technique and law derived from the study of world history, the common comparisons of Napoleon with Ceasar or of Athens with Paris are fragmentary and misleading. Spengler therefore hoped to make an investigation on a scale hardly attempted by previous historians, an investigation that would show deep uniformities "between the differential calculus and the dynastic principle of politics in the age of Louis XIV, between the classical city-state and the Euclidean geometry, between the space-perspective of western oil-painting and the conquest of space by railroad, telephone, and long range weapons, between contrapuntal music and credit economics." By investigating these deep uniformities, "things such as the Egyptian administrative system, the classical coinage, analytical geometry, the cheque, the Suez Canal, the book printing of the Chinese, the Prussian Army, and the Roman road-engineering, can, as symbols, be made uniformly understandable and appreciable."[6]

When one looks beyond the confines of Europe, that peninsular appendage to Asia, and studies all history, one can see that history is not a linear process. Instead of a straight line, the clue to the understanding of history lies in a biological analogy. A culture is like an organism with its life cycle. No one says of an oak tree that just now, at the present moment, it is about to enter upon its true and proper course. But optimistic exponents of progress often viewed past history as so much stupidity and misery and confidently asserted that now the true purpose of history has begun to be realized. It is better to think of a culture as an organism: it is born, it grows strong, it deteriorates, and dies. The oak tree has a long life cycle; the caterpillar a short one; the other particularities of their existence also differ; but both have the same general phenomena of birth, life, and death. In this sense,

6. *The Decline of the West*, Vol. 1, p. 7, (A. A. Knopf, 1947).

the life cycles of cultures are parallel, though the specific characteristics are dissimilar.

Trained morphological insight can see how an event in one history can be "contemporaneous" with an event in another history. The two events occur in exactly the same relative positions in their respective cultures. Thus Pythagoras is the contemporary of Descartes; Polygnotus pairs in time with Rembrandt; and Hannibal with World War I. The application of this morphological principle will aid both in predicting the future and in reconstructing long vanished and unknown epochs.

Spengler burst into popularity not by reason of any reconstruction of vanished epochs but by reason of his prediction of the collapse of western civilization. Prediction is possible when one has learned the signs of senility that are common to all by-gone cultures. Spengler makes a distinction between culture and civilization. Culture is full of life — it is youth and vitality; civilization is the hardening of the arteries that indicates approaching death. Civilizations are the most external and artificial of all human productions. They are the rigidity that follows expansion and are the inevitable conclusion of life. The Greeks had a culture; the Romans had a civilization. The Romans were the unspiritual barbarians, devoid of art, intent on tangible success, who closed a period of culture. In the western world, as Spengler views it, the transition from culture to civilization occurred in the nineteenth century. Of the many signs of an approaching death and of the multitude of comparisons among various epochs, perhaps the most infallible indication is the growth of large cities. It is a recurrent theme in Spengler's work and one which he elaborates in great detail. Culture is found in provinces and towns. Orphism and the Protestant Reformation, both of which were full of life, considered every hamlet important. But city people are traditionless, matter of fact, religionless, clever, unfruitful, and contemptuous of the gentleman, especially of the country gentleman. Civilization must expand. It drains the countryside of people, tearing them up by the roots to produce the megapolis. This is not a matter of choice either of individuals or of classes. It is a doom that grips mankind and brings the inevitable results. There is no use of hoping for impossibilities. We may deplore the present, but it cannot be otherwise. If one says that fatalism is discouraging, the reply is that false hopes are not to be encouraged. One must learn what is possible. Western men will never again produce great music, art, or poetry. Kant was the last systematic philosopher. Those who are able to avoid wishful thinking can see the handwriting on the wall. We of today face — we of today are — the decline of the west.

Professing to be more optimistic than Spengler, Arnold J. Toynbee has recently written *A Study of History* of gigantic proportions. His method of procedure and the laws he discovers are conspicuously different from those of his German predecessor. The first and most obvious difference to be observed lies in the type of information amassed and its more orderly arrangement, for Toynbee manages to give the impression that his method is completely empirical. Spengler may have seemed to be subject to flashes of erratic genius; but Toynbee accumulates a mass of sober facts and claims to discover the laws in the facts themselves.

The facts, however, are not the facts that Spengler uses. While a few may be found in both authors, it is surprising that works of such ample proportions overlap so little. But of course history itself is rather ample. From the innumerable events that constitute history each has selected the facts that suit him and discovers in them the law of history. But is it *discovery?* Are the results empirically established? One may entertain serious doubts as to the empirical objectivity of the procedure. This is not to insinuate, as a young student of philosophy might at first suppose, that either of these men was consciously dishonest; and Toynbee especially makes a great effort to base his views on facts. But, rather, the point is that empirical history is inherently impossible. If a person with a completely unbiased mind should try to study history, the thousand and one events that happen every minute the world over would foredoom him to speedy failure. To make any progress at all, he would have to select some of these events and pay no attention to others. In doing so, however, he would have to use a principle of selection not found in the events themselves. Unconsciously, and in spite of himself, by an unrecognized psychological law, and by the nature of history and the world, Toynbee or any other student of history must select his facts and in the selection begin to impose his interpretation upon them. But at any rate there is no doubt that Toynbee has collected six volumes of exceedingly interesting information.

Both Spengler and Toynbee assume that history must be divided into units, and the intelligible units of historical study, Toynbee says, are neither nations, nor periods, but societies. England, for example, can be understood only as a part of Western Christendom; and Christendom grew out of the now defunct Roman society. It is to be noted that this intelligible unit is larger than that of Spengler. At least Spengler gives the impression that the Middle Ages and modern times are two different units, for he speaks of the Reformation as a time of culture and therefore as the beginning of a new society. This is indeed plausible, for is it not true that the customs and activities, the ideas, the interests, and the general outlook on life are markedly different in these two ages? If medieval culture and modern culture are not two different cultures, if the changes that took place in the sixteenth century are insufficient for distinguishing between two societies, one may begin to wonder whether the problem of units in history is not an illusory one. However, Toynbee dates our present society, not from the renaissance but from the end of the Roman empire. The society in question is not the modern civilization that delighted the eighteenth century optimists, but it is Christendom, or more exactly western Christendom; and he would argue that the renaissance and the Protestant Reformation cannot be understood apart from the Middle Ages. No doubt this is true; but, then, as Toynbee admits, Christendom grew out of the Roman civilization, and it would seem difficult to understand Christendom apart from the Roman empire. Of course, a tolerable knowledge of Christendom can be had without paying too much attention to antiquity; but it is similarly true that some understanding of modern civilization can be acquired without much reference to the Middle Ages. The point is this: if a relatively elementary knowledge is satisfactory for one's purposes, the units of study may be relatively short; but the more thorough the understanding needed, the further back in time one must go. The same consideration that led Toynbee to suppress the division between modern and medieval society would, if pressed, remove the division between Christendom and Rome; or, conversely, the need to distinguish between Christendom and Rome, when uniformly recognized, requires a division between medieval and modern societies. This problem of determining the limits of each historical unit is a very perplexing one. The historian cannot look into the year 1066 or 1517 or 410 and see a sign inscribed "Leaving one Society, entering the next." Before one can set the chronological limits of societies, even before one can conclude that there have been several historical societies and not just a single, all-inclusive, human society, it is necessary to know what a society is. And empirical evidence does not produce the needed definition. The problem of chronological limits therefore must be postponed until society is defined.

Toynbee, however, making the natural assumption that there have been several societies, proceeds to formulate the basic law of history. It is to be found in the uniform process by which a later society arises from an earlier one. Since the study of history aims at discovering universal laws, Toynbee wants to show that these successions, these apparentations and affiliations, always occur in the same way. The parent society, split into numerous political divisions, experiences a time of trouble and develops a universal state. Under these conditions an alienated internal proletariat forms a new Church, and an influx of barbarians, the external proletariat, ends the political form of the older society. As an example of this regular process, other than that of the familiar sequence of Roman and Christian societies, the Babylonian-Syriac sequence may be chosen. Toynbee, significantly, is in doubt whether Babylonian society is a separate society or whether it is an epilogue of the Sumeric society; but he gives it the benefit of the doubt. Its time of troubles was the seventh century, issuing in a universal state and a universal peace in the sixth century. Then the new religion, Zoroastrianism, and the Medo-Persian barbarians, as the external proletariat, began the Syriac society. With a church and a barbarian irruption as the criterion of apparentation and affiliation between two societies, it is possible to enumerate nineteen (or twenty-one) civilized societies. Six of these societies are supposed to have emerged from primitive life; the other fifteen arose in the manner just described.

Toynbee's account of how the first six societies emerged from primitive life suffers from an inherent defect, for it seems to depend on the assumption that primitive life is faithfully represented by the savage tribes known in recent times. This is a precarious assumption; at any rate the story of such an emergence, based on analogy, lacking the usual documentary and archaeological evidence, falls short of being a study of history. His general solution, however, is that societies develop because of a challenge and a response. The particular challenge that produced a society directly from this unknown primitive life may have been the increasing aridity of what are now the Arabian and Sahara deserts. Some of the primitive residents of these regions continued to live there, but to do so they had to alter their way of life. Thus they developed a nomadic civilization. Others maintained their way of life by changing their location: these retreated southward into the jungles of Africa and remained primitive. Still others changed both their location and their manner of living: they entered the Nile valley and originated Egyptian civilization. In the case of the fifteen affiliated societies, however, while climatic or geographical conditions sometimes contribute to the result, it is usually the human environment that produces the challenge. A ruling class becomes oppressive and provokes a reaction in the external and internal proletariats.

Society, therefore, is the result of adversity. Ease is unproductive. Toynbee describes in extensive and interesting detail the adversity of tropical climates, of bleak shores, of military defeats, or class penalizations. But there is a limit. The Vikings responded successfully to the challenge of Iceland but failed before the extreme adversity of Greenland. Massachusetts was a severer challange than the Carolinas and evoked a better response, but Labrador proved to be too inhospitable. Now, all this may be true, and yet Toynbee may not have satisfactorily explained the genesis of a society. He notes that the Mayan civilization was a triumph over the tropics, but he does not explain why this adversity no longer stimulates a successful response. A similar question can be asked concerning the Polynesian civilization of Easter Island or the Indic civilization of Ceylon. The adversity remains, but there is no response.

Apparently a response must depend on some human quality — intelligence, morale, or something of the sort, and not alone on geography. Now, if in general the proportion of possible leaders is about the same in all populations, why is there no longer a response? It is true that Toynbee has something to say about creative minorities, and even creative individuals, so that the point is not completely avoided. But in the meantime the inquiry has advanced from the genesis to the growth of civilization. Some civilizations, such as the Eskimo, and Nomad, and the Spartan remain static instead of growing. Others show growth. The question is, Why? Or, perhaps, it is first necessary to show what is meant by growth. Geographical expansion is not growth. Toynbee produces instances of geographical expansion that he considers signs of decay. Nor does growth mean technological improvement and mastery over nature, as other examples show. Instead, growth is a progressive, inward self-determination, a streamlining of the civilization's material and intellectual tools, an "etherealization" of social values. The difficulty with this definition of growth may be seen first of all in a comparison with the rejected definitions. The notion of geographical expansion is clear and distinct: if European customs are being adopted in China, for example, it is obviously a geographical expansion. Similarly, technological improvement and mastery over nature are not too vague for identification. But phrases such as "progressive, inward self-determination" and "etherealization of values" do not permit an easy decision as to whether a given society is still growing or whether it has broken down. Toynbee asserts that the breakdown of Hellenic-Roman civilization occurred at the Peloponnesian War; but is it quite clear that there was no improvement of material and intellectual tools, not to mention etherealization, between 431 B.C. and A.D. 410? Against the less important objection that he puts the end of growth at too early a date, Toynbee defends himself more effectively by remarking that men cease to grow at an early age: after a man reaches twenty or twenty-five, he stops growing — though he may continue to deteriorate for fifty more years before shuffling off this mortal coil. But what growth is, remains unclear. And though it may be granted that nonetheless growth is a fact, is it not important to know what growth is and to determine its empirical limit?

Not only should growth be clearly defined, but also if a successful response to adversity depends on human qualities as was indicated above, it is essential to fix the respective roles of society and of the individual. Which is the more important factor? Which is the basic entity?[7] What precisely is a society? Above it was seen that the chronological limits of societies could not be assigned until a definition of society was accepted. Will this part of Toynbee's argument, approached from the somewhat different angle of the antithesis between a society and an individual, satisfy the previous requirements?

---

7. If anyone should argue that individuals are not real or basic because they cannot exist apart from society, he might be asked whether society is basic because it can exist apart from individuals.

Spengler was taken to task by a reviewer[8] for having neglected to define culture; but he made it abundantly clear that he considered culture or society analogous to an organism. The individual person is little more than a cell in the body social. This biological analogy, so fundamental in Spengler, Toynbee rejects. Sociology, he argues, should invent and employ a terminology proper to itself. When it accepts an analogy from physics and speaks of society as a mechanism, or from biology as Spengler does, or from some forms of psychology or philosophy and speaks of society as a person, or from religion and confuses it with God, it is shutting its eyes to its own ignorance. Analogies, he says, are myths. Unfortunately, however, Toynbee's criticisms apply with equal force to much of his own work. The section now under review concerns the *growth* of civilizations; other sections refer to *abortive* civilizations, *fossilized* relics, and civilizations that are *dead* or *dying*. Moreover he has defended himself against the charge of dating breakdowns too early by appealing to the fact that human organisms do not grow much after their twentieth year. Not only is biological analogy as prevalent in Toynbee as in Spengler, but Toynbee also appeals to physical, electro-magnetic, and mathematical analogies.

However, he does not apply his analogies as Spengler did. Though he sometimes seems in danger of losing the individual, not as a cell in an organism, but as a point in universal space, on the whole he appears to be more individualistic than Spengler. He says,[9] "A human society is in itself... a particular kind of relation between human beings who are not only individuals but are also social animals in the sense that they could not exist at all — or at any rate not humanly — without being in this social relation with one another.... Indeed, societies themselves are simply institutions.... The study of societies and the study of institutions are one and the same thing." It might seem that this account still submerges the

---

8. C. M. Chase, *Sociology and Social Research,* May 1928, pp. 414-420.
9. Arnold J. Toynbee, *A Study of History,* Vol. III, p. 223 (Oxford University Press, 1935).

individual like a cell in an organism. While it is true that human beings cannot exist at all without having had parents, and presumably having parents is a social relationship, beyond that it is not true that men cannot exist at all without being in a social relationship to one another. Let us make a comparison. A red blood corpuscle lives ten days in the blood stream, perhaps one can live thirty days; but if it is removed from the blood stream (and not placed in an equivalent solution), it will die quickly. On the other hand, a man, even though he is removed from society to an uninhabited island (hardly an equivalent solution), can live out his normal span.[10]

On the other hand, it is only just to note that Toynbee continues with a less extreme statement.[11] "The source of social action cannot be the society, but can only be each or some or one of the individuals whose field of action constitutes a society on the ground where they coincide. . . . The society is not and cannot be anything more than a medium of communication through which the individual human beings interact with one another. It is human individuals and not human societies that make human history."

How does this explain the growth of societies? Toynbee holds that the individuals who initiate the growth of a society are more than mere men: they are "superhuman in a literal and no mere metaphorical sense." These superhuman creators of societies are identified as the mystics. Their creative personalities are impelled to recreate ordinary men in their own image. Some of them fail and are martyred. Others succeed and make life intolerable for those who prefer the old customs. A civilization grows therefore when the uncreative majority is willing to follow and imitate the creative personality. Mimesis is one of the ordinary faculties of primitive man, and it is by this that the superior personality is able to drill and regiment his inferiors.

---

10. Conversely, a cell's life can be extended for a great length of time in a solution; but Robinson Crusoe could not have doubled his life span by avoiding Friday and refusing to return to England.

11. *Ibid.* pp. 230-231.

But if civilizations grow, it is also true that they decline and die. Of the twenty-six civilizations, including the arrested civilizations in the number, sixteen are already dead, nine have broken down, and only our own civilization remains alive. Must it too die? In view of the intense interest this question elicits, it will not be amiss to study the argument with a little care, particularly since Toynbee himself gives much more space to the breakdown and disintegration of societies than he does to their growth.

Toynbee professes to be more optimistic than Spengler. Spengler was a determinist: the decline of the west is inevitable. Toynbee, on the other hand, rejects all the deterministic views of the breakdown of societies and tries to allow room for some hope concerning our own. "One of the perennial infirmities of human beings," he writes,[12] "is to ascribe their own failure to the operation of forces which are entirely beyond their control and immeasurably wider in range than the compass of human action." This sentence is a psychological and sophistic preparation for the rejection of inevitability. In expanded form it would run: Men frequently place the blame for their own failure on other factors; the breakdown of civilization is a failure; therefore no factor beyond man's control can have had a determining role. Obviously this invalid argument does not dispose of determinism. Each type of deterministic theory must be examined on its own merits, and this Toynbee proceeds to do.

The theory of cosmic senescence, adopted by Lucretius in his *De Rerum Natura,* to the effect that civilization is breaking down because the world is growing old, is sufficiently refuted by the fact that at least one civilization has been born and has attained stature since Roman times. And, although modern scientists may predict the end of the solar system, the date of that event is so remote that there will be time for the rise and fall of many civilizations. Cosmic senescence is not the cause.

---

12. *Ibid.* Vol. IV, p. 7.

Toynbee also disposes of the dual theory that the rise of civilization is caused by the influx of new barbarian blood and that its later collapse is due to the decadence of an inbred race. The lack of fresh blood in the later Roman empire, so this theory has it, was the cause of social decay; and the earlier vigor of the Roman people came from the racial intermixture at the beginning of Hellenic civilization. Similarly the glories of the Italian renaissance resulted from the infusion of Goth and Lombard blood in the preceeding centuries. In opposition to this theory Toynbee presents empirical evidence. After the Italian renaissance had subsided into a period of decadence, another Risorgimento took place in the nineteenth century without the infusion of any new blood. Its cause is to be found, not in the mixture of races, but in the challenge of military and national humiliation at the hands of Republican and Napoleonic France. Somewhat unfortunately for Toynbee's argument nineteenth century Italy is not a new civilization, and therefore cannot strictly be considered a case in point. Be that as it may, he continues to suggest that the decline of the Roman empire was not due to inbreeding but to militarism, and the renaissance should be traced to mystic supermen like St. Benedict and Pope Gregory the Great instead of the Goths and Lombards. And the original rise of the early Roman people was their response to the challenge of Etruscan colonization. But if Spengler's "eloquence. . . nowhere amounts to proof," one may ask, Does Toynbee's? Or, if Toynbee's assertions are to be accepted, there is another question. What was it that caused the Roman people to respond to this challenge? To say that a civilization arises and grows because of responses to challenges, is to say that the Romans decided to make this latter response. Why did they decide? Did they decide to respond to Etruscan colonization because the inferior majority decided to imitate the superior personalities? This seems to fall a trifle short of explanation for the reason that in some cases majorities do not imitate and the responses do not occur. If the natural potentialities of leadership and imitation occur roughly in the same proportions among all peoples, then a factor must be found present in some cases and absent in others to account for the response. If this factor cannot be found, the explanation amounts to saying that civilizations grow and die because they grow and die.

Although Toynbee has made a good case against attributing cultural breakdowns to cosmic senescence, and has perhaps damaged the idea of physical deterioration due to inbreeding, this refutation of two or three types of determinism does not suffice for a general refutation of determinism. It does not disprove the inevitability of western collapse. Particularly interested in physical deterioration, he seems to have over-looked or minimized the possibilty that civilizations are predestined to die because of moral deterioration. Toynbee's chapter therefore fails to establish its conclusion that we are not confronted with any *Saeva Necessitas* and that our society is not inexorably doomed. Of course the fact that twenty-five civilizations are dead or dying does not *prove,* as Toynbee jubilantly insists, that the twenty-sixth must die; but the empirical evidence hardly constitutes "a message of encouragement for us children of the Western Civilization as we drift today alone . . . with none but stricken civilizations around us."[13]

The net result of the discussion so far may seem somewhat discouraging. Determinism has not been refuted, nor has it been established. Spengler has made plausible and stimulating remarks and Toynbee has contradicted him in a most impressive and persuasive manner. Neither of the two seems to have proved anything. Analogies cannot be trusted and empirical evidence is not decisive. Perhaps then one should not entertain too great hope that Toynbee, after rejecting all deterministic solutions, can successfully explain the breakdown of civilizations.

Since the rise and growth of civilization is to be explained by the mass imitation of the leaders, the breakdown of civilization is caused by the refusal to imitate. This will occur when the leaders impatiently exchange the pipe of persuasion for

13. *Ibid.* Vol. IV, p. 38.

the whip of compulsion. They thereby produce a resentful proletariat, and the society loses its capacity for self-determination.
The change in the attitude and methods of the leaders, is,
strange to say, a natural result of their former successes. A
victorious group seldom is victorious again. South Carolina
and Virginia, leaders before the Civil War, failed to recover;
while the previously undistinguished North Carolina took their
place. Or, sometimes the leaders may exhaust their energy
in military conquest. The Assyrians were ruined, not because
they allowed their armor to rust, but because they wore it out.
And similarly in the non-military sphere, the Hildebrandine
Papacy, after raising itself from the depths to the heights,
failed because, intoxicated with its own success, it used its
political weapons in pursuit of inordinate aims. But once
again, is not this merely a statement that civilizations decay
because they decay? Is not the change of attitude on the part
of the superior social leaders itself decay? Is not the pursuit
of inordinate aims a result rather than the cause of a breakdown? Is it not at least the early stages of the breakdown?
And if so, must not some deeper cause be sought? Racial inbreeding and the need of new blood may not be that cause, but
could there not be a psychological or moral flaw in human
nature itself that causes some to rest on their oars and others
to pursue inordinate aims? And if this is a possibility, is it
not also possible that societies, whose source of activity lies
in individuals, are fated to die by reason of their constituent
elements? And then, if so, Western Civilization must inevitably collapse like the rest.

Determinism and inevitability often elicit an emotional
antipathy. And it is said that a belief in the inevitable collapse
of western civilization results in supine apathy. But at any
rate there is no reason to believe that pessimism, if this is
pessimism, is any more paralyzing than optimism. If it is
asserted that the belief in the inevitable is inconsistent with
effort, the belief in inevitable perfection may prove more en-
ervating than the belief in inevitable cultural defeat. The
theory of progress could easily acquire popularity by an appeal

to men's good opinion of themselves. Inevitable collapse cannot make that appeal, and because of western civilization's love of material comforts, there is an unwillingness to face unpleasant realities.[14] People want to shut their eyes to collapse, but the signs have so multiplied that, inevitable or not, there is a growing belief that collapse is a fact. Perhaps some of the blindness to the fact of collapse is the picturesque quality of our language. When a building collapses, it falls down, altogether, suddenly, in one grand crash, and its dust soars upward and slowly settles. Society is not so spectacular. As long as there is food in the grocery store, as long as the utilities function, as long as the police keep a semblance of order, the society has not evidently collapsed. But if this is what is meant by collapse, no society has ever collapsed. There has never been a time when the entire population was without food and water, or when there was a complete absence of order. At times civil war and barbarian invasion have seriously disturbed the order, but, to quote a less than profound statement, "Society has always survived." The human race has always survived — so far; but the integrated society, in the sense that there have been several different societies in history, has not always survived. All but one or a few have collapsed. Like a building, providing we can escape the evils of analogy, society is bound together by many girders, beams, joists, and planks. Some of these may loosen without an evident crash; and even after the crash the debris may reveal a number of jointed combinations. The termites on one of these jointed pieces may still optimistically believe there has been no collapse. It is this condition that the mid-twentieth century seems to be facing.

An Appraisal

The most obvious evidences of a present social breakdown are of course the two world wars and the rumors of the third.

---

14. Winston Churchill, in *The Gathering Storm,* underlines this unwillingness and stupidity on the part of the British and Americans after World War I. It is nothing to be compared with the stupidity and blindness, particularly of America, following World War II.

However, the physical destruction of cities, factories and homes, the casualties not only in battle but by disease and famine, and the dislocation of populations are by no means the only or even the most important evidences of the end of western civilization. They are merely the most obvious to astigmatic believers in progress. Not every war, to be sure, heralds the end of a civilization, and some people are willing to suppose that our present troubles are no more serious than the Franco-Prussian War or the conflict between England and France during the Middle Ages. Can one be safe in such a comfortable opinion? Pitirim A. Sorokin, professor of sociology at Harvard University, has endeavored to compare the degrees of destruction caused by 967 wars from 500 B.C. to A.D. 1925. His bases of comparison are the casualties per million of the populations, the size of the armies, and the duration of the conflict. By these means he calculates a numerical indicator of war magnitude for every century.[15] The results show that the first century of our era was the most peaceful of all; thirteenth century Europe was also an age of peace; and the nineteenth was a notable improvement over the two preceeding. But the first quarter of the twentieth century, by itself, was more warlike than any hundred years except the third century B.C. in Italy; and if the second quarter should be figured in, even the third century in Italy would seem relatively peaceful. On this showing, our present troubles are no ordinary troubles. Wars and brutality are not new to mankind; on the contrary they seem to result from a permanent element in human nature. Roman slavery, the Spanish Inquisition, and the Thirty Years War are ugly commentaries on man, but at least some of these evils occurred when a society was apparently in vigorous growth. It is therefore not the mere fact of war, but its much deeper bite into the social organism that is evidence of the end of an age.

War, however, is only one example of a more general condition. War is a species, as it were, of a wider genus, and that genus is brutality. Accordingly one may list widespread bru-

---

15. *The Crisis of Our Age*, pp. 213 ff. (T. P. Dutton & Co. 1942).

tality as an evidence of social disintegration.[16] War is always brutal, and the civilian population usually suffers; but a large amount of twentieth century brutality lacks all claim to military necessity. So much has occurred that the individual instances are quickly forgotten — new and worse brutality makes the earlier cases stale news. The rape of Nanking was described in *The Reader's Digest* of July 1938. The depravity of the 'superior' and scientific Nazis filled the newspapers at the time of the Nürnberg trials. Communism has been consistently worse from the first, far surpassing the more trivial and more stupid brutality of the Czars.[17]

Americans naturally think that Americans are better. And it may be gratefully admitted that the same amount of brutality has not been perpetrated here yet. But the pathway of brutality has been entered with the consequent weakening of laws and order. Membership in labor unions sometimes has been recruited by organized violence. Some strikes have approached the proportion of insurrection. Unions have even defended violence in the courts, until in the case of the Southern Cotton Oil Co. of North Little Rock, Ark., the United States Supreme Court ruled: "It is no abridgment of free speech or assembly for the criminal sanctions of the state to fasten themselves upon one who has actively and consciously assisted in promoting, encouraging, and aiding an assemblage the purpose of which is to wreak violence."

But if the philosophy of history shows that there are signs of decaying civilizations, and if violence and brutality are symptomatic of the end, then the thoughtful observer is in a position not merely to describe the ancient past but to make a plausible prediction as to the near future.

There are evidences of civilization's imminent collapse other than physical brutality, for brutality is a species of the wider genus of coercion. Many people, though strongly opposed

16. Lewis Mumford, *Saturday Review of Literature*, June 26, 1948, makes this point by comparing this century with last century, in an interesting article that painfully understates the case.

17. *Cf.* William C. Bullitt, *The Great Globe Itself*, pp. 50, 76, 80. (Charles Scribner's Sons, 1946).

to armed revolution, view with complacency the accomplishing of the same results by means short of violence. By this attitude they condone a coercion that is equally destructive of the best phases of western culture.

Socialistic coercion and the destruction of freedom in the United States is following the more advanced programs of the European nations. In the nineteenth century the memory of autocracy was vivid, and after several nations had rid themselves of tyranny, the acknowledged aim of government was to maintain order so that free individuals could arrange their personal, social, business, and religious affairs as they saw fit. Today, however, the disadvantages of absolute government have been forgotten, and so-called liberals, who are truly reactionaries, aim to establish a so-called democracy on the principles of Louis XIV. To this end taxation is imposed, not so much to pay for legitimate governmental expenses, not on the basis of services rendered and received, but with the avowed aim of impoverishing one class of people and of enriching another class. One might say that taxation is becoming legalized theft. These apostles of absolutism propose the reconstruction of society according to their own superior ideals. And one by one the liberties that were gained a century or two ago are being lost to governmental coercion. The public school systems are being used more and more as propaganda agencies for this reactionary totalitarianism. Even such a scholarly journal as *The American Political Science Review* has contributors[18] who want the state supported schools to indoctrinate their pupils.

As the love of liberty grows dim under socialistic suffocation, as coercion increases, the more brutal it will become. The basic methods of procedure were stated by Karl Marx, and they have been accepted, in varying degrees, by many who are not conscious of their origin. Marx was deeply interested in progress, and for him misery is a powerful instrument for

18. Feb. 1948, p. 74; June 1948, p. 542; *cf.* the concrete proposal to use the schools as propaganda agencies for Proportional Representation in New York City, Dec. 1948, p. 1148.

gaining one's goal. Tension and antagonism, the result of misery, are forces of progress. For this reason a clever social planner will provoke violence and bloody conflicts. Happy men are weak, but if they can be made wretched, they can be stirred to action. Class must be played against class and hatred must be stimulated. The economy of nations must be ruined by huge governmental expenditures that lead to bankruptcy. Demagogues, willing to be looked on as God, will deceive the people with impossible promises of freedom from want and freedom from fear. Then a dictator can liquidate the remaining opposition and take control.

The evidences of social decay in western civilization have been listed in an order proceeding from the more specific to the more general, from the more obvious to the less obvious, and from the more derivative to the more original. The next and nearly the last of these, the widest genus of all, is immorality. The word immorality frequently directs attention to sexual offenses; and while this is not the only sense intended, the sexual aspect need not be overlooked. One of our most serious calamities, more deadly to civilization than any ordinary war, is the destruction of the family by the growing rate of divorce. Some people view divorce as a sign of the emancipation of woman and as an evidence of progress. And the accompanying promiscuity, both result and cause, would be another step in the evanescence of evil. Edwin A Burtt[19] refers to some members of this humanistic school of thought who regard sex as an essentially harmless pleasure which should be regulated only by personal taste. Divorce and promiscuity are empirical facts, but there are other interpretations besides that of humanism. Sorokin, believing that the family exercises a powerful social function, and that the destruction of the family by divorce is an equally powerful factor of opposite tendency, writes:

"An illiterate society can survive, but a thoroughly antisocial society cannot. Until recently the family ... was the principal school of socialization for the new-born human

19. *Types of Religious Philosophy*, p. 382 (Harper & Brothers, 1939).

animals, rendering them fit for social life. At present this vital mission is performed less and less by the family ... because the young are turned over at a very early age to such agencies as nursery schools and kindergartens, and because an increasingly unstable family is a poor school of socialization. Instead of inculcating in its offspring a strong sense of moral and social integrity, it teaches them lessons of moral laxity and loose relationships. ... If outside agencies performed efficiently the former functions of the family, the defect might be remedied. Unfortunately, they have not successfully replaced the family in this mission. Even an illiterate mother, endowed with kindness and common sense, appears to have been a better moral educator of children than most of the highly trained educators of schools and correctional institutions. The result is a rapidly mounting juvenile delinquency, an increasing number of people without moral integrity ... who swell the ranks of criminals ... from common murderers to the praetorian guards of the dictators."[20] Corroborating Sorokin, F. B. I. reports released in 1948 include these data:

Fifteen million sex magazines read monthly by a third of the nation,

One million girls infected with social disease.

One hundred thousand girls enter white slavery each year.

One million babies born illegitimately yearly.

One in five marriages ends in divorce.

More barmaids than college girls.

One murder every forty minutes.

One major crime every twenty-two seconds.

One hundred thousand unapprehended murderers walk the streets.

Seventeen-year-olds represent the largest criminal group.

Sixty suicides every day.

Suicide is also a moral problem, a form of immorality, and it is a sympton of the whole situation. Sorokin is particularly thorough in his attempt to show the breakdown of western civilization in many phases. He notes that popular religion

20. Sorokin, *op. cit.* pp. 190-191.

has degenerated into a second-hand social gospel, a sort of political creed. He analyzes contemporary art and compares it with the past; he examines the course of philosophy; and he tries to make clear the significance of the present rate of insanity and suicide. In the United States from 1860 to 1922 suicide increased from 3.1 per hundred thousand population to 11.9. And since 1922 the rate of suicide has doubled and tripled. With suicide, and with the breakup of the family, there is the increase of mental disease. "This means," he says, "that western society is progressively becoming mentally deranged and morally unbalanced."[21]

When the citizens of a nation are immoral, it is not surprising that the government becomes immoral. And turning again from the basic individual decay to its more obvious results, we may once more quote Sorokin.

"There exists scarcely a single government in any of the western countries which has not broken most of its solemn pledges to the citizens — which has not changed the fundamental laws (whether constitutions or statutes) or repudiated its obligations respecting the gold currency, gold certificates, and bonds, the inviolability of the courts, and countless other matters."[22]

Under these conditions mutual trust becomes less and less possible; respect for just government tends to be replaced by fear of force; and the majority begins to seize the temporary advantage of the day. In other words, society has collapsed. There are many people, naturally, who will disagree with all this. They will point out that through this discussion some moral preferences have been discerned between the lines. The facts may have been relatively accurate, but a non-empirical interpretation has been placed upon them. It is exactly this interpretation that is the most serious matter of dispute. One party calls it the breakdown of society; the other hails it as the fulfilment of their hopes. The one idealizes freedom; the other idealizes tyranny. The one allows each

21. *Op. cit.*, p. 225.
22. *Op. cit.*, p. 201.

individual to make his own most important decisions; the other is sure the leader knows best. A decision on these two interpretations cannot be settled by an appeal to facts. There is involved a moral and normative judgment; and before a philosophy of history can be satisfactorily established, it will be necessary to erect some system of morality as its foundation. No theory of history rests on an empirical basis; no theory of history can dispense with the underlying phases of philosophy. And the phase to which attention has now been directed is that of morality or ethics. But this crucial subject must be postponed to a later chapter.

The Significance of History

In the meantime, within the narrower scope of a philosophy of history, there is another problem more important than morphology and breakdown. The discovery, if such it be, that societies rise and fall in similar stages is interesting enough, but what does it signify? What does it all mean?

Significance should be sharply distinguished from description. A watch, a radio, an auto can be accurately described in a blue-print; but the blue-print tells nothing of the value, the importance, or the use of the object. In the preceding pages there has been some description of contemporary conditions. No one is likely to quarrel too much with the description; but the significance of the facts, the implications that were drawn, the interpretation that was imposed on the description may have evoked vigorous opposition. It is clear, therefore, that so long as Spengler and Toynbee describe the similarities of cultural change, their writings may be stimulating, their descriptions may be accurate, and yet the really important questions may remain unanswered. Suppose it is true that one society gives birth to a second and then dies. Is this any more important than the fact that one generation of mosquitoes gives birth to another generation of mosquitoes, and then another, and another? What is the end of all this? Is there any end? The question, Does history repeat itself? must therefore give way to the deeper question, Does history have any significance?

Karl Marx and Bertrand Russell give an essentially negative answer. Russell in eloquent, rolling periods prophesies the cosmic death that will extinguish all human hopes and fears. It is one of the impressive passages in literature, and one of the most dismal. [23]

"That man is the product of causes which had no prevision of the end they were achieving; that his origin, his growth, his hopes and fears, his loves and his beliefs, are but the outcome of accidental collocations of atoms; that no fire, no heroism, no intensity of thought and feeling, can preserve an individual life beyond the grave; that all the labours of the ages, all the devotion, all the inspiration, all the noonday brightness of human genius, are destined to extinction in the vast death of the solar system, and the whole temple of Man's achievement must inevitably be buried beneath the debris of a universe in ruins — all these things, if not quite beyond dispute, are yet so nearly certain, that no philosophy which rejects them can hope to stand. Only within the scaffolding of these truths, only on the firm foundation of unyielding despair, can the soul's habitation henceforth be safely built. . . .

"Brief and powerless is Man's life; on him and all his race the slow, sure doom falls pitiless and dark. Blind to good and evil, reckless of destruction, omnipotent matter rolls on its relentless way; for Man, condemned today to lose his dearest, tomorrow himself to pass through the gate of darkness, it remains only to cherish, ere yet the blow falls, the lofty thoughts that ennoble his little day; . . . proudly defiant of the irresistible forces that tolerate, for a moment, his knowledge and his condemnation, to sustain alone, a weary but unyielding Atlas, the world that his own ideals have fashioned despite the trampling march of unconscious power."

Brief mention should also be made of the more optimistic views of the Stoics of antiquity and of Nietzsche of the last century. In neither of these philosophies was cosmic death to wipe out the human race. They held that after world

---

23. Bertrand Russell, *Mysticism and Logic,* pp. 47-48, 56-57 (Longmans, Green and Company 1925).

history is completed, the show, like a reel of motion pictures, will be given over again with every detail just as it was before, and so on for endlessly recurring cycles.

But is a theory of eternal recurrence any more optimistic than cosmic death? Can history have any significance either in Russell's view or in Nietzsche's? Whether we shall dissolve into atoms with nothing remaining of human hopes, fears, joys, and sorrows, or whether we fight World War I and World War II and World War III, only to fight them over again next time — in either case history can have no purpose. Neither view is entirely inspiring.

Now it may possibly be that pessimism is the final word. And, since the theory of endless cycles is not popular in contemporary thought, it may possibly be that the human race exists only to meet complete and ultimate frustration. It may possibly be that history is devoid of significance. At any rate, the twentieth century is producing a number of pessimistic philosophers.[24] But before adopting this dreary view of things, before basing one's life on unyielding despair, would it not be wise to ask whether there are any other possible theories? Should it not at least be asked what is assumed or presupposed by a theory that gives significance to history? How could it possibly be known whether human life has meaning and value, unless the more hopeful as well as the more pessimistic view be considered?

This is not yet the place to decide whether pessimism or optimism is true. The precise question at this point is merely, What must be true if history and humanity are to be meaningful? What is the presupposition of significance?

An approach to the solution of this problem can be made by noting what denials led to the position that life is meaningless. The pessimistic theories deprived man of significance by denying that history has a goal. In the philosophies canvassed,

24. W. T. Stace, *Man Against Darkness*, The Atlantic Monthly, September 1948; Jean-Paul Sartre, the existentialist, as well as Bertrand Russell, both of whom Stace mentions; Joseph Wood Krutch, *The Modern Temper* and other writings. Such a list of pessimists could be considerably extended.

the human race was doomed to extinction and oblivion, or else it was condemned to repeat and repeat the events of this world in cycles without end. Conversely, therefore, if significance is to be assigned to human history, extinction and oblivion cannot be the end. Nor will a theory of cycles suffice. There must be a goal. Significance requires a purpose for which history takes place, and a purpose or a goal is the prerequisite for assigning a value to life. This was argued somewhat in the discussion on progress. Progress is possible only when there is a goal. Whether the world has made progress or not, and whether the nineteenth century notion of progress is to be accepted or some other very different notion of progress, the point here is that if there is to be progress of any sort whatever, there must be a goal toward which someone is progressing.

This goal cannot be merely the end of a cycle that is to be repeated again. It is foolish to assert that Sisyphus was making progress. A true goal is final, ultimate, and permanent. Accordingly, if history is to be granted significance, something must happen once for all. The end is a unique event, and the whole historical process that leads up to the end consists in a series of unique events. There may be similarities in history. One civilization may very well pass through stages that are similar to the stages of another civilization. In this sense history may repeat itself. But Cyrus, and Alexander, and Caesar, and Napoleon lived only once. And it is only an end or goal that can give significance to these unique events.

The implications of this conception should not be overlooked, for there is involved a basic point of division between two radically different types of philosophy. One type of philosophy centers its interest on sameness, similarity, and repetition. It is often called a "scientific" viewpoint. As science describes the similarity among all pendulums — that their periods are proportional to the square roots of their lengths — and disregards their differences — the weight of the bob and the thickness of its string — so this type of philosophy considers unique events unimportant and endeavors to formulate "laws" that describe the similarities and repetitions in its subject matter. Spengler makes a point of distinguishing this "scientific" view from what he calls the "historical" way of looking at the world, and he notes that the Greeks, who were so thoroughly scientific, paid no attention to a theory of history. Some of them, like Plato and Aristotle, were interested in theories of politics, and when they traced the development of political institutions they perforce mentioned historical antecedents. But they had no theory of history. So lacking in an historical sense were the Greeks that their best historian, Thucydides, asserts that nothing of importance happened prior to the Peloponnesian War. This scientific, non-historical viewpoint has also dominated modern times. One of its best expressions comes from Spinoza, who is interested in showing its implications for religion.[25]

"The truth of a historical narrative, however assured, cannot give us the knowledge nor consequently the love of God, for love of God springs from knowledge of him, and *knowledge of him should be derived from general ideas,* in themselves certain and known, so that the truth of a historical narrative is very far from being a necessary requisite for our attaining our highest good."

It is because of this very basic judgment that modern times have been slow in producing a philosophy of history. While Hegel may be credited as the first to study history philosophically, and while Marx had some definite ideas on the laws of history, they barely made a beginning. The serious and detailed study of history awaited the twentieth century. But the hidden presuppositions of these studies necessitated the repulsive conclusions of the previous discussion. It was assumed that a description of similarities would be a satisfactory philosophy of history. It was assumed silently that there is no goal.[26] And although Spengler rejects the scientific view

---

25. Spinoza, *Tractatus Theologico-Politicus*, chapter IV.
26. Hegel may be said to have had a goal, and even Marx set a goal of political and social evolution; but later views became more "scientific."

in favor of the historical view, he as well as Toynbee provides no basis for assigning significance to a unique event.

A Christian Philosophy of History

If it now be wise to compare these conclusions with an opposing theory, the quotation from Spinoza provides a hint as to where to look. It was the scientific secularism of Spinoza, of Marx, of Russell that assured men of final frustration. If this is the result of secularism, the opposing philosophy must be found in religion; and the religion must be an historical religion. Spinoza and the ancient Greeks both had a religion. The word is very broad. It can include the melancholy fervor of Russell and the brutal frenzy of Marx. The argument requires a particular type of religion, best exemplified in Christianity. The argument does not aim to *prove* or *demonstrate* that Christianity is true and that Russell is wrong. The precise aim is to show in both cases what assumptions and what conclusions are consistent with each other. The aim is to compare the theory that begins with the denial of value to unique events and ends in despair with the theory that assumes a goal and on this basis asserts the significance of history. Which assumption is true is another matter; and if they are really first principles, neither of them can be demonstrated. Each person must look at the two world-pictures and make his choice.

In contrast to secular philosophy, Christianity has always emphasized history. Of course the events of the gospel story have formed a large part of Christian preaching, and the events of the Old Testament too. But in addition to a recital of events, Christianity has taught a philosophy of history. The events are emphasized because in them Christianity finds the clew to all significance and value. It could hardly be otherwise. If the second person of the Triune God actually became flesh and dwelt amongst us, and died on the cross for men, that event would naturally overshadow every other aspect of the world, scientific or historical. And such a descent of Deity into human affairs would not only involve a theory of history logically, but must psychologically provoke some general reflection on history. Both logically and actually therefore Christianity has a philosophy of history.

Prior to an exposition of this philosophy, a preliminary statement should be made as to what Christianity is. Various definitions of this religion are current, some of them in fairly sharp contrast with others. One popular statement is that Christianity is a life, not a doctrine. But if Christianity has no doctrine, that is, if it has nothing definite to teach, can it even teach that one sort of life is better than another? A life without doctrine verges on insanity; at best it would be a desultory life without conviction or purpose. This has not been characteristic of the outstanding Christian leaders through nineteen centuries. It may then be suggested that Christianity is the life and the doctrine of the people who today call themselves Christians. And they call themselves Christian because they have historical and cultural ties with people in earlier centuries who called themselves Christian. To be sure the doctrines that were held in the fifth or fifteenth century may now be largely discarded, but the historic continuity of the Christian church as an institution justifies, so it is said, the use of the term Christianity to designate the life and doctrine of the twentieth-century church, regardless of its differences from other ages and regardless of the differences that exist among the churches today. Historical continuity is the criterion.

A similar situation is found in the history of Platonism. Plato founded an Academy that continued in corporate existence for nine centuries. The doctrine with which Plato made his Academy famous was the theory of Ideas. He asserted the existence of unchangeable, supersensible realities beyond this visible world of flux. Knowledge, he taught, is a grasp of these Ideas. The physical world, on the other hand, is constantly changing, and therefore science is not knowledge but opinion — it is tentative, not fixed. Both in the relatively early dialogue *Meno,* 98 b, in the middle masterpiece, the

Republic, 478, 508, 534, and in the late dialogue *Timaeus,* 28 a, 29 b-c, Plato insists that the distinction between knowledge and opinion is no bare conjecture with him, but a basic principle. But two centuries later the Platonic Academy under Arcesilaus and Carneades had decided that the theory of Ideas was not essential to Platonism: the essential value of Platonism was to be found in its skeptical tendencies in physical science. Truth, they argued, cannot be attained; and no definite assertions should be insisted upon. This skeptical Academy of the second and first centuries was undoubtedly the corporate successor to Plato and his pupils. There had been unbroken continuity. But to call their skeptical views Platonism would empty the word of all meaning — except that of historical continuity. To some people this seems legitimate, but to others Platonism is a definite theory of Ideas. Wherever that theory is found, with or without institutional continuity, it is Platonism; and wherever it is not found, particularly wherever skepticism is professed, there is no Platonism, no matter how strict the apostolic succession.

Similarly, if the term Christianity is to have any definite meaning, if it is not to be applied to theories or to manners of life that are in direct opposition to each other, some criterion must be chosen other than the historical continuity of socal groups. There are people who deny that Christ is the second Person of the Trinity, and yet they call themselves Christians. Following the assassination of Gandhi, various religious editors called him the outstanding Christian of the age — and this in spite of his Hindu beliefs and background. Such shifting and confusion does not aid clarity of thought. A criterion must be chosen on the basis of which Christianity can be distinguished from Hinduism and every other form of paganism. The problem is both difficult and easy. But the part that seems easy to one person seems difficult to another. When C. E. M. Joad[27] attempts to define Christianity, his approach may seem easy, and no doubt he thinks it is the only reasonable one. He argues, "Unfortunately, as the critic of Christianity

27. *God and Evil,* p. 285. (Harper & Brothers, 1943).

quickly finds to his cost, whatever statement he does take
[as definitive of Christianity] is certain to be assailed by objections from some quarter on the score that it is not an
accurate representation of Christian doctrine.... How is he
to avoid this difficulty? Since with the best will in the world
he cannot avoid it completely, he must make do with the
best contemporary statement he can get." This easy solution,
however, faces two difficulties, one of which may prove insuperable. The lesser of the two difficulties is the choice of
a contemporary statement in preference to a fourth- or six-
teenth-century statement. Wherein lies the compulsion to
choose a twentieth century statement when the older ones
have been so much more carefully prepared? The second and
greater difficulty is how to determine which of the many contemporary and contradictory statements is the best. One
eminent, contemporary archbishop said that if his views were
the views of another eminent contemporary archbishop, he
would in simple honesty leave the ecclesiastical body of which
they were both members. Is it not obvious that before one
can choose between two incompatible contemporary statements
of what Christianity is, one must have a criterion by which
to judge? Joad's solution therefore, is not an easy solution;
it is difficult, one may say impossible.

There is another solution that is also easy and difficult.
It is easy because it is reasonable both systematically and
historically. It will not be universally accepted, for as has
been shown, the most antithetical views are labeled Christian;
but it does not shock common sense or historical sense; it is
plausible; and it avoids the difficulties of the other definitions.
Christianity, then, is simply what the Bible teaches. The
volume of objection to this definition swells before one can
examine its implications. The voices ask, Have not the
churches differed very materially on this point? Was not
that the exact difficulty with all the contemporary statements?
Now, it must be admitted that this easy solution is difficult.
But though there are difficulties, they are not the exact difficulties that condemned contemporary statements. The previous

difficulty was that the contemporary statements — of Gandhi, of Oxnam, of Manning, of Walter A. Maier, and of two archbishops — are mutually contradictory. What the Federal Council of Churches calls Christianity, and what the American Council of Churches calls Christianity are two radically antagonistic religions. But if Christianity is all these things, the term has no definite meaning at all. This method of attacking the problem is therefore not merely difficult, it is logically impossible. To define Christianity as what the Bible teaches, has its obvious difficulties; but it is not logically impossible. The difficulty is of another kind. To use Plato again as an illustration: Platonism is reasonably defined as what Plato taught. The contemporary scholars present various opinions as to the meaning of several passages in the dialogues. These disagreements may not be so radical as are the disagreements among contemporary statements of Christianity, for the issues involved are not so vital; but none the less the views on dialogues like *Timaeus* or *Parmenides* vary considerably. In such a situation the contemporary scholar attempts to show from Plato's text that he has caught the meaning, and he stands by his arguments. Is it not similarly the scholarly thing to do to work out the detailed exposition of Christianity by a careful study of the text? The difficulties should not be minimized; but neither should the responsibility be shirked, for only by this method can the contradictions and confusions of contemporary statements be authoritatively evaluated. While the Christian position on history, politics, and ethics, here pictured to form a contrast with secularism, does not reproduce all the details of exegetical study, the general argument is based on this procedure.

Christianity, thus defined, not only contains a philosophy of history, but so prominent is this theme in the Bible that few members of the Christian Church have been unaware of it. It was therefore as natural as it was fortunate that early in the history of the Church one of the greatest Christian scholars undertook the exposition of the Biblical theory of history.

Prompted by the pagan reproach that the sack of Rome in A.D. 410 was a punishment for having forsaken the old gods in favor of Christianity, St. Augustine worked for thirteen years to produce his massive *City of God.*

While it was an historical event that first called forth the effort, and while the situation required an interpretation of history, St. Augustine did not consider his work as narrowly confined to the philosophy of history. Its immense scope enabled him to examine the presuppositions of this theory of history and thus to produce a general defense of Christian philosophy in most of its divisions. The first of these presuppositions, in fact the first of all Christian principles, is the Being and Nature of God. A philosophy that is based on the existence of God will differ throughout from a philosophy that has no place for God; and similarly two systems that do not agree as to what sort of Being God is, will also differ in all their details. Augustine therefore had to distinguish the Christian conception of God from the popular Roman polytheism and from the philosophic One of Neoplatonism.

The different conception of God begins to affect the philosophy of history with the doctrine of creation. None of the Greek philosophies had any notion of creation. Aristotle earlier and Plotinus[28] later both argued for the eternity of the world. Christianity on the other hand teaches that God created the world out of nothing at a point in the finite past. This is an event which happened just once and forms the temporal basis of all those unique events of history to which Christianity attaches so much significance. The concept of creation therefore produces a worldview in which humanity plays the central role while nature is the stage setting, as opposed to Greek and all other naturalism in which man is a minor detail.

Since God created Adam and Eve as the one original pair, the human race would normally form one society. But because Adam sinned, the condition of man is not now normal. Sin

28. *Cf.* the author's *Plotinus on the Eternity of the World,* The Philosophical Review, March 1949, pp. 130-140.

warps human nature with the result that all men become more or less antisocial, making coercive civil government necessary; and the race, instead of forming one society, is divided into two *cities,* the city of this world and the City of God. These two societies, though they have certain temporal conditions in common, differ in their motives, their aims, and their principles; the destinies of the two cities are likewise different.

"Accordingly, two cities have been formed by two loves: the earthly by the love of self, even to the contempt of God; the heavenly by the love of God, even to the contempt of self. The former, in a word, glories in itself, the latter in the Lord. For the one seeks glory from men; but the greatest glory of the other is God, the witness of conscience. The one lifts up its head in its own glory; the other says to its God, 'Thou art my glory, and the lifter up of mine head.' In the one, the princes and the nations it subdues are ruled by the love of ruling; in the other, the princes and the subjects serve one another in love, the latter obeying, while the former take thought for all. The one delights in its own strength, represented in the persons of its rulers; the other says to its God, 'I will love Thee, O Lord, my strength.' And therefore the wise men of the one city, living according to man, have sought for profit to their own bodies or souls, or both, and those who have known God 'glorified Him not as God, neither were thankful, but became vain in their imaginations, and their foolish heart was darkened; professing themselves to be wise,' that is, glorying in their own wisdom, and being possessed by pride, 'they became fools, and changed the glory of the incorruptible God into an image made like to corruptible man, and to birds, and four-footed beasts, and creeping things.' For they were either leaders or followers of the people in adoring images, 'and worshipped and served the creature more than the Creator, who is blessed for ever.' But in the other city there is no human wisdom, but only godliness, which offers due worship to the true God, and looks for its reward in the society of the saints, of holy angels as well as holy men, 'that God may be all in all.' "[29]

Only under one of two conditions, neither of them actual, could the human race be considered one society. If Adam had not sinned, all men would have been members of a universal brotherhood. Presumably also there would have been but one society, had not God graciously established his better City. Every system of philosophy that views all men as brothers must either be blind to sin or ignorant of God's grace. At any rate, the popular contemporary statements about the universal Fatherhood of God and the universal Brotherhood of Man are the antithesis of Christianity. Far from teaching that God is the Father of all men, the Bible poses as a most important problem how men may *become* the children of God. The authority or power to become the children of God is a gift, and this gift is given to those who believe on Christ, and to believe requires a new birth, not of the will of man, but of God.[30] In other places entrance into the family of God is explained under the figure of adoption. Naturally men are born children of wrath and stand in need of the Spirit of adoption who enables them to call God Father.[31] And Jesus himself pointedly asserts that God is not the Father of the Pharisees and that the devil is.[32] In view of Jesus' many statements about outer darkness, weeping and gnashing of teeth, the worm that dieth not and the fire that is not quenched, the great gulf that separates the rich man from Lazarus, and in view of Jesus' own statement of what he himself shall say at the day of Judgment, to wit, "Depart from me, ye cursed, into everlasting fire prepared for the devil and his angels,"[33] in view of such repeated statements, a theology of the universal Fatherhood of God, denying as it does the reality of hell, is even farther removed from Christianity than the skeptical

29. *The City of God*, XIV 28.
30. John 1:12, 13. *Cf. City of God* XII 21-23; XIV 1.
31. Ephesians 2:3; Romans 8:15; Galatians 4:5.
32. John 8:42-44.
33. Mt. 8:12; 22:13; Mk. 9:44; Lk. 16:19-33; Mt. 25:41.

Academy was removed from Platonism. The two cities therefore are most clearly distinguished in their separate destinies.

The special people who are citizens of the City of God derive their rights as citizens through their personal relationship to the person and work of Christ. Again, as was said before, the incarnation, the crucifixion, and the resurrection of Christ are unique events, and on them the significance of history turns. Quite in opposition to Spinoza, Christianity is not a religion of universal, abstract propositions alone. Christianity indeed requires the assertion of several eternal, unchangeable truths, but the greatest distinction between Plato and Christ is not some theory of Ideas or some philanthropic platitudes. The great difference lies in the fact that Plato himself is not, and Christ himself is, a part of his message. The truth contains a unique historical element — the works but especially the person of Christ. In the sermon on the Mount, Jesus' teaching is not confined to general abstractions; but, as Plato never said, Jesus insists, "Blessed are ye when men shall . . . say all manner of evil against you falsely *for my sake*." And, "Whoever therefore shall be ashamed of *me* and of *my* word in this adulterous and sinful generation, of him also shall the Son of Man be ashamed when he cometh in the glory of his Father with the holy angels." And, "Depart from *me* . . . *I* never knew you." It is not possible to examine the complex of ideas that go by the name of the Messianic consciousness, but its relation to a philosophy of history, as opposed to Spinozism, is unmistakeable.[34]

Since Augustine's *City of God* touches on so many points, not all immediately connected with the philosophy of history, it might be better to go behind Augustine to his source and, more by way of summary than by way of addition, formulate from the text of the Bible the most general and most important historical principles. No doubt the material can finally be put

---

34. *Cf.* J. N. Figgis, *The Political Aspects of St. Augustine's City of God*, p. 34; J. Gresham Machen, *The Christian Faith in the Modern World*, pp. 160-187; Geerhardus Vos, *The Self Disclosure of Jesus*, pp. 61-62 and *passim*.

in one completely general formula, but it is convenient first to divide it into three closely related statements.

First, God controls history. This is indicated in great detail by explicit statements relative to particular events.[35] There are also many statements of limited generality.[36] And there are numerous statements of complete generality, such as "The Lord bringeth the counsel of the heathen to nought; he maketh the devices of the people of none effect. The counsel of the Lord standeth forever," and, "I form the light and create darkness: I make peace and create evil: I the Lord do all these things," and, "all the inhabitants of the earth are reputed as nothing; and he doeth according to his will in the army of heaven and among the inhabitants of the earth; and none can stay his hand, or say unto him, What doest thou?"[37] These few out of a large number of similar passages suffice to justify the formulation that God controls history. How else could the Bible be understood when so much of it concerns the prophecies of and the preparation for the coming of the Messiah?

The second principle is not logically distinct from the first: it is a special application of it; but the application is of such importance that it deserves to be mentioned separately. God has not only controlled history so far, but he will bring it to its end and culmination. The Messianic function of Christ was not exhausted in his past work, but he is to return to earth again, 'in flaming fire taking vengeance on them that know not God and that obey not the Gospel."[38]

The third principle, instead of being subsidiary, makes the previous two subsidiary to itself. God not only controls history and brings it to its culmination; God himself acts in history. Other philosophies beside Christianity assert that God acts in some sense. Hegel's Absolute Spirit acts in history. It

35. Gen. 50:20; Ex. 12:36; I Sam. 16:12; II Sam. 16:10; II Sam. 24:1; Isa. 10:6, 7.
36. Dan. 2:21; Acts 17:26.
37. Psa. 33:10-11; Isa. 45:7; Dan. 4:35. *Cf.* Neh. 9:6; Rom. 8:28; Eph. 1:11.
38. II Thess. 1:8. *Cf.* Acts 1:11; Acts 3:19-21; Rev. 1:7 and a hundred other verses.

comes to consciousness in mankind, particularly in Hegel; it expresses itself in art; it has its finest manifestation in the Prussian State. But this Absolute Spirit is not a personal Being independent of the world. It is more correct to say that the Spirit is the world itself. An immanentism or pantheism may talk of Divine action, but in reality the action is simply the world's action. On the other hand, Aristotle, who distinguished with some clarity between the world and his divine Thought-Thinking-Thought, while he tried to maintain that his ultimate principle is a cause of motion in one sense, left little opportunity for that First Mover to act in history. Indeed, not only is this divine principle ignorant of the future, he knows little of the present either. Hegel and Aristotle therefore have conceptions of God that make action in history an incongruity. From a different quarter action may be denied to God, even though God is considered as possibly personal. The Deists of the eighteenth century granted that God made the world and established its natural laws, but then God left it alone. It was argued that a machine in need of constant tinkering is no compliment to its maker's skill. And if God is supposed to be supremely wise, he could not have made a world in which he would have to interfere. But this analogy fails to do justice to the Christian view of the world because Christianity does not regard the world as an automatic mechanism that runs itself once somebody pushes the button. If the world were altogether a machine, the Deists would have had a point. But if God created the world for the purpose (not necessarily the only purpose) of having personal relations with his creatures, the idea of a Deistic God who does not need to "interfere" makes no sense.

There is, however, another objection to the principle that God acts in history. Again the quotation comes from Joad.[39]

"The claim seems to me to be topographically parochial; it seems, that is to say, unlikely that the particular set of events associated with Christ's life should be so uniquely important in space, as the claim asserts. Space is very large,

---

39. *Op. cit.*, p. 294.

Palestine is comparatively small. Why am I expected to believe that what happened in Palestine is of such unique importance?"

When one stops to think of it, this is a remarkable objection. It says in effect that God could not possibly have acted in history because Palestine is such a small country. In order to act in history God would need a very large country, Russia perhaps; or he might need the solar system, since space is large and our planet is small.

The objection can therefore be reduced to this: God cannot possibly act in history because if he did, he would have to act at some particular place; but God cannot act at any particular place because every particular place is too small; therefore God cannot act in history. The manner in which Joad presses his objection is still more remarkable. He asked the question, "Why am I expected to believe that what happened in Palestine is of such unique importance?" He replies, "The answer would seem to be, that it is because I happen to live spatially to the west of Palestine, and belong, therefore, to a civilization-culture which derives its religion from Palestine. If I had lived equally near to Palestine, but to the east of it instead of to the west, if, in other words, I had been born in a bedroom in Delhi and not a bedroom in Durham, no such expectation would have been entertained in regard to me. I should not, that is to say, have been expected to take, and should not in fact have taken, this view of uniqueness in space of Palestine, and in Palestine of Bethlehem."

Just how this amazing answer is obtained is a mystery. Joad is trying to prove that Christianity is incredible; and to this end he seems to argue that the unique events of Christ's incarnation, crucifixion, and resurrection are important *because* we live to the west of Palestine. If we lived to the east of Palestine these events would not be important. But by what process of reasoning can one come to the conclusion that the location of an Englishman's residence is the cause of the importance of these events? Peculiar as it sounds, yet this seems to be the argument Joad's conclusion requires. But

Joad does not actually use this argument. What he says is, I am *expected to attach* importance to these events because I live to the west of Palestine. People who live to the east are not *expected to attach* importance to these events. But if this wording is stressed, the argument retains little cogency. It achieves a certain amount of plausibility by reason of the ambiguity of the word *expect*. To avoid this ambiguity one must specify both *who* expects, and *on what grounds* he expects. If the person is a Hindu who has never heard of Christ, of course he does not expect his neighbors to believe in Christ. In this situation residence is a factor only in so far as it is the cause of ignorance and social custom. These are the real grounds of the expectation. On the other hand a humanistic philosopher in London does not expect his intelligent friends to believe in Christ, either. But once again, the place of residence is incidental; the grounds are whatever arguments the humanist thinks sound. On the other hand, the Christian missionary *expects* the Hindus to whom he preaches to believe in Christ, not because of residence, and in spite of social custom, on the grounds that the events actually occurred and are as a matter of fact important. The whole situation in all its ambiguity would be reproduced if it should be asked, Is a Hindu expected to believe that Plato taught in Athens or are only westerners expected so to believe? These several objections have therefore failed to show any internal inconsistency in the Christian philosophy of history. The view hangs together. God not only controls all history and brings it to its culmination, "working all things after the counsel of his own will," but he also acts or "intervenes" personally at particular junctures. This results in the formation of a new society on earth whose history, though entangled in the history of the rest of mankind, has different principles, motives, means, and ends.

In conclusion one may ask, what has all this discussion proved? The answer is, the discussion has *proved* nothing. The philosophy of history, however interesting or even important it may be, is only a derivative aspect of philosophy, and before a view of history can be established, either by strict demonstration or even by persuasive argument, there are underlying problems that must be settled. These problems have not been faced in the preceding discussion. Therefore neither the secular nor the Chritsian view has been "proved."

The two views, however, have been sketched as two pictures in outline. If the secular standpoint is chosen, history has no significance; human hopes and fears are to be swallowed up in oblivion; and all men, good, evil, and indifferent, come to the same end. Anyone who chooses this view must base his life on unyielding despair. If however, he chooses the Christian view, then he can assign significance to history; human hopes and fears in this life contribute to the quality of a life after death, when two types of men will receive their separate destinies. Anyone who chooses this view can look at the calamities of western civilization and say, "We know that all things work together for good to them that love God." There has been no proof, but there is a choice.

III

THE PHILOSOPHY OF POLITICS

CHAPTER III

The Philosophy of Politics

THE study of history presented problems of such large dimensions that even those with the poorest vision could hardly fail to see them. It was this grand scope that made history such an inviting introduction to philosophy. But to those who have spent a little time reflecting on history, this grand scope may seem to turn into the disadvantage of requiring an immense amount of information. One must be conversant with Egypt, China, Rome, and Israel. And not only must their kings and battles, their dates and boundaries be studied, but it is even more necessary to understand their social customs, their philosophical outlook, and their religions. This would be quite a task. Then, too, these countries are remote, not simply in geographical distance, but in time, in temperament, and in immediate relevance. For a while our interest in the possible collapse of western civilization may stimulate the study of Babylonia, but after a bit we seem to have lost our way in the sands of the desert. The clay tablets, the nomads, the crumbled empires are unreal; the here and now, the twentieth century, the coming elections usurp our attention. For this reason the chapter on politics might have preceded the chapter on history. However, if the inspiring vistas of universal history lead to a dry archaeological desert, a study of the coming elections brings us even sooner to the thorny intricacies of political science. From the standpoint of one who has not made much progress in philosophy, a vast expanse is easier to see than microscopic patterns. And for this psychological reason the chapter on history came first.

Logically, however, if the order progresses from the more specific to the more general according to the main plan of this volume, the philosophy of politics should have preceded. Politics is a subdivision of history. Just as the general laws of botany apply to heliotropic plants as well as to the others, so the laws of universal history include the phenomena of politics. What may at first seem antithetical to this, but which in reality is an inference from it, is that assertions relative to the species presuppose certain views concerning the genus. If a scientist[1] explains heliotropism on a strictly mechanistic, physico-chemical basis, he has implicitly denied the theory of vitalism in all botany and presumably in all biology as well. Similarly, it is logically impossible to adopt any political theory without presupposing some view of history. The student of politics who asserts any definite opinions may be unconscious that he is assuming a certain position with reference to the course of history as a whole; but it would not be too difficult to show that on some view of history his particular theories of politics could not be true. The most obvious case in point, and the least that a political scientist could assume, is the theory that history has some significance. When he stops to think, he could not logically maintain that politics is important and that history in all its scope is only a tale told by an idiot. Political theory therefore presupposes that history is in some sense significant or rational. The only way to divorce the two — and it would not be a divorce at that — would be to assume that history is meaningless. If life has no goal, if the world is a blind and purposeless mechanism, if human actions are void of sense, then the political scientist need not bother with history. But neither need he any longer bother with politics. This intellectual nihilism leads logically to suicide, to alcoholism, or to any other irrational reaction as the emotions of the individual dictate. And it may be noted, parenthetically, that these reactions, with their judgment that life is futile, presuppose ethical judgments that are to be discussed in the following chapter. History, politics, and ethics are all interrelated: the subsidiary divisions presuppose definite

---

1. Jacques Loeb, *The Mechanistic Conception of Life,* (University of Chicago, 1912).

solutions to the more general, more fundamental problems, and the more fundamental studies imply definite results in the more particular fields.

But whether politics should have come first or second, and even though it may be as possible to lose oneself in the details of politics as in the debris of ancient Babylon, the subject is no less interesting and is even more inescapable than the study of history. We can easily stop thinking about the laws of universal history, but we can scarcely avoid noticing the present situation. Our daily life is largely made up of political matters. As a result of social upheavals governments regulate a man's work and fix his rent and wages. The bureaucratic restrictions imposed by the Labor government in Britain between 1945 and 1951 were unbelievably detailed and extreme in their severity. In the United States during the same years potatoes became a symbol of the useless, destructive, and expensive results of subsidies. Restrictions are placed on business and removed from government spending.

Religion is no more exempt from politics than the carpenter, the farmer, or the housewife. Cases concerning religious freedom and religious education have been carried to the Supreme Court. Some state governments have banned the Bible from the public schools as a board of censors might ban an obscene novel. And the question of an ambassador to the Pope has been raised.

In this situation the most unphilosophic workman and even the most impervious college student, though their interest in ancient Egypt may be slight, cannot fail to see the importance of contemporary politics. Whereas polite conversation used to ban the discussion of religion and politics, the turbulent twentieth century, polite or not, gives the impression that not much else is worth talking about.

And everybody is talking. Every columnist and every special group knows exactly what to do. The communists in their fifth columns call for dictatorship of the proletariat in the interests of atheism. Opposed to them is Roman Catholicism which, in the papal encyclical *Immortale Dei,* declares that "the uncontrolled power of thinking and publicly proclaiming one's thoughts has no place among the rights of citizens."[2] The largely Protestant World Council of Churches, at its organization meeting at Amsterdam in 1948, condemned both communism and capitalism without indicating what third possibility there might be. Previously in the United States the Federal Council of Churches advocated pacifistic principles which weakened the United States prior to World War II, and since then it has opposed universal military training. And there are the American Legion, the C.I.O., the N.A.M., the National Association for the Advancement of the Colored People, and the farm lobbies. In these days, if one talks at all, one must talk politics.

Normative *versus* Descriptive Politics

Since political science can no more examine every legislative proposal than can physics measure every pendulum, the first philosophic task in this welter of opinion is to reduce the material to some recognizable form. Unity must be introduced into the chaos. Is there not lying beneath the embarrassment of detail one basic issue? Or, if not one, at most a very few? History consisted of an infinite number of events: the assassinations of Caesar and Lincoln, the battles of Agincourt and the Marne, the election of Hitler and of Chamberlain; but the philosophy of history tried to formulate a single all-embracing law and to answer a single all-inclusive question: Has history a goal? Likewise, among the various tax and tariff proposals, the labor laws, lynching, and the foreign policy, is there not to be found a pervasive and decisive issue? A philosophy of politics presupposes that there is. Underlying and comprehending all these items is a very general question, *viz.*, What form of state is best? If this question is not itself the basic question in politics, it will upon examination be found to merge into the basic question. At any rate it is an indispensable introductory question, both important and

---

2. *Cf.* Ryan and Bolan, *Catholic Principles of Politics,* pp.. 298-300, 316ff. (Macmillan, 1940).

popular. People ask it in various forms: Is Fascism better than Communism? Is Democracy better than either? What kind of government do we want? If these questions could be answered, then automatically one would know that detailed legislative programs would be good if they conserved, advanced, or brought in by revolution the best form of government. But how can this general question be answered? What method must be used and what arguments can be found?

Suppose a study were made of the various forms of government. Monarchy, absolute and limited, oligarchy or aristocracy, representative governments with different provisions for franchise — all these could be examined, their various parts, functions, institutions, methods, and effects could be listed. It would be noted that stability in monarchical government depends largely on a clear and undisputed law of succession; while in republics the methods of elections must be popularly understood and there must be a general willingness on the part of the defeated party to accept the verdict of the polls. Such an examination could be pursued into the alleys of city politics and into the torture chambers of secret police. And one might obtain a vast knowledge of the intricate workings of several systems. But no amount of factual information will imply that one form of government is better than another. Monarchy and socialistic bureaucracy sustain special privileges. This is a fact, but is special privilege good or bad? Communism and Fascism liquidate the opposition. This is a fact, but the fact by itself does not imply that liquidation is better or worse than something else. All this factual, descriptive knowledge may be useful and necessary; courses in political science examine in great detail the administration of various types of government; but while all this is a part of political science, it hardly constitutes a philosophy of politics — it does not answer the underlying question.

Political philosophy must aim to say what form of government is better. If a description of how governments work does not suffice, what further is needed to frame an answer?

What is the missing element? And toward finding it, one may first ask, What do *better* and *best* mean?

Whenever a comparison of this sort, a judgment of value, is made between two forms of government, it is necessary to use a norm or standard. The government of Russia and the government of the United States are equally in existence: they are equally facts of history. If now one of these governments is to be judged superior to the other, it must be on the basis of some ideal. Usually it is granted that the ideal does not exist as an historical fact; but it will be said that the one government more closely approximates the ideal and is making greater progress toward the ideal than the other. But how is the ideal determined? Some theorists say that the ideal is economic security, and to this end everything else must be sacrificed: depressions are the worst things that can possibly happen, and to avoid them a totalitarian control of money, prices, labor, education, and religion is justified. Two centuries ago there was a species of political bird, now apparently extinct, that held political freedom to be the ideal. For men like Jefferson and Patrick Henry, tyranny was the worst of governmental evils, and a little economic competition was a small price to pay for liberty. Which of these two asserted ideals is ideal? No listing of facts can answer the question. Facts are statements of what *is;* ideals or standards are statements of what *ought to be.* One phase of political science is descriptive: it enumerates the various forms of governments and their workings. Another phase of political science will be normative: it will judge among other things which form is better. That is, if there are such things as standards, there will be a normative phase of politics; but if it is impossible to determine any standard, description will exhaust our powers.

It may be suggested that the problem has been oversimplified. Could it not be that one government has one ideal, and another, another? Would it not be surprising if the ideals of the United States today were applicable to ancient Egypt? In one sense this is true enough, but if it merely means that ancient people believed one form of government was best, and that modern people put their faith in another form, the suggestion simply amounts to a description of belief. It is not necessary to go to ancient Egypt to find differences of opinion: there is a violent clash in the modern community. And just as a description of forms of government cannot establish what is desirable, so too a description of the variety of opinion cannot decide which opinion is best. Both in politics and particularly in ethics, sociological theories have gone awry by neglecting the distinction between the descriptive and the normative. This neglect takes the form of mistaking the description of norms for normative theory. An interesting example is found in one of Sorokin's arguments.[3] The eminent professor of sociology is in process of analyzing sensate or empirical philosophy. To many minds, he says, it is unthinkable that our present materialistic, sensory, scientific philosophy should ever be replaced by any other type. New laws may be discovered, and greater accuracy may be obtained, but the form of science will never again be altered. This in fact was a basic proposition in the positivism of Auguste Comte. But Sorokin considers this belief erroneous. "Its first fallacy," he says, "is the illusion that there can be only one valid system of truth — that of the senses. We have seen that, as a matter of fact, there have been at least three fundamental systems: ideational, idealistic, and sensate." In these lines Sorokin confuses a description of past beliefs with the truth of the belief. Sorokin no doubt has shown that fundamentally different systems of philosophy have been popular at various times. It takes no sociologist to tell us that. But the fact that these three fundamentally different systems have been popular in different ages is no proof whatsoever that there is more than one valid system of truth. The fact that a theory *has been,* or *is* popular does not make it true. A description of norms is not a normative theory. On the following pages Sorokin lists the brilliant ideas that came like a flash to Newton, Galileo, Poincaré, Pascal, Mozart, Buddha, Zoroaster, Mohammed, Paul, and others. The conclusion based on this enumeration is startling: "The foregoing discussion affords

---

3. *The Crisis of our Age,* p. 103 (E. P. Dutton & Co., 1942).

unequivocal proof [italics mine] that all three systems — the sensory, the rational, and the intuitional — are sources of valid cognition; that each of them when adequately used, gives us knowledge of one of the important aspects of true reality; and that none of them, accordingly, is wholly false."[4]   Far from being unequivocal proof, the facts that Sorokin lists prove nothing at all.   No doubt all these men were struck with bright ideas; but if Pascal's great idea is right, then Zoroaster was wrong; and if we believe what Buddha or Mohammed said, we reject Paul's theology *in toto*.   It may be admitted that each of these men had great ideas, but even Sorokin's escape clause 'when adequately used' does not allow the conclusion that all these ideas are knowledge of true reality. But to bring the illustrations back to the field of politics: no doubt Louis XIV and Charles I believed that autocracy was ideal.   No doubt ninety percent of the American populace believes that democracy is ideal.   But these assertions are strictly descriptive.   They may seem to be normative because they state what certain people believe to be of value.   It does not automatically follow that what is believed to be ideal is in fact ideal.   Therefore political theory must find some method of determining a standard that is not a mere description of belief, if one government is to be rightly considered as superior to another.

There is another sense in which it is sometimes said that ideals change from age to age, and that the forms of government that are good today would not have been suitable in antiquity.   We might fondly say that our traffic laws or our corporation laws are ideal and yet recognize clearly that they would have been nonsense to the Aztecs and Athenians. Conditions are different.   But while this is true enough, and while failure to recognize this truth would cause confusion, it is only a superficial avoidance of the basic question of norms. The factors of a civilization which no longer remain applicable after its collapse are, by and large, means to more important ends.   They are not so much the ideals of a culture as they

---

4. *Ibid.*, p. 112.

are the methods of actualizing the ideals. For example, certain traffic laws may be called ideal because they promote safety and convenience. Safety and convenience, however, could be regarded as the more ultimate values, applicable to the Athenian agora as well as to Times Square, so that in this case the ideal would not have changed although the means of achieving it would have. This sort of change in 'ideal' traffic laws does not therefore remove the logical possibility that some more ultimate ideal may be valid for all men at all times. It would be only the methods that would change with the density of the population, the technology and temper of the age, and other factors. Of course the other logical possibility, that there is no universal ideal, still remains; the analysis was intended merely to show that the existence of a norm was not disproved by the obvious changes throughout the history of law. And it may be that all human action is a means and that there is no end. It may be that there are no norms, but only a belief that there are. Possibly everything is in a constant flux. This belief has been held by philosophers in many ages: the ancient Sophists and the modern instrumentalists.

The preponderance of evidence would seem to confirm this theory of flux. There is little similarity between the Asiatic nomads and gentlemen farmers, or between the ancient oriental despotisms and modern parliamentarianism. Of course we are all human beings, and Aristotle relied on this similarity to maintain an identity of end for all men and a fixed norm for all governments. But others have denied even the similarity of a human nature common to all men. Spengler, in stressing the cultural impenetrability of organic societies against the notion of a universal society developing through the Greek, Roman, Medieval, and modern periods, explicitly asserts that *man* does not exist — only *men*. And the school of progress argued that governments can mold men to any desired pattern because human nature is pliable. Clearly then the theory of flux has its exponents. While the resolution of this contest awaits, and while we remain in doubt whether to cast anchor on dogmatic norms or to drift with the skeptical tide, we may yet see that if there are no norms, then one government cannot be better than another. The majority of Americans want something they call democracy, and they may possibly know the techniques and propaganda that will efficiently get them what they want; but the Nazis wanted something else, and the communists want something else. Without standards or norms no one state can be said to be better than any other.

The Function of Government

A discussion of flux, however, and of norms, of fixed and eternal truths, goes beyond politics. Flux is often considered in relation to physical science; norms usually introduce questions of ethics; fixed and eternal truths concern epistemology and theology. If the factual description of the forms of historic governments was too purely political and not sufficiently philosophical, these matters are too generally philosophical and not sufficiently political. The details of politics do not solve the problem, but the solution of the problem is not politics. Such is the dilemma, and this chapter must straddle, or balance, between its two horns. Part of the balancing, assuredly, is to show how politics is related to and dependent on other divisions of philosophy.

The basic problem of political philosophy can be approached by again facing the question, what form of government is best? The very asking of the question may assume that there are norms; but though this has not been proved yet, it remains a descriptive fact that the great works on political theory grapple with this problem. The significance of the question can be better appreciated, if a subsidiary question be appended. When one asks, which government is better, one must explain the *better*: better for what? The German government was pretty good at waging war, but the American government was better. The British government is pretty good in stability, but the French government has been better at alternating premiers. Perhaps the problem should be expressed in other words. The clearest expressions may be, What is government

good for? What is the purpose of government? And this
is the question that underlies many of the most controversial
issues of our legislative chambers. Tariff, states rights, TVA,
as well as socialism and laissez-faire, raise the question of the
purpose of government. Whether it is simply the purpose
which the majority of voters choose and force upon the minority, or whether it is an ideal purpose that some philosophic
argument proves to be valid for all societies, the detailed proposals will be tested by an appeal to this end. Those that
accomplish the aim are efficient or good; those that delay or
prevent the accomplishment are inefficient and bad. The basic
question therefore is, What is the purpose of government?

Aristotle gives a most explicit answer to this question. His
work on Politics opens with a definition of the state, and for
Aristotle a definition is in reality a statement of purpose. For
example, a lyre is an an instrument that produces a certain type
of music, and the purpose of a lyre is to produce this type of
music. Further, a good lyre accomplishes its purpose well.
Thus, an object is what it is good for; and when Aristotle
tells us what the state is, he has defined its purpose.

The terms in which the definition is framed have as their
background the various associations of everyday life, such as
the family and business corporations. The persons who form
these associations have certain interests in common. The
family exists for certain goods, and a business partnership
aims at certain other goods. Now, says Aristotle, a city or
state or government is a sort of partnership. Its members
have certain interests in common and hence they may be called
a community. The difference between the family or other
partnerships and the state lies in the fact that the state is the
partnership that includes all partnerships, and the good it
promotes is the good that includes all goods. Whereas the
members of a family have a few or even many interests in
common, the citizens of a state have all interests in common.

Aristotle expands on the all-inclusive nature of the state
in Book VII of the *Politics*. He prescribes that the citizen

should be molded to suit the form of government under which he lives. By a system of public education the government is to impress its own type on each of the citizens. Parents are not to be permitted to educate their children. Private schools would be made illegal, and everybody would be indoctrinated by the State Board of Education. The reason is that no citizen belongs to himself; all citizens belong to the state; and the care of each one is inseparable from the care of the whole.

Elsewhere[5] Aristotle argues, "If then there is some end of practical action, an end we desire for its own sake, other things being desired as a means to this end, and if we do not choose everything for the sake of something else — for this would result in an infinite regress so that desire would be ineffectual and in vain — obviously this must be the good and the best. . . . [The knowledge of this supreme good] is admittedly the province of the most authoritative and architectonic science. And this is Politics. For Politics determines which of the sciences are to be studied in the state, which students are to study them, and up to what point they shall study them."

Not only is the education of youth to be controlled by the state, but since no citizen belongs to himself even the size of the family is determined by the same authorities.[6] Sickly children must be killed, and if the state is threatened by over-population, even healthy children are to be exposed on the mountainside and births are to be reduced by abortion.

These provisions, the implications of Aristotle's definition of the state as the partnership that includes all partnerships, are sufficient to show the totalitarian character of Aristotle's ideal government. It is true that Aristotle did not approve the communism that Plato advocated. Plato so exalted the role of the state that the family and presumably all lesser partnerships were to be abolished. No one was to have any private property, no one was to have any private family, but on the contrary, with the possible exception of the lowest class of society,

5. *Ethica Nicomachea*, I 2.
6. *Politics*, VII 16.

everyone was to be devoted solely to the state. With this Aristotle does not agree. He defends the necessity of the family, and in fact the definition itself implies that there must be other partnerships to be included in the state. Now, if Plato's theory is a form of communism, perhaps Aristotle could be called a fascist. The important point is that they are both totalitarian. Today's popular demand for democracy arises from opposition to the regimes of Mussolini and Hitler; the tacit assumption seems to be that a government by elected officials is the highest desideratum. But it may be suspected that this popular mentality does not see clearly, as Thomas Hobbes did, that a congress or parliament can be as autocratic as an individual emperor. How many the officials are who exercise authority is not the point.

Whether there is a dictator, an absolute monarch, or an elected convention, is immaterial. The basic fact is the extent to which the state regulates the lives of individuals. And Aristotle's state regulates totally.

The reason for this totalitarianism can be made a little clearer by stating the purpose of the state in slightly different words. Aristotle would have been shocked, had anyone suggested that the state ought not to be concerned with the good of the citizens. Is the state — so he would have argued — to concern itself with the relatively unimportant matters of property and neglect the really important matter of morality? Is the state to guard the external possessions of people and neglect the people themselves? Are not human rights superior to property rights? Does the state have no interest that the citizens should be good men and women? Surely a good man is worth more than a good house; and surely a state populated with good men is the best state. It is therefore the function of the state to make men moral. Aristotle says,[7] "We stated that the end of political science is the best end, and political science spends most of its pains on making the citizens to be of a certain character, viz., good and capable of noble acts."

---

7. *Ethica Nicomachea*, I, 9.

Later he continues the same theme:[8] "Lawgivers make the citizens good by training them in habits of right action — this is the aim of all legislation, and if it fails to do this, it is a failure."

Parenthetically, it is interesting to note how a contemporary thinker,[9] outstanding in the field of ethics and politics, returns to the position of Aristotle. T. V. Smith writes, "Aristotle seems always to be saying between the lines of his great work on ethics — a wise saying it is — 'What we Greeks agree upon as moral *is* moral,' as indeed it was for the Greeks. Let our assumption be that 'what we Americans have come to pre-suppose as ethical *is* right,' as indeed it must be for us Americans. . . . Among all that must be taken for granted in order to live at all, patriotism is the most completely presup-posed (i.e., loyalty to some community and if to 'some,' why not to the larger and then the largest?)." T. V. Smith, unlike John Milton, does not consider the possibility that the larger and especially the largest society may be wrong or inferior and that some smaller group may be right. In fact, this is what he castigates as 'sectarianism,' and he suggests that this "is not easily, perhaps not safely to be allowed in a democratic world." Consistent with this notion of democracy that would suppress dissent, he seems also to assume that morality is a matter of loyalty to a social group, rather than loyalty to a set of principles or to God; and this seems to imply that truth, at least truth about right conduct, can be determined by popular vote. It is true that in some paragraphs he pays respects to the freedom of religion (as he defines religion); and in making patriotism the supreme virtue he tries to insist on his form of patriotism and to avoid chauvinism; and no doubt he would dissent from some of the harsher elements in Aristote-lian ethics. But it is a serious question whether consistently in theory or actually in practice he could maintain his gentle-

---

8. *Ibid.* II, 1.

9. T. V. Smith, *Constructive Ethics*, pp. 5, 6, 94-96, (Appleton-Century-Crofts, 1948).

manly ideals on his position that "what we Americans have come to presuppose as ethical *is* right."[10]

Analysis and Criticism

By this time it must appear that the double question, What is the state? and What is the purpose of the state? is as important to ask as it is difficult to answer. No doubt morality is of greater value than wealth, and nearly everyone would prefer a state with good citizens to a state of immoral citizens. Aristotle speaks plausibly when he says that the legislator should improve the morals of the people. But then some anti-social sectarian may ask who will improve the morals of the government officials? If politicians had an unexcelled record of personal morality and supreme wisdom, there might be some show of reason for the proposal to put the training of citizens into their hands. It is not because morality is unimportant that some people object to making moral indoctrination a function of government. Quite the contrary, a Federal Bureau of Thought-Control is opposed precisely because the issues of morality are far too important to be decided by majority vote or administrative decree. In the light of Hitler's attempt to guide the thoughts, control the conduct, and set the ideals of the German people, one might be willing to look at competing views on the extent of the government's authority. Instead of defining the state, or the World Government, as the partnership that contains all partnerships and asserting that its good includes all goods, perhaps the purpose of the state does not go beyond the preservation of life, liberty, and possessions.

10. It is significant that T. V. Smith quotes frequently and with approval the late Justice Oliver Wendell Holmes. Ben. W. Palmer, *Hobbes, Holmes, and Hitler,* in the American Bar Association Journal, 31: 569, Nov. 1945, underlines the nature of this philosophy. He quotes Holmes as saying, "truth was the majority vote of the nation that could lick all the others." And, "I am so skeptical as to our knowledge about the goodness or badness of laws that I have no practical criticism except what the crowd wants." Holmes approved Holland's statement, "That which gives validity to a legal right is, in every case, the force which is lent to it by the state. Anything else may be the occasion, but not the cause, of its obligatory character." From these and other quotations the author concludes that Justice Holmes' political theory is indistinguishable from that of a storm trooper proclaiming the supremacy of the blonde beast.

This discussion of the theory of politics has centered around a few aspects of a basic question. First it was asked, Which form of state is the best? An examination of the forms of the state, considered merely as so many historical facts, was seen to provide no answer to the question. An answer could be obtained only by the establishment of norms, standards, or ideals in terms of which the best could be distinguished from the worst. This normative theory is chiefly a matter of ethics and was postponed to the following chapter. Then the question was rephrased: What is the state good for? What is the purpose of the state? Since no norms had been established, it was possible to proceed only hypothetically. Aristotle's definition of the state as the partnership that includes all partnerships, or the community that includes all communities, with a brief reference to the modern world-community, was examined for the purpose of tracing out its implications. If the morality behind this type of definition can be accepted, the implications must be accepted with it; but if anyone should refuse to accept the implications, he is prevented from choosing the premises.

There is still another way of phrasing the original question. When the question is put, Which state is better? instead of asking, Better for what? one may ask, Better for *whom*? This too can be discussed only hypothetically, but it gives rise to additional considerations. Then too it has the advantage of seeming to be more concrete: it applies more obviously to the people governed than the abstract notion of the purpose of the state.

There have been states in the past that have openly been managed for the good of the rulers. The oriental despotisms certainly were not run for the good of the people at large. Similarly, the tyrannies of Greek times, the absolute monarchy of pre-revolutionary France, and the Russian Czarist government favored the ruling classes to the great detriment of the masses of people. Such states are better than others, only if better means *better* for the rulers.

But the revolutions came and democracy developed. It was assumed that the better state was the state that was better for the people. And a school of thought proposed the political and ethical slogan of the "greatest good of the greatest number." This slogan contains two elements: the good, and the people. No further emphasis will be put on the fact that the concept of the good still remains unknown and the problem of norms unsolved. This is reserved for the chapter on ethics. But it must never be forgotten to what extent one topic, like politics, depends on more basic studies, like ethics. This extent is not limited to the notion of good; it also includes the other element of the slogan — the people. And the investigation of people may bury us under philosophical profundity even deeper than the normative discussion of the good.

The greatest good of the greatest number obviously cannot be ascertained without first determining the good of one man. And what is good for a man can be determined only after one knows what man is. That is to say, the definition of good depends on the nature of man. If human nature is one sort of thing, the good and the good state will correspond; but if human nature is actually a different sort of thing, another good and another type of state will be indicated. Something of this has already been seen. When Aristotle says that the citizen belongs to the state, he is not far from Spengler's view that society is an organism and that each man is only a corpuscle in its blood stream. If this should be the case, the sacrifice of a man's life for the good of society is a light matter. When Stalin liquidates his opposition, when he sends dissident elements to perish in Siberia, he is acting wisely and morally. Anyone will squeeze poison out of a wound; anyone will cause the blood to flow freely; and if a number of corpuscles are lost beyond the bare, necessary minimum it is no great loss. In fact the shedding of blood is legitimate even as a preventive. If there is fair reason to suspect that certain men are likely to cause trouble, it is better to assassinate them beforehand. This is for the good of the greatest number. A corpuscle has no rights that conflict with the body as a whole. It exists solely to preserve the body. And if its expenditure accomplishes this aim, the cost is small. Of course, if society is not an organism, and if man is not a corpuscle, these expedients may not be justified. Again, suppose that human nature is positively good. Then it would follow that the officers of government could be trusted with wide discretionary powers. Government regulation and bureaucracy would be efficient and honest. Or better still, the country, that is, the people, could be entrusted to a benevolent dictator. If, on the other hand, human nature should not be so benevolent as this theory maintains, some people would be suspicious of these proposals.

The study of human nature is of course not the province of political science. One would expect discussions of the nature of man under the title of psychology, or perhaps ethics, or possibly theology. A book on politics that spent most of its space on the goodness or wickedness of mankind would be judged to have been misnamed. But — and this is the all-important point — the questions of politics cannot be answered without assuming some particular answer to these deeper questions. A writer on political science may be unaware, or just dimly aware, of his assumptions; but the theory of politics that he advances reflects his opinion of what man is.[11] One may study the details of dictatorship, and thoroughly explore the workings of Jeffersonian democracy; but before a reason can be given to favor one of these above the other, it is necessary to pass far beyond the limits of political science.

However, though the record be one of repeated failure, let us make another attempt to keep on the subject. Underlying the previous discussion was the assumption that even if some states are bad, other states are not so bad, and any state is better than none. It was tacitly presupposed that anarchy would be actually worse than despotism. How could man manage merely to exist under the condition of anarchy? The

---

11. Holmes said, "When one thinks coldly, I can see no reason for attributing to man a significance different in kind from that which belongs to a baboon or to a grain of sand." And, "I wonder if cosmically an idea is any more important than the bowels." Cf. note on p. 111. *Hobbes, Holmes, and Hitler,* by Ben. W. Palmer.

strongest and most brutal thug would be the first to kill the unprotected and expropriate his wealth. Even Stalin guarantees some security to his loyal subjects.

Anarchy, however, has had its exponents, both in philosophical debate and in political programs. Like the communists anarchists have been enemies of captialism, but unlike the communists they argue against the centralization of authority. Some of their best work bares the evils of a strong centralized bureaucracy. Their mildest proposals call for the establishment of voluntary associations that will take over many and finally all state functions. To begin the destruction of capitalism, they will establish banks that lend money at one per cent or less. People will then borrow, buy homes, and rent will be abolished. An exchange of labor by mutual agreement will produce the comforts of life in abundance, and a greatly increased leisure may be devoted to education and art. Such are some of their proposals. But, one may ask, what means will be used to insure the repayment of loans to this mutual bank, and how can the voluntary exchange of hours of labor be continued on a scale sufficient to support large communities? Is it true that human nature is so dependable that voluntary promises will enforce themselves?

Besides these literary anarchists there has been a more vigorous contingent whose dislike of the state was expressed in the I.W.W. labor movement during World War I, and in the assassination of kings and presidents. If it is true that the existence of a state provokes these anarchists to violence, it still is not clear that the abolition of the state would put an end to violence. Competent thinkers have asserted that government is the greatest of all temporal blessings and that no condition of man is worse than anarchy. This may not be quite true. Possibly the communistic dictatorship with its conscious and resolute purpose to do evil is less tolerable than the irregular and unplanned violence of anarchy. Be that as it may, it is at least plausible that some sort of state is needed to regulate some human affairs to some degree.

Justification of Coercion

The contrast between this plausibility and the theory of anarchy brings into accurate focus the question which, without qualification, may be labeled the basic question of politics. If a state is necessary for the prevention of violence, an explicit answer must be found to the question, What justifies violence or coercion on the part of the state? This is essentially, if not verbally, the same question as those relating to the nature, purpose, and definition of the state; for when one asks what form of state is best, the reply could be that no form is best; accordingly the justification of civil government is the basic question of politics. It was this question that was so pointedly put by J. J. Rousseau.

In addition to the intrinsic importance of this question and the influence that Rousseau actually exerted on subsequent developments, there is another reason for discussing his theory in connection with that of Aristotle. The reason is contrast. As the details of a study of history would show, eighteenth century France and the Greece of Alexander and Aristotle supported widely divergent civilizations. Even if with Spengler we take the two ages as almost "contemporary," still they are the same only as the maturities of an oak tree and of a caterpillar are the same. Concretely and particularly their philosophies were not the same. Then too Rousseau's personal temperament was as nonaristotelian as modern symbolic logic. The theories of politics that the two men produced seem, at least at first, to have nothing in common. If, now, with all this diversity, an analysis can discover a deep rooted agreement, that factor, whatever it might be, ought to prove to be a significant characteristic of a very general type of worldview.

After a few sentences of introduction, Rousseau begins his *Social Contract*[12] with this question: "Man is born free, and everywhere he is in chains. . . . How did this happen? I do not know. What can justify it? I think I can answer

---

12. *The Social Contract and Discourses,* J. J. Rousseau, p. 3, (Everyman's Library, E. P. Dutton & Co., 1946).

this question." A better formulation of the political problem is hardly possible, and certainly no other political problem is so basic. The church, the family, and business associations are voluntary organizations; but the state is coercive. By what right therefore does the state exist? How does a government get, not the power, but the authority to coerce its people? This is a question that does not ordinarily occur to the average newspaper reader. Anarchy is either so utopian or so repulsive, and government is such a familiar institution that people are not predisposed to suspect its legitimacy. There have been troubled times, civil wars, or contests of authority during which people did not know to which claimant they should pay their taxes; there have been disputes concerning *de facto* governments and governments *de jure;* but doubt as to the justification of government as such has been a luxury reserved for political philosophers. It was precisely this matter that stimulated Rousseau.

Immediately he rejects an easy answer. Coercion, or force, does not justify itself.[13] If force were the whole story, there would be no difference between a legitimate government and a *de facto* government; and a people would always be justified in a successful rebellion. In spite of Rousseau's hatred of the French monarchy, he was not an anarchist; and if he was intent on preparing the people for a revolution, it was because he believed that the government was not legitimate, even though at the moment it possessed force to coerce. Force is a physical power, he argues; to yield to force is an act of necessity, or at most an act of prudence, but it cannot be a duty. If people obey a government perforce, there is no need for them to obey because they ought. Does a brigand on the highway have a right to rob me because he has the force to do so? No, force cannot create morality.

Since no one has a natural right to rule, and since force creates no right, all authority must be based on conventions.

---

13. *Cf.* notes on pp. 111, 114. Holmes wrote, "Sovereignty is a form of power, and the will of the sovereign is law because he has the power to compel obedience or punish disobedience and for no other reason."

Only by some voluntary agreement can a social order be established, and it is the social order that is the basis of all other rights. When a people chooses a king, it should be noted that it is first a people; and one must explain how all these individuals became a unified people engaged in choosing a ruler. Further, since the election was probably not unanimous, one must explain by what right the majority coerces the minority. "The law of majority voting is itself something established by convention and presupposes unanimity, on one occasion at least." This occasion arose when the obstacles to self-preservation became too great for the resources of each individual singly. A concourse of people, thus threatened by natural conditions, faced the problem of framing a social contract by which the group would "defend and protect the person and the goods of each associate, and in which each, while uniting himself with all, would obey himself alone and remain as free as before." The chief clause of this contract is "the total alienation of each associate together with all his rights to the whole community; for, in the first place, since everyone gives himself entirely, the condition is equal for all; and since the condition is equal for all, no one has any interest in making it burdensome to the others. Moreover, since the alienation is without reserve, the union is as perfect as possible, and no associate has anything more to ask; for if the individuals retained any rights, as there would be no common superior who could decide between them and the public, each one, being his own judge on some point, would soon claim to be his own judge on all points; the state of nature would therefore remain, and the association would necessarily become tyrannical or useless."[14]

It is this unanimous agreement that creates a public body, a city, or a state. When this union is formed, it becomes impossible to offend against one member without attacking the body or to attack the body without offending the members. Duty and interest therefore coincide. Under these conditions the state cannot have any interest contrary to that of

14. *Ibid.* I, vi. p. 12.

the citizens; it cannot wish to hurt all its members, and it cannot hurt anyone in particular. The sovereign association is always what it should be. But if there are no misgivings as to the state, there are as to individual members. In spite of the common interest, an individual as a man may have a particular will contrary to the general will which he has as a citizen. He may believe that his contributions to the state are more of a loss to himself than they are a gain to others; he may come to regard the state as a fictitious Person and refuse to fulfil his duties as a subject. Such a man by the terms of the contract, should be coerced: he must be forced to be free. Thus coercion is justified.

To strengthen this position Rousseau adds an elaborate argument concerning the general will; but it is an argument that may produce more confusion than clarity. "The general will is always right and always tends toward the public good; but it does not follow that the deliberations of the people always have the same rectitude. . . . There is often a great difference between the will of all and the general will: the latter has regard only to the common interest, the former has private interests and is nothing but a sum of particular wills; but remove from these same wills the pluses and the minuses that cancel each other, and the general will remains as a sum of the difference."[15] Later he says, "The citizen gives his consent to all the laws, including those which are passed in spite of his opposition, and even those which punish him when he dares to break any of them. The constant will of all the members of the state is the general will. . . . The general will is found by counting votes."[16]

Since interpreters of Rousseau have uniformly found difficulty in his conception of the general will, it may be suspected that he has not helped his politics by introducing it. Even at first sight the paragraphs are puzzling, and more study increases rather than diminishes the perplexity. At any rate, Rousseau teaches that the social contract creates a new en-

15. *Ibid.* II iii, pp. 22-23.
16. *Ibid.*, IV ii.

tity, "a moral and collective body," a "public person."[17] In an earlier work he expresses the idea more clearly: "The body politic therefore is also a moral being possessed of a will; and this general will, which always tends to the preservation and welfare of the whole and of every part is the source of the laws. . . ."[18]

One strand of Rousseau's thought is that the general will is determined by a majority vote. This is easily understood. Only, if it is a majority decision that determines the general will, how can it be said to be always right and always tend to the welfare of each citizen? Is it true that majorities are always right? Is it true that the sovereign association is always what it should be? Majority voting is a procedure easily understood, but it does not correspond to all that Rousseau has said of the general will. And Rousseau was not so insistent on majority voting as some of the phrases already quoted might seem to imply. In the *Political Economy* he says, "the most general will is always the most just also, and the voice of the people is in fact the voice of God. [But] it does not follow that the public decisions are always equitable."[19] And a few pages below he argues that even if the whole people were assembled to decide a question, "it is by no means certain that its decision would be the expression of the general will . . . [this method] is hardly ever necessary where the government is well intentioned: for the rulers well know that the general will is always on the side which is most favorable to the public interest, that is to say, most equitable; so that it is needful only to act justly to be certain of following the general will." This sounds almost naive. If then we are forced, as we certainly are, to distinguish a majority decision from the general will, we shall probably have to identify the latter with the unknown common good. The common good is always right, it cannot harm any citizen, it is always as it should be, and in fact the common good always tends toward

---

17. *Ibid.*, I vi, p. 13.
18. *Political Economy* (*Ibid.*, p. 236).
19. *Ibid.*, p. 238.

the common good. It might even be said that if the pluses and minuses of particular goods be cancelled, the common good remains. This interpretation will make many of Rousseau's apparently false statements true; but their new truth, tautological as it is, does not advance political science.

There is still another interpretation to be obtained by stressing Rousseau's assertion that the social compact creates a new moral person with a will of its own. This person could possibly be identified with Hegel's Absolute Spirit that controls the course of history, or with the Universal Reason of later ethical writers who wish to substitute an altruistic utilitarianism for individualism. But whether this is mysticism, nonsense, or profundity, it cannot be Rousseau's conscious meaning. The most promising explanation of Rousseau's actual words is that he confused an ideal construct with an actual political reality. He seems to be torn between an infallible general will that cannot express itself and an expressed majority vote that is not infallible. And in general it may be said that political scientists have frequently found it difficult to preserve a sharp distinction between their normative ideals and their real descriptions.

However, the value of the social compact theory should not be judged by any confusion that one author may have fallen into. If the chief interest is in political science and not in Rousseau as an individual, it is the essential elements of the theory that require evaluation. The confusion of the general will is by no means essential; that part of the discussion could have been omitted to the benefit of the social compact as a whole.

There are certain other confusions or even contradictions that lie nearer to the heart of the matter. At the beginning Rousseau had said that "the social order is a sacred right which is the basis of all other rights; nevertheless this right does not come from nature, and must therefore be founded on convention." This assertion that all rights are founded on the social compact seems to be inconsistent with the compact itself, for if man in his natural state has no rights because all rights are founded on the social convention, how can Rousseau consistently assert that in the social compact each associate alienates all his rights to the community?[20]   A man surely cannot alienate or surrender what he does not possess.   And if there are natural rights, then Rousseau's original statement basing all rights on convention must be put aside as incorrect. It would seem to follow therefore that a social compact theory presupposes the existence of natural rights, and these rights would require an explanation that is of course lacking in Rousseau.

In the next place, if men had natural rights, did they, would they, and could they alienate them? Rousseau has answered these three questions affirmatively in the terms of his social contract.   But at the same time he uses phrases which, superficially at least, imply a negative answer.   "To renounce liberty is to renounce being a man, to surrender the rights of humanity and even its duties. . . . Such a renunciation is incompatible with man's nature; to remove all liberty from his will is to remove all morality from his acts."   These words, in addition to presupposing natural rights, seem also to imply that some rights, particularly liberty, are inalienable.   And this would be in contradiction to the social contract.   To this Rousseau might answer that he has not contradicted himself because his denial of the alienation of liberty refers to slavery and not to the social contract.   Since there is no *quid pro quo* in slavery, there is no contract or agreement, and therefore the slaveholder's right to his slaves is illusory.   If one reply that the slave contracts to sell himself for his food, security, and tranquillity, Rousseau minimizes the *quid,* promises tranquillity in jail, and calls it a bad bargain.   Let it be assumed that a bad bargain is not a bargain and that a man cannot alienate his liberty to a slaveholder.   The social contract is still very different from slavery.   In the social contract men surrender all their rights; but, since Rousseau wants to have it both ways, they do not lose their liberty because "each man in

---

20. *Ibid.,* I i, vi, pp. 3, 11-13.

giving himself to all, gives himself to nobody."[21] This "nobody," however, by social convention becomes a moral person
with a will of its own, and when, for Rousseau's successors
the convention became The Convention and the "nobody" instituted a Reign of Terror, the reassurance of the line just
quoted begins to seem specious.[22] It will quickly be said that
neither Rousseau, the individual nor the social contract theory
can fairly be charged with the practices of Robespierre. This
is a point that calls for more consideration; perhaps the practices of Robespierre are indeed legitimate conclusions of the
theory.

The question whether men could have alienated all their
rights may be left unanswered, for a more important question
is, Would they have done so?

Since some men do very foolish things it is virtually impossible to guess what men would have done in framing a
social contract. All that need be said in answer to this question is that some men, at any rate, would not. The signers of
the Declaration of Independence spoke of inalienable rights and
exercised their right to rebel. Caesar and Napoleon, though
not regarded with the same honor, are equally pertinent instances of men who would not have surrendered all their rights.

But perhaps it is fruitless to ask whether men would have
surrendered all their rights and whether they could have.
The most important question is, Did they? If they did, the
other questions receive their answers automatically; and if they
did not, then the social contract theory does not justify any
actual government.

Rousseau asserts that on one occasion at least there was a
unanimous vote establishing the body politic. On that occasion
all men agreed to surrender all their rights. No one dissented
and no one retained any right for himself. It is usually considered an unfair philosophic practice to press the question of
historicity in this matter. Rousseau could not, and he knew

21. *Ibid.*, I vi, p. 12.
22. How specious it is may be seen in Rousseau's distinction between
"natural liberty" and "the conventional liberty in favor of which he re-
nounced it" (I vi).

he could not give the date and place of the compact that established the French people. And it is assumed that since he was aware that he was not writing history, the critic ought not to raise that question. John Locke also faced the objection that there is no historical justification for a social compact theory. He disposes of this inconvenience first by noting that government antedates written records, and second by claiming that the governments of Rome and Venice were initiated by a free compact. This, however, is an insufficient reply to the objection. For, first, the absence of written records does not prove that there was a contract; second, though Rome and Venice may have been so formed, these two instances do not justify the governments of London and Paris; and third, Locke does not specify the terms of the contract.

Had Locke and Rousseau lived to see the influence their theories exerted, they could have pointed to an instance far more convincing than Rome and Venice. Is not the government of the United States exactly what this theory describes? The question should not be taken rhetorically as if an affirmative answer is tacitly understood. For, contrary to Rousseau's requirement of an initial unanimous vote, not all of the thirteen states adopted the Constitution. Rhode Island did not even send delegates to the Convention. And when the Constitution was submitted to the people for ratification, there were at least some individuals, even in the states that adopted it, who voted against it. Therefore, if unanimous action is required to establish a legitimate government, the United States has never had a legitimate government. This point of unanimous initial agreement cannot be dismissed like some others as an unhappy oversight of the author. On the contrary, it is essential to the theory. John Locke, who differs in many particulars from Rousseau, was quite explicit on this point. "Men being, as has been said, by nature all free, equal, and independent, no one can be put out of this estate and subjected to the political power of another without his own consent, which is done by agreeing with other men to join and unite into a community.... This any number of men may do because it injures not the freedom of the rest."[23] Nor need dependence be put simply on the statements of Locke and Rousseau. Unanimous consent is essential to the theory because the main question is, By what right can a majority coerce a minority? This question cannot be dodged, and it was precisely because this is the essential question of political philosophy that Rousseau took his stand on an initial unanimous action. Since Rome and Venice were probably no more unanimous than the thirteen states, we must either do without an historical justification of the theory or place our faith in some ancient government unknown to written records. In either case, on this theory, governments now existing, including the government at Washington, have no right to coerce a dissenting minority.

On the other hand, neither Locke nor Rousseau was willing to admit that a dissenting minority could prevent the formation of a body politic. What right do dissenters have to coerce the majority into not having a government? Were not those who voted to adopt the Constitution unanimous? Not only did Locke say that any number of men may enter such a compact because it injures not the freedom of the rest; but Rousseau also is equally explicit. He writes,[24] "If then there are opponents when the social compact is made, their opposition does not invalidate the contract, but merely prevents them from being included in it." These statements would give the government authority over those who adopted it, even if it had no authority to collect taxes from the others. Such an unreal condition is highly unsatisfactory, and Rousseau tries to overcome its unreality by appealing to a tacit agreement. "When the State is instituted," he says, "residence constitutes consent; to dwell within its territory is to submit to the Sovereign." But this is equally unsatisfactory. By what right did the new state acquire territory? Presumably the associates previously owned some land in private, and surrendered their land to the new moral person. But how could these associates surrender the land of people who did not participate or who voted against

23. *Of Civil Government,* Second Essay, VIII, 95.
24. *Ibid.,* IV ii, p. 88.

surrendering their property? And even if the dissenter owned no land, and therefore found himself residing in the territory of a new state against his will, how can residence be construed as consent? He would of course have no rights to land, and the state could control all land as it saw fit; but there are other rights that the dissenter holds from nature — how does he lose them by residence? Rousseau himself saw some difficulty here and appended this footnote: "This should of course be understood as applying to a free state; for elsewhere family, goods, lack of a refuge, necessity, or violence may detain a man in a country against his will; and then his dwelling there no longer by itself implies his consent to the contract or to its violation." And when the World State shall have been formed, to which planet may the patriot emigrate? It should therefore be clear, by argument, by Rousseau's hedging, and by history that no actual government can be justified on the basis of an initial unanimous vote.

Also damaging to the historical support of the contract theory is the fact that those who voted to adopt the United States Constitution (no longer to speak of dissenters) did not intend, as Rousseau's terms dictate, to surrender all their rights. They very deliberately granted certain specified rights to the federal government and reserved all others to the several states.[25] While the Constitution does not repeat the phrases about natural and inalienable rights that are found in the Declaration of Independence, it is still quite clear that those who voted in favor of the Constitution did not intend to alienate all their rights. They were even unsatisfied with the explicit delegation of certain rights only, and required a gentleman's agreement that as soon as the new government was in operation the Constitution should be amended by the addition of a Bill of Rights. The American government therefore furnishes no historical support for Rousseau's theory and leaves the basic question still unanswered.

---

25. Nor did they suppose that they had previously surrendered all their rights to the states.

And next, can any social contract, whether its terms alienate all rights or some only, bind those people who did not participate in the Convention? These non-participants are not only the citizens of Rhode Island, they are all the succeeding generations. Can the father's contract bind the children? What right does a father have to do so? The children certainly did not give him that right. And Rousseau admits that "even if each man could alienate himself, he could not alienate his children. . . . Before they come to years of discretion, the father can, in their name, lay down conditions for their preservation and well being, but he cannot give them irrevocably and without conditions; such a gift is contrary to the ends of nature, and exceeds the rights of paternity."[26] How, then, even if a govenment had been once unanimously constituted, could it continue? Theoretically there would have to be a unanimous vote in every generation, and oftener. Rousseau seems to require a repetition of the unanimous vote at every session of Congress. He says, "The opening of these assemblies, whose sole object is the maintenance of the social treaty, should always take the form of putting two propositions that may not be suppressed. . . . I am here assuming what I think I have shown, that there is in the state no fundamental law that cannot be revoked, not excluding the compact itself."[27] But if a unanimous vote could not be obtained in 1789, would it be more possible today?

The Consent of the Governed

The social contract theory can be made more plausible by discarding some of Rousseau's particularities and by attempting to see its value in the notion that a legitimate government depends on the consent of the governed. This phrase, so frequently used since the time of Rousseau, seems to provide a less vulnerable defense of coercion than does a unanimous

---

26. *Ibid.*, I, iv, pp. 7-8.

27. *Ibid.*, III, xviii, p. 84. Rousseau is not clear whether it would require a unanimous vote or only a majority vote to break the social contract. If the people have alienated all their rights, possibly a minority would have no rights, and a unanimous vote would be required to restore them.

vote. But while the phrase has more propaganda value, it is nonetheless an obscurantist slogan. The reason that this phrase obscures the issue is that 'the governed' is usually conceived collectively instead of individually. The people of the thirteen colonies withdrew their consent to the British crown and rebelled. But of course many people did not withdraw their consent. They enjoyed life or suffered obloquy as Tories, and eventually many of them fled to Canada. The result was that the majority finally consented to a new government. So to treat the notion of the consent of the governed is to ignore the basic question: By what right does the majority coerce the minority? It cannot claim a prior compact because there has been none. Can it claim a present implicit compact that binds the sons as well as the fathers? What evidence is there of any implicit compact?

There is to be sure some evidence. Perhaps it will be possible to show that implicitly the men of 1789, without intending to, surrendered all their rights. It must be insisted upon that the contract is implicit and that the framers of the Constitution were unaware of what they were doing. What they thought they were doing is clear enough. The Federalist, Essay X by Madison, shows that they wanted to establish a government that would avoid "a rage for paper money, for an abolition of debts, for an equal division of property, or for any other improper or wicked project." Evidently they did not believe that they were endowing the government with unlimited rights. However, it was necessary, both for the Bill of Rights and for any later improvements, to include in the Constitution a provision for amendments. Suppose, now, that some improper or wicked proposal be adopted by Congress and by three-fourths of the states, and become a part of the Constitution. It is not beyond possibility that some form of taxation, some social legislation, or some regulation of commerce, deeply repugnant to Madison or Hamilton, be incorporated in the highest law of the land. In fact this is exactly what has happened. A graduated income tax, previously declared unconstitutional, has become by the process of amendment a most important form of federal revenue.   It will not be seriously doubted that Hamilton would have opposed such a proposal.   But now that it is a part of the Constitution, what view can Hamilton take of the matter?   Although the purpose for which the Constitution was framed has in his eyes been nullified, and an opposite purpose has replaced it, yet Hamilton, by agreeing with the provisions for amendments, had pledged himself to consent to the results of that process.   Does this not mean that Hamilton, and Jefferson all the more, implicitly, unconsciously, and contrary to their intentions, surrendered all their rights?   Is a constitution that provides for amendments logically consistent with the theory of inalienable rights?   And furthermore, to stretch plausibility, but not to go beyond possibility, if American citizens humbly consider recent events in Europe, anti-semitism may become such a force that the Constitution will be amended for the consignment of Jews to concentration camps.   Such an amendment, happily, would not poll enough votes in 1950, any more than an income tax amendment could have won in 1800.   But a century brings changes.   It follows therefore that if an amendment to exterminate the Jews (may I be forgiven for the use of this illustration) is adopted, the government, on this theory, will then have not merely the force but the right to exterminate them. Is not the voice of the people the voice of God?   Does not the majority rule?   And has not everyone, or nearly everyone, consented to the section on amendments?

So it would seem; but there is one further consideration. Did those people who adopted the Constitution reserve the right to terminate the contract?   Or did they bind themselves and their children to acknowledge the right of any amendment and the legitimacy of any governmental action whatever?   As a matter of historical fact a large number of people never consented to continue the contract regardless of alterations in its terms.   Not only could amendments be improper or wicked, but the acts of officials could so nullify the contract that secession would be imperative.   Accordingly a number of states seceded.   They gave evidence that they did not consent.   But the majority won by a long and bloody war.   These rebellious southerners had to be forced to be free.   By marching through Georgia the sovereign power, which is always what it should be, would coerce them to consent.   And because the minority consents, coercion by the majority is not force only, but right also.

Before going on, one may note how the arguments on political theory often shift from historical appeal to ideal ground and back again without an author's seeming to be aware of it.   If Rousseau wishes to argue simply that the consent of the governed is the justification of government, it would be hard to refute him; but then he would have to admit that no actual government rules by right.   If on the other hand he wishes to justify any actual government, he will have to relinquish the social contract theory.   He cannot have it both ways.   Somewhere along the line his answer must have lost contact with the question.   And since this probably occurred at the very beginning, another type of view will be considered. This theory, worked out by Spengler,[28] appears to avoid the inconsistent mixture of ideal and actual and to stick to the facts better than Rousseau's theory did.   It may seem to do so too well, for someone is sure to remark that it sticks so closely to facts that there is no theory at all.

It is true that Spengler deprecates political theory.   Great statesmen like Caesar or Napoleon act immediately on the basis of a flair for facts.   Their action is not sicklied o'er by the pale cast of thought.   If indeed there are any general principles of politics, they never enter the heads of great men.   Political theory is the work of professional pedagogues so remote, inwardly, from political action that they have spun webs of myth about justice, virtue, and freedom.   The problem of politics is not to describe what might or ought to have been, but to penetrate the meaning of the actual events.   All living is politics.   The blind cosmic drive to power, obvious in plants and animals, appears in human life as politics.   War is the primary politics of everything that lives: life and will to battle

_____
28. *Op. cit.*, Vol. II, Chap. XII.

are one. Even when diplomats attempt to substitute intellectual weapons for the sword, the character of battle remains. In every war the essential question is which life power will govern. To be the center of action, to bring one's own family or people to the top of events is the scarcely conscious but irresistible impulse of every person who has an historical vocation. It is not a matter of what laws or system there shall be, nor of what ideals shall be pursued; the sole question is, *Who* shall rule? Revolutions are no exception to this rule of war, for phrases, such as the sovereignty of the people and the consent of the governed, only express the fact that the ruler has assumed the title of people's leader instead of king.

The born statesman has no theory — he judges the situation at a glance and does the right thing without deliberation. Beyond the true and false, never confusing the logic of events with the logic of systems, he may have private convictions, but he is never tied to them in action. "The doer is always conscienceless," said Goethe, "no one has a conscience except the spectator." The essential thing therefore is to understand the time for which one is born. He who does not sense the secret forces, who does not feel himself driven forward on an undefined path, who believes in the surface, public opinion, large phrases and ideals of the day — he is not of the stature for its events; he is in their power, not they in his.

Politics is the art of the possible. Every doer is born for a time, and thereby the ambit of his attainable achievement is fixed. Rarely is a fine politician unaware of his limitations, and rarely does he overlook anything realizable within them. On the other hand political idealists create out of nothing; their castles of the mind, constructed of airy concepts like wisdom and righteousness, liberty and equality, are built from the top story downward. The master of fact, for his part, imperceptibly directs what he sees and accepts as plain reality. The secret of all victory lies in the organization of the nonobvious. By this means Tallyrand could go to Vienna as ambassador of the vanquished and make himself master of the victors.

What needs to be done must be done opportunely. Political forms are living forms whose changes inexorably follow a definite direction, and to attempt to prevent this course or divert it toward some ideal is to confess oneself a careless athlete, 'out of condition.' In the period of mounting democracy, as in France in 1789, there is a fatal moment after which it is too late to grant necessary reform as a free gift for the purpose of buying confidence; at that time the reform which should be refused with the sternest energy is given as a sacrifice and as a sign of dissolution. Declining democracy today repeats the same error of trying to hold to yesterday's ideal. On the path toward Caesarism, a Cato is always found.

A statesman, no matter how great, possesses virtually no control over the methods available. One who would seek a more ideal form, who would permit his tastes or feelings to overpower the pulse within him, immediately loses his grip on realities. The present political methods are parliamentary — elections and the press; the politician may respect or despise them, but he must command them. These outer forms of statecraft are merely a disguise. An extension of the franchise (granting the Negro a vote in the South) is quite unimportant in comparison with the technique of operating the votes.

The art of politics is to maintain one's own nation inwardly in form for events outside. Internal politics exist exclusively for international politics. Internal reform, economics, and social policy are for the purpose of buying the trust and confidence of the people, of giving them a sense of power, contentment, and on occasion enthusiasm. But the future of the nation will not be decided by internal measures; it will be decided by international power politics. And since the masses are not so clear-sighted, a ruling minority must possess this quality on behalf of the rest. This is the basic principle, not of an aristocratic regime only, but of government itself. Anyone who should genuinely feel himself as the delegate of the people instead of their master would not remain in office for one day.

In the early politics of all cultures, the form of government is preestablished and unquestioned. The connection with the mother soil, the feudal tie, or the aristocratic privilege is so strong and self-evident that politics in a Homeric or Gothic age is limited to plain action within the given form. Struggles among minorities or factions proceed on the premises of these forms; the forms themselves are never objects of contention; and any change in form is unplanned and spontaneous. A struggle over form begins only when the bourgeoisie and the city become conscious of their opposition to the Estates. Then the powers of intellect and money set themselves up against blood and tradition. The organized replaces the organic; the party replaces the estate. Forms of the governing minority develop steadily from estate through party towards that of an individual's following. The period of party politics has covered two centuries in our own case, and since World War I it is well on the decline; for the outward sign of the end of democracy and its transition to Caesarism is the disappearance of the party. Democracy made the naive assumption that the mass of the electorate could choose men capable of managing a nation's affairs. Indeed, this is possible at the start when not even the rudiments of group organization exist. But as soon as parliament assembles, tactical units form within it, whose cohesion depends on the will to maintain a dominant position. These tactical units use all the expedients of agitation to make the people their tool and in turn the organization becomes the tool of its leader. The will to power is stronger than any theory.

Whether theories are true or false, continues Spengler, is a question without meaning for political history. But whether they are effective, and how long a belief in theories is a real force in affairs, are important matters. For this reason documents like the *Social Contract* and the *Communist Manifesto* are engines of power in the hands of men who know how to use the convictions of the dominated masses. The end of such theories comes, not from academic refutation, but from boredom. Rousseau is no longer interesting; soon Marx will suffer the same fate. Men finally abandon, not this or that theory, but the belief in theory of any kind. The result of attachment to theory can be seen in the ruin Plato brought upon Syracuse. Similarly the doctrinaire Jacobins with their love of liberty put the country into the hands of the Army and the Bourse. Socialism blazes new paths for capitalism. Theories are threadbare school-exercises; power alone matters.

Spengler's frank appeal to power as an explanation of politics is exactly what Rousseau in his opening chapters of the *Social Contract* set out to deny. But Rousseau has apparently failed. An analysis of his theories sweeps away every factor but force. Majorities persecute minorities, patriots replace tyrants, and Caesars are replacing democracies, all because they can. No inalienable rights are recognized. It was seen that Aristotle was totalitarian: he denied the right of parents to educate their children or even to have children; the state was to select exactly which courses a student would be permitted to take in college; and in general the partnership that includes all partnerships because its good includes all goods would regulate everything. Rousseau came to the same conclusion: men must give up all their rights to the state, and then the majority rules, determining everything that it thinks needs determination. In some situations a few trivial matters may escape bureaucratic control; but nothing important will escape. "The right which the social compact gives the Sovereign over the subjects does not, we have seen, exceed the limits of public expediency. The subjects then owe the Sovereign an account of their opinions only to such an extent as they matter to the community. Now, it matters very much to the community that each citizen should have a religion. . . . There is therefore a purely civil profession of faith of which the Sovereign should fix the articles, not exactly as religious dogmas, but as social sentiments without which a man cannot be a good citizen or a faithful subject. While it can compel no one to believe them, it can banish from the State whoever does not believe them — it can banish him, not for impiety, but as an antisocial being, incapable of truly loving the laws and justice, and of sacrificing, at need, his life to his duty. If anyone, after publicly recognizing these dogmas, behaves as if he does not believe them, let him be punished by death."[29]

Rousseau has quite a facility for mis-expressing himself. The tone of the paragraph suggests that the State makes very few demands on the citizens — just what is expedient, some opinions only, no really religious demands, only some social sentiments, and there will be no compulsion about believing them; the disbeliever will be banished, of course not for impiety but because he is antisocial, or if he remains in the state and behaves as if he does not believe, he will be put to death. "Whoever dares to say: 'Outside the Church is no salvation,' ought to be driven from the state." And so in the name of patriotism, Rousseau, Nero, Tojo, and apparently T. V. Smith, would discourage the religions they do not like and establish their own.

Aristotle and Rousseau, not to mention Spengler, have come to a common conclusion in politics: totalitarianism. Since these men had such different backgrounds, this agreement seems to be more than a coincidence. It must be the result of a common presupposition held, perhaps unconsciously, by them all. This underlying presupposition seems to be a nontheistic world view. If there is no source of rights other than the state, whether with Rousseau it is based on a social convention or with Aristotle it is as natural a development as the family, if there is no force more powerful than the state, if there is no God who controls states, then totalitarianism is the conclusion to be expected. Both Aristotle and Rousseau made some profession of belief in God, but neither of them thought of God as a real factor in political science. Theism cannot properly be regarded as a mere belief in some sort of divine principle: a God who is worth anything is a God who makes a difference in politics and in every phase of philosophy. What is the difference? The discussion turns therefore to a theistic

---

29. *Op. cit.*, IV, viii, pp. 113-115.

and particularly to a Christian view of human rights and civil government.

A Theistic View

The best starting point for an exposition of the Christian view of politics is the Pauline statement on the authorization of government: "Let every soul be subject unto the higher powers. For there is no power but of God: the powers that be are ordained of God. Whosoever therefore resisteth the power, resisteth the ordinance of God: and they that resist shall receive to themselves damnation. For rulers are not a terror to good works, but to the evil. Wilt thou then not be afraid of the power? do that which is good, and thou shalt have praise of the same: For he is the minister of God to thee for good. But if thou do that which is evil, be afraid; for he beareth not the sword in vain: for he is the minister of God, a revenger to execute wrath upon him that doeth evil. Wherefore ye must needs be subject, not only for wrath, but also for conscience sake. For for this cause pay ye tribute also: for they are God's ministers, attending continually upon this very thing. Render therefore to all their dues: tribute to whom tribute is due; custom to whom custom; fear to whom fear; honour to whom honour."[30]

This statement, while it is subject to limitations expressed elsewhere, gives the general Christian position. The basic thought is that government is a divine institution. The authority of magistrates does not derive from any voluntary social compact, but it derives from God. In view of the Roman system, corrupt and tyrannical as it was, under which Paul and the Christians lived and suffered, it is absurd to suppose that Paul was satisfied with the empty phrases of the consent of the governed and the surrendering of rights by agreement. All human rights are gifts from God, who out of the same lump of clay can fashion one vessel to honor and another to dishonor. It is not to be assumed that any man has a right

---

30. Rom. 13:1-7.

to surrender any right given to him. At any rate, God is the source of all rights. He is sovereign in dispensing them, and the rights of magistrates are given to them by God. These rights are best exemplified in the powers of capital punishment and taxation. Without these no government could continue in existence. It is the essence of government to coerce, and capital punishment, or more generally the power of life and death, the power of the sword, used both against crime and in war, is the most conspicuous form of coercion. Similarly, coercive taxation is needed for the government's support. In singling out these two items as ordained of God, Paul gives a quite sufficient basis for governmental authority.

Naturally this theistic justification of governmnet is co-herent with the Christian view of God's sovereignty in history. The Old Testament had taught that God sets up kings and casts down kings; it had taught that heathen rulers, iike Cyrus, fulfil God's plan though they are unconscious of it; and Paul is merely applying the same general principle to the field of politics.

It may be noted too that the Christian theory of politics avoids certain disjunctions that non-theistic thought takes as complete. From Aristotle and Rousseau it would seem that government is either a natural product like the family or a social convention. Non-theistic thought might add a third possibility as well: government is a matter of force, of will to power, alone. And without considering the Christian position, one might suppose that there are no other possibilities. That Paul did not consider government as based on social convention has already been mentioned. That it is not merely a matter of Spenglerian force is also clear from the quotation. And it is equally true that government is not a natural in-stitution like the family. There is to be sure a very important sense in which the family also is a divine institution. On the Christian position everything is ultimately to be referred to God. And if the word *natural* were to be understood in some antitheistic sense, then nothing would be natural. However, Christianity makes a distinction between the family and government that would not have appealed to Aristotle. The family is a divine provision with respect to man's original nature. Before the fall of man into sin, God gave Adam a wife and commanded them to "multiply and replenish the earth." But there was no provision for civil government before the fall. When man was created God gave him "dominion over the fish of the sea and over the fowl of the air, and over the cattle, and over all the earth," but there was no dominion given over other men. In this natural state of innocence there was no need of civil government. But the situation changed when man fell. Sinful man needs to be restrained, and it is in connection with man's acquired evil nature that the ideas of master, servant, and ruler enter. St. Augustine made a point of this.[31] "Sin therefore is the mother of servitude and first cause of man's subjection to man: which notwithstanding comes not to pass but by the direction of the Highest, in whom is no injustice, and who alone knows best how to proportion his punishment to man's offenses. . . . But take a man as God created him at first, and so he is neither slave to man nor to sin." In thus avoiding the disjunction between Aristotle's natural government and Rousseau's conventional government, the Christian theory of politics is consistent with its view of human nature as it now actually is. All the nontheistic systems assume that the present condition of man is normal; the Christian system views actual humanity as abnormal. This answers a question which is occasionally raised in political discussion as to whether the state is a positive good or essentially an evil. The Christian answer is that the state is not a positive or unconditional good, but rather a necessary evil. To do justice to the Christian view one must insist on both adjective and noun. The state is an evil not only because of the abuse of power by the magistrates, but also because it interferes with freedom and introduces an unnatural superiority among men. But the state is also necessary under actual conditions because without civil government each man's evil

31. *The City of God*, XIX, xv.

nature would turn his freedom to intolerable actions. The existence of the state is a partial punishment and cure for sin.

When the several factors of the theistic position are kept in mind, it appears to possess a greater degree of coherence than the humanistic view. Not only does Christianity succeed and humanism fail to solve the basic problem of the justification of government, but also in the subsidiary details of the so-called 'liberal' humanistic proposals there appears to be self-contradiction. Those who espouse socialistic principles or who advocate communism without openly professing an attachment to violence sometimes produce strange combinations of ideas. They frequently insist on the evils of capitalistic monopoly, they picture little Red poor people as in mortal danger of big bad business, they furnish the impetus of soak-the-rich campaigns; and yet they often combine with this the doctrine of liberal theologians that men are essentially good. But if men are essentially good, how is it that when they pass from psychology or theology to politics only the poor remain good and the wealthy become evil? Further complications arise from the demand for more and more governmental regulation. This demand seems to imply that not only are poor people good, but politicians are even better. Since politicians are immune from evil, temptation, and the profit motive, they can be trusted to regulate all our affairs. In this humanistic, socialistic view, it seems that wealth corrupts but power does not. But if men are essentially good, not even wealth should corrupt; and in this case government regulation should not be necessary. This lack of coherence seems to spring from two basic humanistic tendencies. The first is the exalted opinion humanism has of man's nature, and the second is the drive of non-theistic political theory toward totalitarianism. Unless the rights of government are given and limited by God, there is no systematic ground between anarchy and dictatorship.

Christianity by its more coherent thought escapes this choice. It holds that all men, poor as well as rich, politicans as well as business men, are sinful and are in need of restraint. And they are in such need of restraint that the Christian is under obligation to obey governments that are in many ways undesirable. When Paul insists that every soul should be subject to the powers that be, he is evidently removing from individual judgment any question as to a *de jure* as opposed to a *de facto* government. Julius Caesar instituted the Roman imperial system by a criminal *coup d' état;* Augustus also had little claim to a throne other than armed force; and Christians, especially the Jewish Christians of the first century, could easily produce arguments against obeying Rome. It will not be forgotten that one of the catch questions put to Christ was, "Is it lawful to pay tribute to Caesar?" Probably most of the Jews secretly believed that it was unlawful. Christ's answer and Paul's statement are justifications of *de facto* government. The powers that be, *i.e.,* the actually existing powers are ordained of God. Their taxes may be, and in those days were exceedingly unjust, but it is the religious, and not merely political obligation of the Christian to pay them. Rebellion or revolution on account of taxation is not condoned by these statements. It does not follow that Christians are enjoined from using all legal and peaceful means toward a just and honest administration. On the contrary the obvious tenor of the Bible is to lay an obligation on men to promote justice in all the activities of life.

To pursue this thought may give the impression of leaving the high plane of abstract philosophy to descend into the sordid details of party propaganda; but, once more, if theism is not to remain a vague and useless fancy but is to be a force in actual life, it must attempt to apply itself to concrete practical affairs, even though the application be less rigorous in logic than generalities are. And taxation is a sufficiently important detail, if one wishes to speak of justice. Economists list three desiderata in tax procedure. The first, ease of collection, is purely a matter of convenience, and need not be discussed except to say that it is unfortunate if considerations of ease crowd out principles of justice. In the second place, a good tax law ought to proportion the tax paid to the benefit received.

A poor family with little property ought not to pay as much for police protection as a wealthy family with a pleasant estate. But if life is an equal value to all, there is something strange, when war comes and large military expenditures are necessary, in requiring the person who has saved for a life insurance policy to lose half its buying power by inflation, while the spendthrift loses nothing and enjoys high wages to boot. In more recent years economists have added to the principle of payment for benefit received a third principle under the title of equality of sacrifice. This is a high sounding name and millions of people are delighted to see that by this principle the wealthy pay enormous taxes while the poor escape. It can easily be seen, however, that the second and the third of these commonly acknowledged desiderata are mutually inconsistent. Not only so, but in the name of this splendid principle of equality of sacrifice, procedures have been put into effect that cannot possibly be called just and that are in fact violations of the principle itself. The graduated income tax,[32] to which Hamilton objected on a previous page, is a conspicious example. The point is not that the wealthy pay more than the poor — there is no injustice in that. A man with ten times the income of another should pay ten times as much, for he receives ten times the protection. But no principle of justice could obligate him to pay a hundred times as much. If this is what equality of sacrifice means, then equality of sacrifice should be repudiated as unjust. If the moral obtuseness of the modern community fails to perceive this injustice, perhaps a violation of the principle itself can be made clear. The present tax procedure requires the wealthy and even the moderately well-to-do to pay, not just a hundred times the amount others pay, but an amount that is infinitely greater, for some people pay no income tax at all. But an infinitely greater tax can hardly be defended as equality of anything. This, however, can be said in its favor: it enables politicians to buy votes with their opponents' money.

---

32. This example, rather than another of the many unjust laws, is chosen because it has been made a part of the Constitution.

The Christian will not try to evade any unjust tax, but in the interest of Christian morality he will advocate its repeal. Beyond taxation and in general, a Christian, since he believes that rulers are as evil as anyone else, would normally oppose the extension of government regulations.   Power is a much more dangerous possession than wealth, and even anarchy is no worse than totalitarianism.   For purely temporal reasons, aside from religious considerations later to be mentioned, anyone who recognizes the evil tendencies of human nature could not consistently encourage a paternalistic, welfare-police state. Nonetheless, injustice, corruption, and fraudulent social and tax policies are not sufficient reasons for revolution.   The powers that be, including Caligula and Nero, are ordained of God.

A careless reading of the Pauline passage and a failure to collect the whole of the Biblical teaching on politics might result in the impression that all civil disobedience is condemned by Christian principles.   And certain Christian authors have in fact argued in favor of such an interpretation, but it is not difficult to show that this is a mistaken view.[33] For the very reason that government is a divine institution with its authority derived from God, it follows that totalitarian governments are without authority beyond the limits set by God.   And if magistrates exceed their authority, no one is under obligation to obey.   This Christian justification of civil disobedience does not depend solely on a bare general principle.   The Bible several times makes explicit statements and gives several concrete examples.   Both principle and example are found in Peter's defiance of the Jewish court[34] when he said, "Whether it be right in the sight of God to hearken unto you more than unto God, judge ye."   This is consistent with Christ's earlier statement, "Render therefore unto Caesar the things which are Caesar's, and unto God the things that are God's," — a

---

33. John Milton, *The Tenure of Kings and Magistrates*, emphasizes the limitations of civil authority beyond what is necessary for the present argument. Milton's interpretation of the Scriptures may not be far wrong, but he entangles himself with the theory of the consent of the governed.
34. The Acts 4:5-21.

statement which presupposes that Caesar's rights are limited. In view of the fact that nearly all of the apostles were executed on charges of religious crime, it is strange to find any Christian arguing against civil disobedience *simpliciter*. The Old Testament also gives instances of disobedience approved and commanded by God. Moses' mother disobeyed the Egyptian government when she preserved Moses alive. Shadrach, Meshach, and Abednego on one occasion and Daniel on another refused to obey the king. And there is little doubt but that this principle justified the disobedience of Niemoeller and his Church in Germany as well as condemned the unprincipled pusillanimity of the Universities. Since totalitarian rulers, like all men, are evil, and since they are usually more evil than other men, it may be expected that they will issue and enforce decrees that conflict with God's laws. Nebuchadnezzar, the Caesars, and the twentieth century dictators show that this is the uniform lesson of history. Accordingly the greatest danger today is not a third World War, disastrous though it will be, but the great calamity is the increasing extension of government regulation. An expanding state must come into conflict with the only authority that limits it.

The purpose of this chapter is to give evidence that Christian presuppositions justify civil governments of limited rights, whereas humanistic principles imply either anarchy or totalitarianism. The person who considers these matters is forced to make a choice. He may choose humanism because he is enamoured of anarchy or of his chances of becoming a dictator; or he may have a desire for political liberty, in which case Christianity will provide him with a coherent worldview. But can he maintain intellectual consistency if he favors political liberty and rejects the Christian presuppositions?

So far as the discussion of this chapter goes it might be maintained that freedom can be justified without Christianity. It will be pointed out that even if Aristotle and Rousseau are totalitarian, it does not follow that other non-Christian systems are. This is a perfectly logical criticism. The implications of two men cannot be blindly imposed on other theories. And to this extent the present chapter is inconclusive. Its defense lies only in the suggestion that if two of the major political authors, differing extremely in their background, motivation, and general philosophy, come to the same totalitarian conclusion, it is less likely to be a mere coincidence than a result of some very basic common principle. This common principle seems to be the denial of any specific application of the concept of God to the problems of politics. For this reason it would not be surprising if further study should find other non-theistic political theories resulting in totalitarianism.

A second objection to the argument of this chapter will also come to mind. It may be true that only in a theistic worldview can both anarchy and totalitarianism be avoided. But though this may be a satisfactory motive for choosing theism, it is not a reason for choosing Christianity. There are other forms of theism. Unitarianism, Judaism, and Mohammedanism are theistic, but they are not Christian. The argument of the chapter therefore provides no sufficient motive for choosing Christianity rather than Judaism. This second objection is not only as formally logical as the first but it is materially more applicable. While there are hints as to how to answer the first objection, it seems there are none that meet this second. And for that matter the chapter fails to motivate anarchists and dictators to choose Christianity or any other form of theism. Its force will be felt only by those who already have a love of freedom. In fact those who desire to reduce men to the condition of regimented robots will be motivated against Christianity — and very consistently so. They make their choice. This simply means that political considerations favoring a theistic worldview constitute only a fraction of the argument. Arguments against totalitarianism must be sought, not in politics narrowly defined but in ethics, or some more general sphere; and similarly the choice between Christianity and other theistic systems requires theological and not just political arguments.

There is a third objection that clashes much more directly with the argument of the chapter. It denies that Christianity avoids totalitarianism, and in fact asserts that only humanism can preserve freedom. This objection has been expressed in varying degrees of vigor by many authors, and a recent statement[35] is taken merely as illustrative. After asserting, with some plausibility, that totalitarian rulers usually base their authority on philosophical absolutism (defined as "the metaphysical view that there is an absolute reality, *i.e.,* a reality that exists independently of human knowledge"), Professor Kelsen apparently tries to convert the proposition and assert further that belief in the existence of a reality independent of human knowledge implies political absolutism. "If one believes in the existence of the absolute, and consequently in absolute values, in the absolute good — to use Plato's terminology — is it not meaningless to let a majority vote decide what is politically good? ... That value judgments have only relative validity, one of the basic principles of philosophic relativism, implies that opposite value judgments are neither logically nor morally impossible. It is one of the fundamental principles of democracy that everybody has to respect the political opinion of everybody else, since all are equal and free. Tolerance, minority rights, freedom of speech, and freedom of thought, so characteristic of democracy, have no place within a political system based on the belief in absolute values.... If, however, it is recognized that only relative values are accessible to human knowledge and human will, then it is justifiable to enforce a social order against reluctant individuals only if this order is in harmony with the greatest possible number of equal individuals, that is to say, with the will of the majority .... What is right today may be wrong tomorrow."[36]

While the earlier citations from the Bible show that Christianity as a matter of fact does not condone political absolutism, it may be that Christianity is inconsistent. In that case the

35. *Absolutism and Relativism in Philosophy and Politics,* by Hans Kelsen, in the American Political Science Review, Oct. 1948, pp. 906-914.

36. The author concludes with a section on the trial of Jesus before Pilate, Jesus being the metaphysical absolutist and Pilate the relativist. The full implication of the passage is obscure. Partly it is intended to show that a Christian cannot approve democracy; does it also imply that Pilate's "democracy" ought to be approved?

author's argument would be that, regardless of what the Bible says, a belief in unchanging truth logically implies absolute government, while relative values justify the majority in coercing the reluctant minority. In this argument it seems that Professor Kelsen has confused and contradicted himself, and that his general intent is almost demonstrably false. While a belief in absolute or unchanging values may render it meaningless to allow a majority to determine what is politically good, in the same sense that it is meaningless to let a majority decide what is mathematically correct, it does not follow that a belief in unchanging truths is inconsistent with majority voting.

Two reasons are pertinent. In the first place, voting is not intended to determine what is good. The aim of a vote is to determine the will of the majority, and it cannot be granted that the majority is *ipso facto* right. Too often the will of the majority has been mistaken or evil. If Professor Kelsen should reply that on this basis a wise dictator could better have decided what was good, and that therefore totalitarianism is implied, he would have to be reminded that human nature is evil. A wise dictator might indeed know what was good for his people or for the world and at the same time choose his own selfish aggrandizement. Politics is not so much a device for discovering the good for the purpose of academic speculation as it is for coercing groups of people. The question is not whether a dictator can know, but whether one man can safely be trusted with power. Democracy is best, not because a majority is wiser than a dictator, but because a large number of evil people working at cross purposes does less harm than a single irresponsible ruler. Then in the second place, a belief in unchanging truth does not imply totalitarianism because something depends on what these truths are. One may believe that it is unchangeably true that human nature is evil and that no man should be trusted with unlimited power. Such an absolute belief is patently inconsistent with totalitarianism. Therefore Kelsen is mistaken when he asserts that minority rights and freedom of speech have no place within a political system based on the belief in absolute values. Quite the contrary, it would seem that the absolute values of political liberty and the unchanging truth of human depravity furnish far more stable opposition to totalitarianism than the position that what is right today may be wrong tomorrow. If value judgments have only relative or temporary validity, and if the opposite value judgments are neither logically nor morally impossible, then even though democracy is good today, despotism may be good tomorrow.

And further, since the author connects politics with metaphysics and epistemology, his consistency here may also be tested. He has stated that coercion is justified only if it is in harmony with the will of the majority, and he asserts that what is right today may be wrong tomorrow. Are these two statements relative, changing, and temporary, or are they absolute, fixed truths? If they are relative, then tomorrow a minority, a minority of one, may be justified in coercing all the rest; and also it will no longer be true that what is right then may become wrong later on. Dictatorship will then be permanently right. In other words, Kelsen asserts philosophic relativism as a philosophically absolute truth. This has all the appearances of the deep-seated confusion with which Protagoras, to whom Kelsen refers with approval, has infected all his modern descendants.

The conclusion therefore is that Christianity is self-consistent in these matters, and that it safeguards human rights and political liberty as humanism and relativism do not.

IV

ETHICS

CHAPTER IV

Ethics

A S the discussion of the nature and authority of government revealed its various complexities, it must have become evident that much of the argument passes beyond the limits of strictly political theory. That there are religious implications in every view was made clear. Other aspects of politics tended to merge either with sociology or with a general philosophy of history. Then, too, it was seen that the problem of politics could not be solved without answering the psychological question as to the nature of man. But of all the subjects to which the preceding chapter led, it is ethics that demands immediate attention. In fact it may have seemed that not a single important decision on politics could be made without choosing between competing moral ideals. Of any particular proposal one had to ask whether it was right or wrong. If the proposal were shown to be a plausible means to an end, one could not avoid the question, Is this end a good end or an evil end? It is therefore impossible to arrive at a satisfactory theory of politics without having first settled the questions of ethics.

Classification of Sciences

This relationship between ethics and politics presupposes the general problem of the classification of sciences, and a short explanation of this matter is required, not so much to clarify the preceding chapters as to prepare for those that follow. The more the various subjects are studied, the more their interrelationships will be seen. Indeed, the breadth of philosophic discipline as opposed to the narrow specialty of a single science depends on these manifold and intricate connections.

For example, the reason that epistemology has been regarded as the crucial point and the most profound part of philosophy is that botany, sociology, physics, and literature furnish it with a common area of investigation.   In a less technical, or at least in a less philosophical setting, anyone who borrows books from a library depends on the results of a particular classification of subjects.   For the convenience of the borrower the librarian has put political books on one shelf, travel on another, while fiction has a room to itself.   Library science, under the compulsion of practical efficiency, autocratically divides all knowledge into ten sections and makes ten subdivisions in each section.   The arbitary character of this procedure witnesses to the difficulty of obtaining an ideal solution, for philosophers have been no more successful than the librarians in working out a detailed classification, and when the implications of the matter are studied, even the larger divisions are difficult to fix.[1]

When the subordination of one science to another is mentioned, or when ethics is said to be basic to politics, it does not mean that the higher, or less independent, science can be reduced to the lower.   It does not mean that politics is ethics.   It means, however, that the terms and principles of the lower science are used in the higher, but the terms of the higher are not found in the lower.   And it also means that nothing in the higher science can violate the more general laws of the lower one.   For example, politics cannot be discussed without the employment of moral principles, although ethics can be discussed without reference to politics.   Or, similarly, zoological terms are not used in physics; but the principle of leverage, strictly a matter of physics, is exemplified in the muscles and bones of animals.   Presumably there could be a physical world without life in it; but there could not be a zoological world without physics.   Zoology depends on physics.   It so depends on physics that it cannot violate the laws of physics.   And this remains true even under the important conditions that life cannot be reduced to or explained by physico-chemical

---

1. See note 26, p. 222.

law.   Similarly, man may exist in such an uncomplicated society that there might be no state or government other than the family.   In such a situation ethics would be exemplified but not politics.   But no condition is conceivable in which there might be politics without ethics.   Ethics therefore is the prior subject.

The warning is imperative, however, that the hierarchy of sciences is not a simple linear arrangement.   Auguste Comte insisted that there were exactly six sciences, and that they could be arranged in a straight line: mathematics,[2] astronomy, physics, chemistry, physiology, and sociology.   At best, this is an extreme oversimplification, as any librarian will testify. A more adequate model of the hierarchy of sciences might be the relationships among the members of the various royal families of Europe.   For the present discussion, however, it must suffice to insist that ethics is basic to politics and to show that ethics is also basic to other phases of other subjects as well.

For example, it might seem that psychology would be a more general and more inclusive subject than ethics, for, it could be argued, ethics cannot be discussed without using such psychological terms as emotion, conation, desire, motivation, consciousness, behaviour, and so on; whereas these psychological functions of man could be described without any appeal to morality.   Theoretically possible though this may be, psychologists as a matter of fact find such restrictions too cramping.   And if psychology is what psychologists write, ethics is found to underlie at least a section of psychological theory.

Two examples may be taken from a recent book.[3]   In a chapter on "Social Proficiency and Leadership" there is a subsection on *Indirect Presentation of Ideas* in which the author gives this advice:

---

2. Strictly speaking Comte did not call mathematics a "science."
3. Fred McKinney, *Psychology of Personal Adjustment*, p. 301, (John Wiley & Sons, N. Y., 1941).

Impute the idea to others.

'I am sure you feel our idea has much merit.'
'As an intelligent man you know better than I
that this view is true.'

Imply the answer in the question.

'Don't you believe every American father should
make sure that his children will receive the
same education as others in their group?'
'Isn't it true that we are basically human...'

Presumably this is presented as a scientific analysis of personality production. Really it imposes the author's views of ethics on the student. A student of good moral character would resent the author's advice, and if he had a knowledge of the Greek Sophists, he would become suspicious of the whole book.

Later in the same book[4] is another example of how ethical theory underlies professions of science. It is an account of psychiatric treatment.

A minister, forty years of age, and apparently satisfactory to his congregation, began to fear that some Sunday morning he would involuntarily swear while preaching his sermon. This fear so unsettled him that he thought he would have to give up the ministry. The psychiatrist advised him to go out in the country where no one could hear him and curse profusely until the fear no longer troubled him.

Obviously the ethics of the psychiatrist made profanity a trivial matter though holding on to a job was considered important. A believer in God would normally think that profanity is wrong and would say, "Thou shalt not take the name of the Lord thy God in vain." If no other cure of this fear could be found, it would be better to resign one's pulpit than to curse God. One's ethics therefore and one's psychiatry are not independent sciences. The theories a given psychiatrist advances are not just the result of disinterested observation;

4. *Ibid.* p. 445.

they do not conform to the popular canon of objective scientific description; on the contrary one's psychology depends on one's religion and ethics. If there are phases of psychology suitable to strict scientific description, and even if psychology as a science ought to be limited to such material,[5] none the less much of what is published under the name of psychology represents the author's religious or irreligious views.

The standards of ethics apply still further, in spheres where they are not well received; for aesthetics, too, must be judged morally. Such a view is not popular. Not only are the Puritans ridiculed, but even Plato is condemned for his moralizing theory of art. Art, it is said, has its own standards: whether it promotes morality or immorality has no bearing on the question of aestheic value. There is undoubtedly some truth in this criticism. Obscene paintings can be as professionally excellent as a Descent from the Cross. And yet it is not with such ease that moral strictures on art are discarded. Aristotle is sometimes represented as having transcended Plato's narrow, moralistic theory of art. Yet Aristotle gives the purpose of tragedy as the purging of the emotions of pity and fear. And this itself is a matter of morality, for one may well ask, Ought pity and fear to be purged; to what degree should they be purged; and is tragedy a proper means to this end? Obviously ethics will not teach one how to paint a picture or how to write a tragedy. Nor will the principles of morality judge the professional techique. On the other hand, ethics and only ethics will judge whether a given painting or a given tragedy ought to be produced. Even the artists and the aestheticians are no longer so enthusiastic about "Art for Art's sake" as they once were. And if it is admitted that art has a serious purpose in the life and culture of people, it will be impossible to rule out considerations of morality.

The science of physics, at least, seems to be independent of ethics; yet in this field, too, a question has arisen whether the atom bomb ought to have been invented. This question may, however, depend on a confusion. Perhaps a distinction is

---

5. Some psychiatrists advocate a non-directive therapy.

needed between the scientist who invents and the political and human being who uses the bomb for military purposes. But it is so hard these days to be only a scientist, only a psychologist, only an aesthetician, and not a man with ethical and religious standards, prejudices, and presuppositions. It may still be maintained that, although a man cannot be so split in two, the science of physics itself is independent of ethical principles. Can the law of the pendulum swing on a moral pivot? To determine the precise relation between physics and ethics, and whether ethics is ultimately autonomous, requires certain intricacies that are to be developed in this and the next chapter. At this point the conclusion is that ethical theory colors many subjects.

The Questions of Ethics

Since ethics covers the entire range of human character and conduct, one might at first be tempted to say that the study of ethics should begin with the question, What actions are right and what actions are wrong? The question seems to be a plausible starting point. Should not a study of ethics disclose to us the types of action that are good and those that are evil? Eventually it should. Of what use would a theory of ethics otherwise be? But two disappointments await the student who begins in this way. The first and very superficial impression would be that everyone or nearly everyone agrees on what is right and wrong. No one seriously advocates theft and murder as conducive to the good life. And if there is a very wide range of agreement, ethics could be of value only in minor or trivial matters where disagreement makes little difference anyhow. On further examination, however, this superficial view gives place to a second disappointment. Soon it is discovered that there is much less agreement, even about theft and murder, than was at first supposed. One source of disagreement lies in the difficulty of knowing what theft is. Contrary to popular and naive opinions, it is very difficult to define theft. Of course we would admit that picking pockets, shop lifting, and embezzlement

are forms of theft. But if a director of a corporation, knowing
that the company is in poor condition, sells his stock, is that
theft? Just possibly it is. Well, is it theft if a broker on the
exchange buys or sells stock for himself? It hardly seems
so. Then, why was it made illegal? Therefore the question,
what types of acts are wrong? must be replaced by the question, what is the definition of such and such a type of conduct?
What exactly is theft? What exactly is murder? But the
second disappointment alluded to is not so much the disagreement about definition as it is the much more serious disagreement concerning the rightness and wrongness of clearly defined
types of action. Various writers have collected interesting
examples of moral standards that differ widely from the ordinary opinions of our time and place. For example, the
Greeks, as Aristotle recommended, exposed sickly infants. Put
aside the somewhat verbal question as to whether this should
be called murder or not. The action of abandoning babies
on the mountains is clearly defined. The essential question,
not a question of mere words, is, Is this action right or wrong?
The Greeks said it was right; the Christians say it is wrong.
There is a sharp disagreement on this material question. It
is also said that the Eskimos kill their aged parents. And some
tribes in the south seas practice cannibalism. These are not
just anthropological oddities to be curiously recorded by a
superior white race: they are deep rooted moral differences.
It is not necessary to collect examples from primitive tribes:
theft, murder, and unspeakable atrocities have been and are
today regarded as legitimate political procedure. Hitler
massacred the Jews in an effort to make his type of morality
supreme, and Stalin has murdered no one knows how many
Ukrainian farmers and has exiled thousands to brutal concentration camps in Siberia. Some who have escaped, like
Trotsky, have been hounded around the globe to be cornered
and murdered. And probably Trotsky too would have murdered Stalin if he could have done so. Such gross moral
differences cannot remain unnoticed. But also within the
limits of western civilization, there are other differences, quite

as important theoretically, even if less obvious and shocking. There are some people who defend so-called mercy killings; others say it is murder and is wrong. Some people oppose capital punishment; others say that "whoso sheddeth man's blood, by man shall his blood be shed; for in the image of God made he man." Some say war is never justified and some have sworn oaths not to defend their country even if and when it is attacked. These problems are not merely verbal. They are real and serious.

But in attempting to solve them we shall find that the discussion has carried us beyond the question, What actions are right? The fact of disagreement discloses a more profound question. When communism approves brutality and when Christianity encourages liberty, it is no longer of any use to ask what is right or what is wrong. Each opposing system has already made its statement on this point, and the next question is, Why?

Why is this act right and that act wrong? What makes an action right? What makes another act wrong? It is no longer the definitions of theft or honesty that are sought, but the definitions of right and wrong. What is the basis of morality?

Teleological Ethics

The problem of the basis of morality has been profoundly studied and profusely discussed by the philosophers of all ages. For purposes of rapid comprehension their theories may be conveniently divided into two groups. There are those who assert that the morality of an act depends on its consequences, and there are those who say the contrary. The former picture the moral motive as a desire for the Good, and an act is virtuous if it is a means to that end. This type of ethics may be called teleological ethics because the moral value of an act depends upon its purpose. The latter type of theory may be called ateleological. An act is virtuous whether or not the consequences happen to be good. Virtue or vice lies somehow in the act itself and not in some far off Good. Since the representatives of teleological ethics have been by far the more numerous, they will be considered first.

At the outset someone might object that this type of theory is not worth while discussing because it is obviously false. The moral value of an act cannot be judged by its consequences for the reason that the agent cannot control them. A man may have the best intentions and he may do what is right, and yet through some accidental, unforeseen circumstance, the consequences are unhappy. For example, he might make a generous donation to a charitable organization that has been highly recommended to him. But because of some recent change in the board of directors or for some other reason of which the donor is unaware, the money is used foolishly or even wickedly. Does this unforeseen consequence make the act of donation evil? Should not its moral value depend on the intention of the donor and not on the consequences of the act? Or, conversely, a wicked man may intend to do harm, but for similar reasons the results turn out to be good. Do not motives, the objector asks, bear on moral values as much as or even more than consequences do? There seems to be real force in such a criticism, for motives in morality have a *prima facie* claim to consideration, and the second type of theory, the ateleological morality that completely escapes this embarrassment, will be given its day in court. But the objection as now stated has little weight because it depends on too limited a concept of consequences. In the example chosen the gift was judged immoral because the charitable organization misused it, as if this misuse were the only pertinent consequence. Teleological ethics, however, instead of taking such a limited view, considers consequences of the widest and most inclusive variety. Not only is the immediate, external result a factor, but involved also are all the consequences to the agent, to his friends, and to all society, of acting on principle. If generosity in ninety-nine cases out of a hundred produces good results both to the benefited and to the benefactor, it would be wrong to cultivate stinginess because of an unknown, possible exception. The teleological view of course will have to admit that the actual evil results of this individual gift detract from the total moral value of the act — and if this gives aid and comfort to the opposition, nothing can be done about it — but this diminution of value may be overbalanced by the positive good of cultivating generosity both in oneself and in one's circle of acquaintances. The effect on the donor of exercising generous impulses and the effect on others of his example are as much a part of the consequences as what the recipients do with the money. Therefore, the objection as stated fails to apply in full force, with the result that teleological ethics, providing as it does for the internal factors of character and motivation as well as for the external and obvious results, cannot be so easily dismissed.

There is a second preliminary objection to teleological ethics. Instead of dismissing this type of theory as obviously false, the objector might brand it as positively vicious. Far from being a theory of morality, one might declare it a theory of immorality. For, it will be said, if we decide on the basis of consequences, and if virtue is only a means, then this theory is reduced to the execrable position that the end justifies the means. And is there anything more vile than this principle — a principle that has justified the worst crimes in history?

But the objector talks too fast. In the first place, the discussion has not yet gone so far as to have identified the crimes of history. There is a fundamental disagreement on the question whether or not murder is a legitimate political or even personal resource. Possibly the poisonings of Renaissance Italy, the massacre of St. Bartholomew's eve, the atrocities of Hitler, and the more efficient brutality of communism are all good — or at least good to the extent they are successful. The objector has really prejudiced the case by his vigorous language: he has assumed the point at issue. If he can show that murder is wrong and explain why, then perhaps he will have grounds for repudiating the principle that the end justifies the means. But not before. Perhaps not afterwards, either; for even if the events mentioned above are assumed to be the great crimes of history, it does not follow that one must reject this principle. It can be plausibly argued that these events were crimes because they were not means to the end. They were, to be sure, means to an immediate end in someone's mind. The Roman Catholics wanted to rid France of the Protestants, and the massacre accomplished this end. But surely the principle does not mean that any end justifies the successful means to it. The theory as it was explained said that the end was the Good, and the successful means to the Good is called virtue. Whether ridding France of Protestants was a good or not, and whether the accomplished riddance was a means to a more ultimate Good, are questions that we have not so far decided. The theory does not require us to justify massacres; it states merely that after we have decided what is the ultimate Good, any successful means to that end is a virtuous action. This is shocking neither to one's common sense nor to one's moral sense — not that either of these senses is the final judge, but that teleological ethics cannot be so easily dismissed without further discussion.

Egoism

Teleological theories of ethics may be divided into two groups. The one group centers its attention on the individual human being and judges conduct by its efficacy in obtaining the individual's good. This is the theory of Egoism. The other teleological theory, called Utilitarianism, considers the good of the whole human race. We shall first consider egoism.

The word *egoism* in the colloquial language has unpleasant connotations, and to the uninitiated it might seem that no thoughtful person would deliberately adopt an egoistic philosophy. That the colloquial connotations have led to an incorrect inference is seen in the fact that both in antiquity and in modern times, egoism has had notable defenders. Some of its defenders have been much maligned on account of it. The ancient Epicureans have been painted in much darker hues than they deserved, and in modern times Hobbes enjoys a doubtful reputation. But Bishop Butler, Bishop Berkeley, and perhaps Samuel Clarke have adopted the egoistic theory and have maintained both their intellectual and personal reputation.

Confusion has arisen first because of unwarranted but popular connotations and second on a higher level because of failure to distinguish between two very different questions.

In the first place egoism has attracted to itself the unwarranted connotation of selfishness. To be sure, this is no objection unless selfishness can be shown to be immoral, and at this point in the argument not even massacre has been proved wrong. However, even a discussion on a superficial level will serve to clarify the meaning of egoism. People think of an egoist as self-centered and inconsiderate. The egoist looks out for his own interest and by shady dealings takes every possible advantage of his associates. There are of course some men who act in this way. And very unpleasant people they are. But they are not egoists in the technical ethical sense, or at least they are not intelligent egoists. Even selfish people are not usually habitual shoplifters or embezzlers, for there is not enough profit in the one, and there is too much danger in the other. Little intelligence is required to avoid these methods of taking advantage of the public. A little more intelligence will suggest that inconsiderateness does not pay, either. Friends are useful and it is quite worth while cultivating them. Further intelligence will make the "selfish" man quite an agreeable gentleman: perhaps more agreeable than the unselfish do-gooder whose virtues stick out like the quills of a porcupine. The theory of egoism therefore does not necessarily inculcate inconsiderateness or "selfishness." It still remains an open question whether to give complete approval to one who is an agreeable gentleman because it is to his interest to be; it is still an open question whether to recommend honesty because it is the best policy; but at any rate the theory of egoism can be distinguished from ordinary selfishness. More than this: does not egoism have a *prima facie* claim to reasonableness? With all due regard to other people, should I not seek my own good? Should I ever deliberately seek my own harm? No doubt I should sometimes inconvenience myself; no doubt I should make certain sacrifices on occasion; but is there any justification for aiming at my ultimate evil instead of my ultimate good?

In the second place, a more troublesome confusion arises from the failure to distinguish two very different questions. Up to this point egoism has been described as the theory whose fundamental moral principle is that one should always seek his own ultimate good. Egoism is thus a method of determining right from wrong conduct on the basis of its effectiveness in producing the good. But in the history of ethics a different problem has been confused with this. It happens, not perhaps by pure accident and yet not by necessity either, that most egoists have identified the good as pleasure. This, however, is a different matter. It should be clear that two thinkers might disagree on what the nature of ultimate good is, and yet be in accord that one ought to seek one's own good. Egoism, regarded strictly as a method of ethics, does not require the good to be identified with pleasure. The theory that the good is pleasure is properly called hedonism. And while most egoists have been hedonists, there is conceivably a form of egoism that is not hedonistic.

Hedonism, however, rather than egoistic method strictly understood, has received the greater attention from writers on ethics, doubtless because hedonism by concretely identifying the Good is thought to provide a definite goal instead of a vague or unknown ideal. Pleasure is something everybody knows. If one is told to seek his own pleasure in all things, he is supposed to have clearer idea of what is meant and of what to do than if he is told simply to seek his own good. And yet the many discussions of hedonism have served to show that even hedonism is not so definite after all. Quite aside from the question whether or not pleasure is really the supreme good in life, it becomes difficult even to make clear what is meant by pleasure and what relation it has to human motives.

One form of the theory is called psychological hedonism. This term is used to designate the view that all people as a matter of fact always desire pleasure and desire nothing else. This is in effect what Hobbes teaches, although in a disguised form. The clearest formulation of the doctrine is perhaps that of Bentham. "Nature has placed mankind under the governance of two sovereign masters, *pain* and *pleasure*. It is for for them alone to point out what we ought to do, as to determine what we shall do. On the one hand the standard of right and wrong, on the other the chain of causes and effects, are fastened to their throne. They govern us in all we do, in all we say, in all we think: every effort we can make to throw off our subjection, will serve but to demonstrate and confirm it. In words a man may pretend to abjure their empire: but in reality he will remain subject to it all the while."[6] Now although this seemed so clear to Bentham, others reflecting on it have found it obscure. Surely the meaning cannot be that everyone always desires only what gives him pleasure at the moment. It is a fact that people desire or will to take bitter medicine, to go to the dentist, and to engage in physical labor. These things do not give pleasure at the moment; they give pain. Hence it is untrue to say that every desire is immediately directed to a pleasure. Of course the reply is quickly forthcoming that these actions aim at a future pleasure. But is it true that the motive of every action is some future pleasure? There are many evidences that this is not true. A drunkard may know that guzzling his liquor will make him sick and give him a headache, but he guzzles. He desires the immediate pleasure and sacrifices the pleasure of tomorrow. He even goes through a voluntary process of self-deception to do so. After a particularly rigorous bout with alcohol, he may have sworn off: "Never again," he says, "it is not worth it." Then toward evening he may meet some of his cronies, and he argues to himself, "One shot of whiskey won't hurt me; tomorrow morning will be different from previous mornings." Why is it, if the only motive of action is future pleasure, that he persuades himself to believe what

---

6. *An Introduction to the Principles of Morals and Legislation*, Chapter I., (*Oxford*, 1822).

he so clearly knew was false? However this question be answered, at least it can no longer be said that every desire is
directed toward a future pleasure as opposed to an immdiate
one. This same illustration is also disastrous to a third interpretation of psychological hedonism. It might be said that
people desire, not the immedate pleasure only, nor the future
pleasure only, but the greatest pleasure whether near or far.
Yet who can soberly maintain that whiskey today and delirium
tremens tomorrow result in a greater amount of pleasure than
abstinence today and good health tomorrow? And in less
extreme and more ordinary situations there are too many examples of foolish choices to maintain even the plausibility that
everyone always acts with the motive of obtaining the greatest amount of pleasure.

Perhaps someone may still maintain that every desire is
for pleasure, not necessarily the immediate pleasure, not necessarily a future pleasure, but one or the other. Such an objector
would not be convinced that anyone desires to go to the dentist: he really desires to get rid of the pain. Apart from the
question of psychological fact, whether the desire to see the
dentist is an unreal desire and does not exist at all and whether the only real desire is to avoid pain — a question that
need not be discussed here — this form of hedonism must
face two objections. The second objection is of general application, but the first is directed specificially against psychological hedonism. The theory under examination asserts
as a fact that there is no motive except pleasure. Now this
may be a psychological theory, but it is not an ethical theory.
The specific province of ethics is the distinction between right
and wrong, good and bad. One life is better than another.
One life is worse. There are differences. But if every desire
is for pleasure, there can be no differences on this score. Psychological hedonism may possibly be true, but it does not
distinguish between a good and a bad desire. If this form
of hedonism be true, ethics must search for its distinctions
elsewhere. Like the theory of gravitation in physics, psychological hedonism professes to describe what is; it cannot

recommend what ought to be but is not. Ethics on the other hand is a normative study. It makes judgments of value; it commends, and condemns; its characteristic verb is not *is* but *ought*. This then disposes of psychological hedonism.

The second objection is of more general application. Instead of asserting that pleasure is the only motive, the hedonist may say pleasure ought to be the only motive: unfortunately people sometimes desire other things; this is foolish and works to their harm; if they are wise they will seek nothing but pleasure, for pleasure is the good. This better form of hedonism, however, is under obligation to make clear what is meant by pleasure. Implicit in the above discussion is the repudiation of one easy solution. It might have been said that pleasure is to be defined as exactly that which is desired. In this view desire is taken as immediately known by experience. and the word pleasure or pleasant is attached to any object desired. The object is pleasant because it is desired: it is not desired because it is pleasant. This treatment of the word pleasure, however, contributes nothing either to psychology or to ethics, and it was not Bentham's view. Bentham took not only desire but pleasure also as known immediately by experience, and held that desire as we know it is always related to pleasure as we know it. But pleasure as we know it is in danger of becoming as vague and unknown as the Good originally was. Hedonism, it was said above, is the most popular form of egoism because it makes the Good definite by identifying it with pleasure. But what is meant by pleasure? There is one form of pleasure so definite that it would escape all charge of obscurity, *viz.*, sense pleasures. Eating roast turkey, drinking rum, and sexual indulgence are pleasures. There is a minimum of ambiguity here. But if pleasure is restricted to the sense pleasures, the plausibility of identifying good and pleasure vanishes. Few people would seriously maintain that the only motive of action is some sense pleasure; few people would maintain that the ultimate good in life is sense pleasure. On this basis hedonism is *prima facie* improbable. On the other hand, if to the sense pleasure there be added the pleasure of chess, the pleasure of philosophy, or the pleasures that are at God's right hand for evermore, hedonism indeed becomes plausible, but the meaning of pleasure becomes as vague as the Good ever was. And if pleasure cannot be more closely defined than "all sorts of agreeable states of consciousness,"[7] it would be better to drop the discussion of hedonism and confine attention to simple egoism.

But in spite of what has been said in favor of egoism, a lurking suspicion may remain that egoism is an unworthy philosophy. The defense against the charge of selfishness may not have been convincing. At any rate, before adopting the egoistic position, it would be wise to examine an alternative view. Comparison might promote clarity. There was mentioned above a second type of teleological theory, which, instead of centering its attention on the individual person, considers the good of the whole human race.

Utilitarianism

Utilitarianism, with which the name of Jeremy Bentham is inseparably connected, has been vigorously defended in one form or another by a number of prominent thinkers. Bentham himself stated and explained the theory as follows.[8] "By the principle of utility is meant that principle which approves or disapproves of every action whatsoever, according to the tendency which it appears to have to augment or diminish the happiness of the party whose interest is in question. . . . I say of every action whatsoever; and therefore not only of every action of a private individual, but of every measure of government.

"By utility is meant that property in any object, whereby it tends to produce benefit, advantage, pleasure, good, or happiness, (all this in the present case comes to the same thing) or (what comes again to the same thing) to prevent the happening of mischief, pain, evil, or unhappiness to the party whose interest is considered: if that party be the community

---

7. Henry Sidgwick, *Methods of Ethics,* 7th ed. pp. 120, 121., (Macmillan and Company, 1907).
8. *Op. cit.* Chapters I, III, IV.

in general, then the happiness of the community: if a particular individual, then the happiness of that individual. . . .

"It has been shown that the happiness of the individuals, of whom a community is composed, that is their pleasures and their security, is the end and the sole end which the legislator ought to have in view: the sole standard, in conformity to which each individual ought, as far as depends upon the legislator, to be *made* to fashion his behavior. But whether it be this or anything else that is to be *done,* there is nothing by which a man can ultimately be *made* to do it, but either pain or pleasure."

These paragraphs show clearly the basic hedonism of Bentham's position: nothing is good but pleasure; nothing but pleasure motivates human action.   But the hedonism is not egoistic. Bentham speaks of the community and the legislator. On this theory the aim of politics is the production of pleasure, or, according to the popular utilitarian slogan, 'the greatest good of the greatest number.' A method of calculation is necessary to determine in any situation what line of action will in fact produce the greatest amount of pleasure on the whole; and the following paragraphs are Bentham's account of his system of moral arithmetic.

"Pleasures then, and the avoidance of pains, are the *ends* which the legislator has in view: it behooves him therefore to understand their *value.*   Pleasures and pains are the *instruments* he has to work with: it behooves him therefore to understand their force, which is again, in other words, their value.

"To a person considered *by himself,* the value of a pleasure or pain considered *by itself* will be greater or less according to the four following circumstances:

1. Its intensity.
2. Its duration.
3. Its certainty or uncertainty.
4. Its propinquity or remoteness.

" . . . But when the value of any pleasure or pain is considered for the purpose of estimating the tendency of any *act* by which it is produced, there are two other circumstances to be taken into account. These are:

5. Its fecundity, or the chance it has of being followed by sensations of the same kind. . . .

6. Its purity, or the chance it has of not being followed by sensations of the opposite kind. . . .

"To a *number* of persons, with reference to each of whom the value of a pleasure or a pain is considered, it will be greater or less, according to seven circumstances: to wit, the six preceding ones . . . and one other, to wit:

7. Its extent; that is, the number of persons to whom it extends; or (in other words) who are affected by it. . . .

"Take an account of the *number* of persons whose interests appear to be concerned; and repeat the above processes with respect to each. *Sum up* the numbers expressive of the degrees of *good* tendency, which the act has, with respect to each individual, in regard to whom the tendency of it is *good* upon the whole: do this again with respect to each individual, in regard to whom the tendency of it is *good* upon the whole: do this again with respect to each individual, in regard to whom the tendency of it is *bad* upon the whole. Take the *balance;* which, if on the side of *pleasure,* will give the general *good tendency* of the act, with respect to the total number or community of individuals concerned; if on the side of pain, the general *evil tendency,* with respect to the same community."

Essentially the same theory, though with some important refinements, was defended by Sidgwick.[9]

"So far we have only been considering the 'Good on the Whole' of a single individual: but just as this notion is constructed by comparison and integration of the different 'goods' that succeed one another in the series of our conscious states, so we have formed the notion of Universal Good by comparison and integrations of the goods of all individual human — or sentient — existences. And here again, just as in the former

---

9. *Op. cit.,* p. 382.

case, by considering the relation of the integrant parts to the whole and to each other, I obtain the self-evident principle that the good of any one individual is of no more importance, from the point of view (if I may say so) of the Universe, than the good of any other; unless, that is, there are special grounds for believing that more good is likely to be realized in the one case than in the other. And it is evident to me that as a rational being I am bound to aim at good generally, — so far as it is attainable by my efforts, — not merely at a particular part of it."

Hastings Rashdall argues similarly against egoism.[10] First he notes that the egoistic hedonist is not just expressing a personal preference, but is appealing to a universal principle when he asserts that every man ought to seek his own pleasure at the expense of the greater pleasure of the community.

First of these points to be discussed is Bentham's popular theme, the greatest good for the greatest number, or more accurately the greatest pleasure for the greatest number. Certainly it would be important to investigate the basis of this principle. Is there any good reason for supposing it to be true? Is it deduced from some more inclusive and more self-evident principle? Is there any argument to justify it? Important though this line of investigation is, it will be replaced by a less important but easier analysis. Instead of searching for the source of the principle, the discussion will try to discover its outcome and results. What does the principle imply? What are some of its concrete applications? Since Bentham stresses the principle of utility for governmental action, let us suppose a nation composed of ninety per cent indigenous stock, blond Nordics, and ten per cent of a despised and hated minority — Jews, for instance. Now, the indigenous, homogeneous stock, having been reared in the rigorous, warlike, and superior virtues of primitive Teutonic barbarism, finds great pleasure, not in scalping white men with tomahawks, but in a more refined and scientific torturing of Semites. It is all

10. *The Theory of Good and Evil,* 2nd ed., Vol. I, pp. 44ff., (Oxford University Press, 1924).

good, clean fun, and very profitable, too. The execution or torture of each member of the inferior race gives pleasure to millions. Even if — the point need not be debated — even if the pain of torture is greater than the pleasure of any one of the superior Nazis, the pain cannot outweigh the sum of the pleasures of the millions. If there should be any possibility of the pain's being greater than the pleasure, the least scientific of a race of scientists could easily adjust the degree of torture; or, better, the national department of education could step-up the courses in torture-appreciation. And the greatest good of the greatest number will prevail.

If anyone deludes himself by thinking that this type of morality was eliminated by the defeat of Germany, he needs only to turn to Latvia, Lithuania, and Estonia. To subdue these tiny states whose immense military might threatened the safety of Soviet Russia, the communists put their victims in soundproof chambers where burning, branding, puncturing the head with needles, and mutilation of organs are regular procedure. In 1941 Red soldiers set fire to the Riga library of 300,000 volumes, and today books of licentious nature are standard in the schools. Free love was actively encouraged, and numerous incidents of rape and immorality occur on school grounds and in the buildings.

Sidgwick, however, guarded himself against these applications of Bentham's phrases. It seemed to him that pleasure should be distributed equally. If at any period of history a definite amount of pleasure is the maximum possible, by reason of the prevailing circumstances, that fixed amount should be divided among all in equal amounts. This doubtless means that no one should own a work of art until everyone owns a bath tub; no one should have a college education until everyone, including those in the interior of China, has graduated from high school. Sidgwick does not discuss in detail the applications of his principle of equality, but it would seem that some such results as these are legitimate inferences from his statement. It should be clearly kept in mind that these consequences, though they may not appear desirable to some overprivileged people, do not disprove or refute the Utilitarian theory. Neither does the outworking of socialistic principles in revolutionary Russia demolish Marxism. If the principles be correct, one ought not to quarrel with the conclusions. The purpose of this part of the discussion is not to show that Utilitarianism is wrong, the purpose is simply to show what it is. Any destructive criticism would have to attack the principles and the basis of the theory; and so far this has not been done.

There is one interpretation of Utilitarianism which, though occasionally disavowed, may have unconsciously sustained some of its exponents in their enthusiasms. If the ultimate good of each individual were in eventual harmony with the good of all others the consequences detailed above would not follow from Utilitarianism. Antisemitism could not be justified because it would harm the Gentile as well as and as much as the Jew. There would be no slave labor camps in Siberia. There would be no diplomatic intrigue or war. At least, these things would not exist in the utilitarian theory. But if the goods of all people perfectly harmonize, what becomes of the distinction between egoism and utilitarianism? Whether one sought the good of all or whether he sought his own individual good, the actions and the outcome would be identical. The difficulty with this happy suggestion is not that egoism becomes indistinguishable from utilitarianism. That one theory supplants two is a loss that can be supported. The real difficulty lies in the supposition itself. Is the universe as a matter of fact so constructed that if Stalin gets what is good for him, Hitler and Churchill must of necessity get what is good for them? Or is the universe so constructed that if Judas gets what is good for him, Barabbas and Jesus cannot get what is good for them? What evidence is there that the pleasures of all people never conflict in the long run? So far as experience can teach us, there are many conflicts. Even in the case of two friends with similar tastes, interests, and ideals, there is no certainty of a perfect and final harmony. And in the case of enemies and enemy nations, all the evidence points to conflict. A theory whose sole support is such an assumption would be in a precarious position. If utilitarianism is to commend itself above egoism, it must argue that an individual ought to sacrifice himself, without hope of future compensation, for the greater pleasure of someone else.

Sidgwick and Rashdall have attempted to meet the situation by appealing to an "impersonal Reason," or by looking at the matter "from the point of view, if I may say so, of the Universe." Their appeal, however, betrays their case. It may be that from the point of view of the Universe, one man's pleasure is as important as another man's, and the only basis of choice is the amount. But it is more likely that the Universe has no point of view at all and cannot choose or approve any pleasure. Even if it could, I am not the universe, and why I should be asked to take the universe's point of view, if it has one, is far from clear. If the good is pleasure, my good is my pleasure. The pleasure of another person is no pleasure at all to me. And to refer to an impersonal Reason, spelled with a capital R, is simply a more poetic way of disguising the confusion. Thus utilitarianism has lost its plausibility, if it has not become entirely untenable.

But egoism still retains a bad reputation. To act only for one's own best interest is selfish. And what is worse is the corollary that one should aim at anothers' good only when it advances his own. Rashdall finds all this very distasteful. He says, "such a doctrine seems to be simply a recrudescence of the old 'soul-saving' view of life, which may so easily degenerate into something considerably more nauseous and offensive than an honest egoistic Hedonism which is naked and unashamed. . . . If I cared for my neighbor's welfare merely as a means to my own edification, I should not be unselfish."[11] But if the consequences of egoism are to be called selfishness, still this does not refute egoism. Consequences do not refute, they explain. If the principle of egoism is correct, then the consequences, provided they are valid inferences, must be accepted. Rashdall confesses to nausea; but whether the nausea should

11. *Ibid.*, p. 40.

be referred to poisonous food or to a diseased stomach has not yet been settled. Let it only be said that egoism has a *prima facie* claim to plausibility. On the surface of things at least, it seems reasonable that every man should seek his own good. It seems unreasonable to tell a man to seek his own ultimate harm. How the good of one individual relates to the good of another may be a difficult problem. But if there is any solution of this problem other than the egoistic solution, it is not utilitarianism.

It is unnecessary to continue balancing at any greater length the respective claims of egoism and utilitarianism, for there is one objection applicable to both that may possibly make any teleological theory of ethics untenable. Ethics, it has been stated, is a normative science. If it is to fulfill its purpose, it must tell men what they ought to do. Although the most basic question in ethics is, What makes an action right or wrong? and not, Which actions are right and which wrong? yet, if this latter question cannot be answered, an answer to the former question will be of no practical importance. Those who are seriously interested in their own lives and their own conduct cannot accept as satisfactory a system of ethics that gives no direction. Specifically with respect to this consideration, teleological theories, egoistic or utilitarian, face what appears to be an insuperable objection. Can these systems give direction to, and particular directions for, conduct? It will not suffice to say that pleasure, or something else, is the goal and that all people ought to proceed in that direction. Babes in the wood don't need to be told they want to go home; they need to be shown the road. Now, Bentham was anxious to show everybody the road. He provided a method of calculation for deciding what procedure would produce the greatest amount of pleasure on the whole. But an attempt to use this calculus, even in a simple situation, shows its impracticability. In our more usual predicaments, which in fact are highly complicated, Bentham's calculus is patently impossible. A father is considering different plans for a vacation for his wife and children; a minister of the gospel is con-

sidering a policy for his congregation or for his denomina-
tion; a president or prime minister is considering national
security; in all these cases what must be done and what must
be known? It would be necessary to know not merely the
immediate results of a given choice, but the more remote, and
the still more remote into an indefinite future. It would be
necessary to know the effects of the proposed action on every
individual who might possibly be involved. And all these effects
in their various degrees would have to be balanced against the
same calculations made for each of the other proposed policies.
Only after all these calculations had been completed, could it
be said that such and such ought to be done. But obviously
these calculations cannot be completed. Therefore a teleological system cannot conclude that one action rather than another
is a moral obligation.

To be concrete: suppose an employee is considering telling a lie to his employer. Can he foresee the results? Can
he foresee whether or not he will be detected? And if detected, will the loss be greater than the immediate gain of lying? And if not detected, will there be other later results, either
good or bad? Will his fellow employees know? And if they
know, will he gain or lose on the whole? It might be argued
that while certainty in these calculations is impossible, we know
well enough that on the whole lying is unprofitable. Probably
it would be best to tell the truth. And probability will suffice
when certainty is beyond reach. This type of reply may be true
enough so far as it goes, but how can the required knowledge
of what is probable be obtained? How could anyone learn that
on the whole lying is unprofitable and that therefore in this
instance it is probably wise to tell the truth? This probability
is in fact more difficult to ascertain than the original problem
was to solve. It would require the original calculation to be
completed in a large number of situations; and only when
these results had been tabulated, could it be seen whether or
not lying is usually unprofitable. It cannot be denied that
probabilty must suffice when certainty is beyond reach — unless probability is beyond reach too. And unless there is some

method of obtaining unquestionable solutions in at least a few instances, there will be no basis for deciding what is or is not probable.

Teleological ethics therefore seems to be a complete failure. It fails in the crucial test of practical, concrete application. Or, at any rate, the case for a teleological theory has become so doubtful that it is wise to turn our attention to ateleological theories.

Ateleological Ethics

If therefore the morality of an act cannot be determined by way of showing that it is an effective means to a good end, it would seem that moral excellence must be found in the act itself regardless of its consequences. And, in fact, this accords with common opinion. That the end justifies the means is widely held to be an immoral principle. Truly moral action should be more spontaneous than a shrewd calculation of consequence. And it should be within the ability of humble and uneducated people, as shrewd calculation is not. An odd theory of morals it is that would tax the genius of the greatest scientist to figure out what ought to be done and would deprive the sincere common man of the possibility of ever determining what is right. Accordingly the moral worth of an action must be sought in the action itself and not in its consequences.

As concrete examples of this temper the history of ethics furnishes the Stoics in antiquity, the British Intuitionists, and Immanuel Kant. For the Stoics and for Epictetus in particular morality must be something within our power. A man cannot be held responsible for anything over which he has no control. The consequences of our acts are obviously not under our control. Even the more immediate consequences such as the health and the reputation we shall enjoy tomorrow are not under our control; and the more remote consequences of next year and next decade cannot possibly be guaranteed. Such matters are therefore external to us. There are, however, in-

ternal actions directly under the control of our will. We may
not be able to control our health or our reputation, but we can
control our thinking, our choosing and refusing; we cannot
control circumstances but we can control our reaction to circumstances. The sphere of morality therefore lies within; it
has to do with the will and not the consequences.

In modern times, too, the British Intuitionists, doubtless
from a somewhat different point of view, removed from ethics
the onus and the odium of calculating consequences. For them
no laborious examination of complicated and remote contin-
gencies was needed to distinguish right from wrong. On the
contrary, the mind of man immediately perceives in itself, or
is innately endowed with, the immutable principles of morality.
A short quotation from Henry More shows how they thought
of the matter.

"II. From this Magazine therefore let us draw forth a stock
of such Principles, as being immediately and irresistibly true,
need no proof; such, I mean as all Moral Reason may in a
sort have reference unto; even as all Mathematical Demonstrations are found in some *first undeniable Axioms*. And because these Principles arise out of that Faculty, which the
Greeks call *Nous,* that signifies the Mind or Intellect; and that
the words *Noema* and *Noemata* derive therefrom, and properly
signify Rules intellectual: we do not therefore improperly
style the Rules that hereafter follow, *Moral Noema's*. But lest
any should fansie them to be morose and unpracticable, I must
here affirm, that they propose nothing for good, which at the
same time is not grateful also, and attended with delight.

NOEMA I

Good is that which is grateful, pleasant, and congruous to
any Being, which hath Life and Perception, or that contributes in any degree to the preservation of it.

Noema V

What is good is to be chosen; what is evil to be avoided: but the more excellent Good is preferable to the less excellent; and a less Evil is to be borne, that we may avoid a greater.

Noema X

A present Good is to be rejected or moderated, if there be a future Good of infinite more value, as to weight and duration to be but probably expected: and much more therefore if such expectation be certain.

Noema XIV

The Good, which in any case in question, you would have another man do unto you; the same you are bound in a like case to do unto him; So far forth as it may be done without prejudice to a Third.

Noema XVIII

If it be good for one man to have wherewithal to be happy; it evidently follows, 'tis twice as good for two men to be happy, thrice for three, a thousand times for a thousand; and so of the rest.

Noema XXIII

However 'tis manifest, that a man may so behave himself, as that what was his own by acquisition or donation, may of right cease to be his own.

"IV. These and such like sayings may justly be called *Moral Axioms* or *Noemas;* for they are so clear and evident of themselves, that if men consider impartially, they need no manner of Deduction or Argument, but are agreed to as soon as heard. And thus we are prepared, as with so many Touchstones, to let the inquisitive know what *Right Reason* is. For in short, *it is that which by certain and necessary Con-*

sequences, is at length resolved into some intellectual Principle which is immediately true."[12]

In this quotation from Henry More it is to be noted that he takes his principles to be immediately and irresistibly true without need of proof, deduction, or argument. Now, to be sure, just before the end of this quotation, More uses the word 'consequences.' But the consequences he has in mind are the logical consequences or implications of the principles. Through the rest of his book he attempts to show how the virtues of prudence, justice, piety, probity, temperance, and so on, are consequences of the noemata. He is therefore not concerned with the amounts of pleasure and pain that an act may produce, but with the logical analysis of immediately perceived truths. For the present purpose it is not necessary to decide whether More's analysis is correct or not. The logic by which he passed from his axioms to his theorems need not be examined. Nor need we consider as an objection to More the theory that denies the very possibility of immediate truths. There are some philosophers who reject any view depending on innate ideas or intellectual intuitions. This epistemological problem would lead too far afield at the moment. Let it be granted that a system may have, if not immediate first truths, at least presuppositions, postulates, assumptions, or axioms. However, these must not be multiplied with abandon. Such primary principles must be restricted to a small number. The ideal in logical systems is to make as few assumptions as possible and to deduce at many theorems as possible. The British Intuitionists, unfortunately, were too liberal with their first principles. If this type of theory is to meet with general approval, it must be worked out on the basis of a single principle, or at most two or three, but certainly not two or three dozen. Immanuel Kant, in his theory of the categorical imperative, closely approximates this ideal.

---

12. Henry More, *Enchiridion Ethicum*, Chap. IV. pp. 21-27. The English Translation of 1690 (The Facsimile Text Society, N.Y., 1930).

Kant

Kant was undoubtedly the most important figure in the history of ethics, of those who sought the test of morality not in the consequences but in the act itself. His basic approach may be seen in the following passages:

"Nothing can possibly be conceived in the world, or even out of it, which can be called good, without qualification, except a good will.... A good will is good not because of what it performs or effects, not by its aptness for the attainment of some proposed end, but simply by virtue of the volition, that is, it is good in itself, and considered by itself is to be esteemed much higher than all that can be brought about by it in favor of any inclination, nay, even of the sum total of all inclinations. Even if it should happen that ... this will should wholly lack power to accomplish its purpose, if with its greatest efforts it should yet achieve nothing, and there should remain only the good will ... then, like a jewel, it would still shine by its own light, as a thing which has its whole value in itself. Its usefulness or fruitfulness can neither add to nor take away from this value."[13]

There seems to be merit in this ateleological position. Can we honestly hold a man responsible for the achievement of results that are beyond his power? Is not the *moral* value of a complex situation to be sought in the will of an agent? That he lacks the physical strength or even the sagacity and political wisdom to accomplish his aim ought not to be held against him. The man whose will is right acts morally regardless of the results of his action. In this way the possibility of morality is retained for the humble, the poor in spirit, and the pure in heart.

The next step in the theory is a criterion by which a good will may be distinguished from a bad will. If one is prohibited from calculating consequences, how in any actual situation

---

13. *Fundamental Principles of the Metaphysic of Morals.* First Section, in *Kant's Critique of Practical Reason and Other Works,* translated by Thomas Kingsmill Abbott (sixth edition) p. 9, 10, (Longmans, Green and Co., 1909).

can one determine what is right? Kant's answer to this question is the categorical imperative. One basic principle is the test in every case. If a particular volition conforms to this principle, it is right; if it does not conform, it is wrong. Kant writes:

"There is therefore but one categorical imperative, namely, this: 'Act only on that maxim whereby thou canst at the same time will that it should become a universal law.' "[14] Kant's most convincing example in support of the soundness of his theory concerns keeping one's promises.

"May I when in distress make a promise with the intention not to keep it? I readily distinguish here between the two significations which the question may have: Whether it is prudent, or whether it is right, to make a false promise? The former may undoubtedly often be the case. I see clearly indeed that it is not enough to extricate myself from a present difficulty by means of this subterfuge, but it must be well considered whether there may not hereafter spring from this lie much greater inconvenience than that from which I now free myself, and as, with all my supposed cunning, the consequences cannot be so easily foreseen but that credit once lost may be much more injurious to me than any mischief which I seek to avoid at present, it should be considered whether it would not be more *prudent* to act herein according to a universal maxim, and to make it a habit to promise nothing except with the intention of keeping it. But it is soon clear to me that such a maxim will still only be based on the fear of consequences. Now it is a wholly different thing to be truthful from duty, and to be so from apprehension of injurious consequences. In the first case, the very notion of the action already implies a law for me; in the second case, I must first look about elsewhere to see what results may be combined with it which would affect myself. For to deviate from the principle of duty is beyond all doubt wicked; but to be unfaithful to my maxim of prudence may often be very advantageous to me, although to abide by it is certainly safer. The shortest way, however,

---

14. *Ibid.*, p. 38.

and an unerring one, to discover the answer to this question whether a lying promise is consistent with duty, is to ask myself, Should I be content that my maxim (to extricate myself from difficulty by a false promise) should hold good as a universal law, for myself as well as for others? and should I be able to say to myself, 'Every one may make a deceitful promise when he finds himself in difficulty from which he cannot otherwise extricate himself'? Then I presently become aware that while I can will the lie, I can by no means will that lying should be a universal law. For with such a law there would be no promises at all, since it would be in vain to allege my intention in regard to my future actions to those who would not believe this allegation, or if they over-hastily did so, would pay me back in my own coin. Hence my maxim, as soon as it should be made a universal law, would necessarily destroy itself."[15]

In other words, moral action is based on a principle that is logically self-consistent, even when universalized; but in an immoral act the agent tacitly contradicts himself. Thus Kant has substituted logical analysis for a calculation of consequences.

Unfortunately one may entertain plausible doubts as to whether logical analysis is a satisfactory substitute. For, if this example seems to support Kant's contention, others produce an opposite effect. Truth telling is right, so Kant argued, because everyone can tell the truth without any logical impossibility arising in the total situation, while lying is wrong because it is logically impossible for everyone to tell lies. But what about suicide? Of course, Kant believed that suicide is wrong. But is it not logically possible for me to commit suicide and at the same time to will that everyone else should commit suicide. If I will to break a promise, I desire to make myself an exception. I want other people to keep their promises to me; I want faithfulness to be universal, with myself an exception. Because of such an exception, argues Kant, the act contemplated is immoral. But no such exception is logically necessary in the case of suicide. I may believe, without con-

---

15. *Ibid.*, pp. 18, 19.

tradicting myself, that life is evil, that suicide is the solution,
and that everyone ought to commit suicide.

Kant was entirely aware of the problem that suicide posed
for him,[16] and he tried on several occasions to produce an
argument that would prove suicide to be wrong. In his early
lectures, apparently before he had clearly formulated the notion
of the categorical imperative, he not only uses general teleological considerations, but explicitly appeals to divine judgment: "But as soon as we examine suicide from the standpoint of religion we immediately see it in its true light. We
have been placed in this world under certain conditions and
for specific purposes. But a suicide opposes the purpose of
his Creator; he arrives in the other world as one who has
deserted his post; he must be looked upon as a rebel against
God. So long as we remember the truth that it is God's intention to preserve life, we are bound to regulate our activities
in conformity with it."[17]

This may be a very good argument against suicide, but its
principles are patently inconsistent with Kant's later views.
On the other hand, his later attempts to show that suicide is
immoral lack the early clarity to such an extent that one won-
ders whether the humble, uneducated, honest man, whom
Kant would save the labor of shrewd calculation, is any better
off than he was formerly.

There is also another consideration which does not seem
to be of much advantage to an ordinary honest man. Kant's
example of prudence or at least convenience pulling one way in
the matter of breaking promises, and duty pulling the other
way, is a well known experience; but what of the case, less
striking perhaps, where duty and interest coincide? While
most of us would no doubt say, 'how fortunate,' and give it
no further thought, Kant uses just such a situation to add
further stringencies. Suppose, as is often the case, that keep-

---

16. Kant also struggles with the notion of an uncivilized life of primitive
ease, and of a callous disregard of other's miseries, both of which seem
capable of being universalized. *Ibid.* pp. 39-41.

17. *Lectures on Ethics,* translated by Louis Infield, pp. 153, 154, (Methuen
& Co., 1930).

ing a promise enhances one's reputation and results in prestige and promotion. Should one do so because it is useful? Kant's answer is, No.

"What is essential in the moral worth of actions is *that the moral law should directly determine the will.* If the determination of the will takes place in conformity indeed to the moral law, but only by means of a feeling, no matter what kind, which has to be presupposed in order that the law may be sufficient to determine the will, and therefore not *for the sake of the law,* then the action will possess *legality* but not *morality* . . . it is even *dangerous* to allow other motives (for instance, that of interest) even to cooperate *along with* the moral law. . . . Respect for the moral law is therefore the *only* and the undoubted moral motive, and this feeling is directed to no object, except on the ground of this law. . . . A maxim therefore is morally good *only* in case it rests simply on the interest taken in obedience to the law."[18]

Thus the man who suspects that honesty is the best policy and has some notion that he will prosper because of his fidelity can hardly escape immorality in his very honesty. Or, if he loves his wife except from a sense of duty, he loves her unethically. To be sure, what he does will be legal, but his will is not good and his action has no moral worth. At this point one may reflect that all this does not help a man to become moral. Even if the theory should be logically flawless, it makes concrete practical problems exceedingly difficult. Not only does the categorical imperative fail to affect one who has no inclination to do his duty; but the prohibition of mixed motives, the rigid exclusion of all self-interest, and the utterly unnatural devotion to a formal principle make actual moral conduct impossible, one might say, to a man with the best will in the world.

Here it will be helpful to pause for an evalution. The criticism of Kant's treatment of suicide has little value as a refutation of his ethical theory. It may indicate only that Kant himself never overcame his earlier theistic repugnance

18. *Fundamental Principles, op. cit.,* pp. 164, 171, 172.

to self-destruction. But the theory does not stand or fall on Kant's emotions. At the most his argument on suicide can be regarded as an inconsistency to be eliminated. If the categorical imperative is otherwise well founded, suicide as its consequence must be accepted as a virtue. When there is no agreement on what is good, when massacre and torture have not yet been proved wrong, and when the inquiry concerns the foundation of morality, any remarks based on an aversion from suicide give but an *ad hominem* argument. The criticism of Kant's prohibition of mixed motives may have more weight. Kant strikes a noble pose in talking about duty and reverence for law; but there is a persistent suspicion that a man who enjoys right conduct, whatever right conduct may prove to be, is a better man than one whose inclinations are evil and whose duty is distasteful.

But perhaps the most weighty criticism of Kant's ethical philosophy is similar to that which broke off the discussion of teleogical ethics. It was previously argued that the impossibility of calculating consequences emptied egoism and utilitarianism of all practical usefulness. Kant faces the same objection with reference to the logical consequences of the categorical imperative. "Act only on that maxim whereby thou canst at the same time will that it should become a universal law." This principle cannot justify a young man in deciding to become a stock broker or in choosing the legal profession for a career; for it is impossible that all people should be lawyers or stock brokers. Similar examples will show that the categorical imperative, though it may sanction generalities, such as, one should earn a living, condemns every particular method of earning a living. And to avoid this disastrous conclusion Kant in his latest writings seems to abandon the strictly ateleological position in favor of a minimum of purpose, as he also includes practical consequences along with the logical deduction. Likewise the maxim may in strict logic condemn the breaking of a promise, but it never shows what promises are to be made in the first place. Or, again, if I have a sum of money for charitable purposes, should

I give it all to a hospital, all to a college, or divide it between them? Theoretically one should be able to deduce the correct conclusion from Kant's basic maxim, but when this is attempted, Kantian deduction appears to be as difficult as utilitarian calculation. What is worse, where deduction is possible, the conclusions are sometimes contradictory. With equally valid reasoning both avarice and benevolence can be proved to be virtues, but it is obviously a logical impossibility to live a life of avarice and of generosity. Kant's theory therefore can hardly be accepted as plausible. And for a parting shot, does the fact that it is possible for everyone to throw three grains of salt daily over the left shoulder or to avoid black cats prove that these actions are commanded by the stern voice of duty and must be performed out of reverence for law?

Another phase of Kant's theory will be mentioned later, but at the moment it may be well to see if anything has been untouched by the destructive dialectic and to translate the failures of both teleological and ateleological ethics into positive desiderata for an acceptable theory. The least plausible element in Kant and the most plausible in egoism were the respective attitudes toward self-interest. The awkwardness, the improbability, the frigid formalism of Kant serves to highlight the fact that the principle of egoism has withstood criticism. The most that was brought against it was an accusation of selfishness and a feeling of nausea. But, as has been said, when massacre and torture have not yet been discovered to be immoral, a little selfishness — if indeed the accusation prove just — is a minor matter. Then, again, although the application of egoism by means of calculating consequences was found impossible, no inconsistency attached to the principle itself. The most trenchant criticism failed to destroy the idea that a man should always seek what is good for him and should never seek evil. Indeed, is not this virtually the definition of a rational agent, for is not he insane who prefers harm to good? Ethical theory therefore must be consistent, not with an unsought happiness that Kant at last introduces surreptitiously, but with an explicit and conscious desire for one's own good.

If this first essential of acceptable ethical theory is the element that escaped destructive criticism, the second is obtained by reversing the failures of teleological as well as of ateleological theory. Earlier in this chapter the field of ethics was roughly delimited by a list of questions. One was, What actions are right and what actions are wrong? Unless this question can be answered, that is, unless there is some specific guidance for the actual circumstances of life, ethical theory can hardly be said to exist. And it was precisely on this point that all the attempts so far discussed have failed. Not one of them could give a satisfactory reason for believing one act to be right and another act to be wrong. This is a situation similar to the dilemmas encountered in the chapters on history and politics. When a group of theories, otherwise incompatible, fail at a given point, it is likely that they have some common element that produces the failure. Consistently therefore with the argument in the previous chapters, the common source of these failures may be sought in their secularism. Even those authors who had some belief in God did not effectively relate God to the problems of human life. If theism, on the other hand, can produce a coherent theory to avoid such failures, its success should commend it to logical thought.

The Ethics of Revelation

Biblical theism advances a theory of ethics that satisfies these requirements. In the first place it provides adequate scope for self-interest.[19] Far from denying the legitimacy of interested motivation, the doctrine of Christ constantly stresses rewards and punishments. The sermon on the mount repeatedly appeals to practical consequences: "Blessed are the poor in spirit: for theirs is the kingdom of heaven.... Blessed are ye when men shall revile you ... for my sake ... for great is your reward in heaven.... Whosoever shall say, Thou fool, shall be in danger of hell fire.... It is profitable for thee that one of thy members should perish, and not that thy whole body should be cast into hell.... For if ye love them which

---

19. *Cf.* Edward J. Carnell, *An Introduction to Christian Apologetics,* Chap. XVIII, (Wm. B. Eerdmans Publishing Co., 1948).

love you, what reward have ye. . . . Take heed that ye do not your alms before men, to be seen of them: otherwise ye have no reward of your Father which is in heaven. . . . And thy Father which seeth in secret shall reward thee openly. . . . And everyone that heareth these sayings of mine, and doeth them not, shall be likened unto a foolish man, which built his house upon the sand: and the rain descended, and the floods came, and the winds blew, and beat upon that house; and it fell: and great was the fall of it."

It is obvious that Biblical theism appeals to self-interest. The gospel of Christ demands sacrifices of men, but it demands no ultimate sacrifice. Although in this world the Christian will suffer tribulation, although like Paul he may five times receive forty stripes save one, be thrice beaten with rods, be once stoned, suffer shipwreck, be in perils, in weariness, in hunger and thirst, still "the sufferings of this present time are not worthy to be compared with the glory which shall be revealed in us." In this sense Christianity is definitely egoistic. Not only will those who meet God's requirements be rewarded with joys unspeakable, but also a conscious desire for those rewards is legitimate motivation.

With this assertion of egoism it should be noted also that Biblical theism does not approve of selfishness as the term is used in ordinary speech. Even if it did, the previous arguments have shown that philosophers like Kant and Rashdall, who reject Christianity on the ground that it is a selfish philosophy of life, cannot justify their opposition to selfishness, or to massacre, either; and hence they have no basis for their rejection of Christianity. But as a matter of fact Biblical theism does not teach selfishness. Documentation is almost superfluous.

One could trace the matter from Abraham who gave Lot the first choice of pasture land; through Moses who refused to be called the son of Pharaoh's daughter, choosing rather to suffer affliction with the people of God than to enjoy the pleasures of sin for a season; through Elijah, Elisha, Jeremiah, and many other unknown saints of whom the world was not worthy; on to Jesus the author and finisher of our faith, who for the joy that was set before him endured the cross, despising the shame.   No doubt the Church contains hypocrites; no doubt also many, yes, all sincere Christians fail to live consistently by their principles; but it is exceedingly strange to charge Christianity with inculcating selfishness.

In the second place Biblical theism gives specific guidance in the actual situations of life.   The Ten Commandments are fairly definite: one should worship God, one should not bow before images, one should not use profanity, and so on.   The New Testament too contains innumerable directions concerning concrete situations that recur in the lives of all people. This does not mean that a Christian is never perplexed.   He can know definitely that murder, adultery, and theft are wrong; he may not be sure that a broker who buys stock for himself on the floor of the exchange is committing theft.   To the extent that the implications and applications of the Ten Commandments are dubious, perplexity will remain; but the difficulty of drawing proper inferences in certain complicated circumstances should not obscure the ease of applying the Commandments at other times.   Only under the most extraordinary conditions could the nature of profanity and adultery be doubtful.   This is quite different from the conclusion of secular ethics that we never have any reason to suppose that any action is our duty.[20]

These considerations show in brief how Christianity escapes the difficulties and the futilities of other systems.   And such an escape recommends the position.   If certain assumptions make the solution of a problem possible, while others make it impossible, it is a reason for accepting those assumptions. But opponents of theism will not be so easily satisfied.   In the first place they will ask, Is there a God?   Perhaps science will disprove the existence of God by establishing a mechanistic worldview; or, even if that should not occur, at least the existence of God has not yet been scientifically proven, so

---

20. *Cf.* G. E. Moore, *Principia Ethica,* pp. 146-164, (Cambridge University Press, 1922). But Moore is more optimistic than his argument allows.

that no conclusion in ethics is possible until the decisions of material science are known and taken into account. This first objection, raising again the problem of the classification of sciences by supposing that ethics and theology are dependent on the results of science, will be considered in the next chapter. To discuss it here would take us too far afield. In the second place, even if there is a God, opponents of Christian theism may deny that he has made any revelation at all, or at least that the Ten Commandments are not such a revelation. A later chapter on religion will touch somewhat on this contention. Then in the third place, it is a question whether ethics should appeal to theology at all. Even if God exists and theology is possible, may it not be that ethics is basic and theology is derivative? This third objection, though it also raises again the question of the classification of sciences, still lies within the scope of a chapter on ethics; and since it not only completes the consideration of Kant but also emphasizes the controlling idea of the present chapter, it may be used as a concluding section.

In order to show the immorality of suicide, Kant in his earlier years had appealed to theology and divine sanctions. What, we may ask, were his later reasons for discarding this theological appeal at the expense of damaging the specific application?[21]

There are two reasons, a positive and a negative. First, positively, the principle which Kant substituted for divine sanctions is the autonomy of the will. "Autonomy of the will is that property of it by which it is a law to itself.... That the principle of autonomy in question is the sole principle of morals can be readily shown by the mere analysis of the conceptions of morality. For by this analysis we find that its principle must be a categorical imperative, and that which this commands is neither more nor less than this very autonomy." If, contrariwise, moral distinctions are to be sought outside the will, in the character of any of its objects, there could be no categorical imperative. In such a case moral

---

21. Abbott, *op. cit.*, pp. 59-63.

action would be merely hypothetical, a means to an end, and it would follow that "I ought to do something *because I wish for something else....* In every case where an object of the will has to be supposed, in order that the rule may be prescribed which is to determine the will, there the rule is simply heteronomy; the imperative is conditional, namely *if* or *because* one wishes for this object, one should act so and so: hence it can never command morally, that is categorically.... The will does not give itself the law, but it is given by a foreign impulse by means of a particular natural constitution of the subject to receive it." Divine sanctions, since they are foreign impulses, and the autonomy of the will are clearly incompatible. Kant identifies a moral command with a categorical command, and with this definition of morality, a theistic view is automatically excluded.

In the second place, the negative reason for removing theological considerations from ethics is that we have no intuition of the divine perfection. If we knew what sort of Being God is, we might deduce from this knowledge what God might want us to do. But the difficulty, as Kant sees it, lies in obtaining a knowledge of God. Kant may not quite say that a knowledge of God is impossible, but if it should be possible, it could only be deduced "from our own conceptions, the most important of which is morality, and our explanation would thus be involved in a gross circle." Obviously, if knowledge of God is based on ethical theory, ethical theory cannot be established on a theological basis.

Kant sees that attempts will be made to secure a knowledge of God without basing it on ethical conceptions. But if ethical material is excluded, "the only notion of the Divine will remaining to us is a conception made up of the attributes of desire of glory and dominion, combined with the awful conceptions of might and vengeance, and any systems of morals erected on this foundation would be directly opposed to morality."

Neither of these two reasons for making ethics basic to theology has much force. The first reason is essentially a definition. Kant defines morality by the categorical imperative, and the categorical imperative by definition depends on the autonomy of the will. Thus not only divine sanctions but all sanctions are ruled out by definition. In other words, what Kant means by morality and what Christianity means by morality are two different things. To choose between these two incompatible definitions, one should examine their implications; and the implications of the Kantian definition, as was shown in the analysis of the categorical imperative, are not choiceworthy.

The second or negative reason also begs the question. It assumes the point at issue, namely, that knowledge of God is based only on independent ethical argument. The converse of this assumption is that God has not revealed himself to man. If God has in fact revealed, say, the Ten Commandments, Kant's assertion would be clearly false. Until the Ten Commandments are refuted, it appears as a *petitio principii*. Apart from the question of revelation Kant further asserted that any system of morals erected on the awful conceptions of might and vengeance would be directly opposed to morality. This brings us back again to Kant's *ipse dixit*. Undoubtedly the sovereignty of God, "in flaming fire taking vengeance on them that know not God," is opposed to Kant's morality; but it is not opposed to specific commandments for human life, nor to mighty sanctions against disobedience, and cannot be disposed of by bare assertion.

This is probably sufficient for a rebuttal of Kant's basic position, though there are other complicating factors in his argument. For example, he achieves ridicule of hypothetical morality, that is, of the thesis that one should seek his own good, by assuming,[22] as many others have done in opposition to egoism, an entirely inadequate view of the good. He describes a man who derives great enjoyment from benevolence and who uses theft as a means to this enjoyment. Underlying this short-sighted definition of the good, there is also the tacit assumption that only human detection, which is often

_____
22. *Ibid.*, pp. 124-125.

avoidable, could ruin such shrewd planning. Such superficial ridicule does not touch theism. The awful conceptions
of might and vengeance, which cause Kant to shudder, protect
theism from this type of objection. A much more profound
complication in Kant's argument is his frequent suspicion that
one must choose between the categorical imperative and
mechanical determinism. He seems to think that this disjunction is complete. Heteronomy of the will gives an object
to the will and determines the will by inclination.[23] This
inclination is thought of as a result of natural or mechanical
causation, so that freedom would be impossible. "What else
then can freedom of the will be but autonomy, that is the
property of the will to be a law to itself?"

But once more the discussion goes beyond the immediate
subject. History and politics drove us on to ethics. The
ethical problems, narrowly taken, have been solved. Biblical
theism satisfies the requirements that other systems cannot
meet. But the solution itself drives us on again, on to theology
and science, on to questions concerning determinism and free
will, on to the existence of God. And if there is a God, we
should expect to be driven on, for would not God so control
the world that every factor would be related to every other
factor? Would not politics depend on ethics, and would not
ethics require some form of science and theology?

---

23. *Ibid.*, pp. 63, 65ff.

V

SCIENCE

CHAPTER V

Science

T HAT theism gives coherence to history, politics, and ethics, whereas naturalism does not, has been the positive argument of the preceding chapters. Both the humanistic denial of God's existence and also that form of agnostic theism, if such a designation be permitted, that fails to apply the concept of God in all phases of knowledge, seem to have reduced history to a tale of human frustration, politics to a system of brutality and torture, and ethics to the lustful conflict of moral anarchy. On the other hand it has been shown that Christian theism furnishes a basis for significance in history, orderly freedom in government, and a life that is still called respectable west of the iron curtain. Therefore, anyone who for some personal motive desires this type of life would, if impressed by the argument, be inclined to adopt a theistic worldview.

Science and Knowledge

This constructive argument can proceed no further without facing squarely some very fundamental objections. The issues of history and politics, it may be said, are so vague and general, or at least the methods employed in those studies are so crude, that any plausibilities derived from them would have to yield to the accurate result of the positive sciences. It is unreasonable to attach much importance to the plausibilities of philosophic speculation when the empirical methods of the laboratory can discover the truth. Furthermore, an appeal to personal desires and comfortable conclusions is a notorious source of self-deception. It may be true that unyielding despair is not so pleasant as a belief in Divine Providence; but if the facts prove the mechanical laws of physics, our wishes cannot alter the matter. Science claims objectivity; no personal or emotional bias contributes to its results; whereas grandiose theories of history are largely, even if not altogether, the products of a fertile imagination. It is only honest therefore, and in the long run it is only wise, to face the facts.

197

Centuries ago it may have been possible to ignore science — in fact centuries ago there was little science to ignore — but today its successes are so phenomenal that it is usually accorded the last word in all disputes.   The younger generation can hardly realize that so simple a thing as the incandescent electric bulb came only yesterday.   Today science receives its praise and respect by reason of the atomic bomb, bacteriological warfare, and the possibility of interplanetary travel.   None of this may be desirable, but truth is not a matter of desire; and the methods that have produced these wonderful products of civilization are capable of answering every question.   As Auguste Comte explained the situation, man began to think under a religious inspiration, and when the concepts of religion became patently absurd, man turned to metaphysical properties; but as progress in clarity is made the concepts of positive science become a permanent acquisition, so that never again will the method of learning and the nature of knowledge change.   Not only does positive science discover facts, but also the classifications of facts are discovered in the things themselves without the admixture of any apriori hypotheses or subjective preferences.   The idea of God, Comte concluded, depends on atavistic mythologizing, and God as a matter of fact does not exist.   Or perhaps the objection will more modestly claim that even if God exists, he cannot be known; or less modestly that he can be known to have no direct interest in human affairs.   The arguments of such an objection to the conclusions of the previous chapters cannot be overlooked.

The compulsion to face these objections, which is laid upon a theist who has stressed the problems of ethics, is all the more stringent because the objectors themselves sometimes contrast their own moral righteousness with the dishonesty of theism. T. H. Huxley asserted that the foundation of morality is to renounce lying and give up pretending to believe unintelligible propositions for which there is no evidence and which go beyond the possibilities of knowledge.   In a similar vein W. K. Clifford said, "It is wrong always, everywhere, and for anyone to believe anything upon insufficient evidence."[1]   The import and context of these statements is a general repudiation of theism in favor of a scientific method that obtains indisputable truth.   Or, reference might have been made to more detailed scientific works, such as *The Mechanistic Conception of Life* by Jacques Loeb, the volumes on behaviorism by J. B. Watson, and more fundamentally the physics of LaPlace, Haeckel, or even Ernst Mach, all of whom in one way or another construct a scientific worldview that makes theism impossible.

To show the bearing of science on theism, some quotations from distinguished contemporary scientists should be made. Without doubt Professor A. J. Carlson is a distinguished scientist, as is attested by his writings and by his presidency over the American Association for the Advancement of Science. Religious ideas and their relation to science have attracted his attention, and his conclusions are found in the twice published article, *Science and the Supernatural*.[2]   One must note what he says on the nature of science as well as what he says on its relation to religion.   He writes, "Probably the most common meaning of science is a body of established, verifiable, and organized data secured by controlled observation, experience, or experiment. . . . The element in science of even greater importance than the verifying of facts, the approximation laws, the prediction of processes is the method by means of which these data and laws are obtained and the attitude of the people whose labor has secured them. . . . What is the method of science?   In essence it is this — the rejection *in toto* of all non-observational and non-experimental authority in the field of experience. . . . When no evidence is produced [in favor of a pronouncement] other than personal dicta, past or present 'revelations' in dreams, or the 'voice of God,' the

1. Whether these authors have sufficient evidence for their fundamental principles of morality has been directly argued in the preceding chapter. The present discussion of science will indirectly support the previous conclusion, and may result in Clifford's having condemned himself by his own assertion.

2. *Science*, 73:217-225, 1931; and *The Scientific Monthly* 59:85-95, 1944. Cf. *Man the Myth Maker,* by Read Bain, in the same periodical, 65:61ff., 1947.

scientist can pay no attention whatsoever, except to ask: How do they get that way?"

Parenthetically it may be remarked that this description of the nature of science somewhat resembles Karl Pearson's statements in his famous *Grammar of Science* to the effect that "The classification of facts and the formation of absolute judgments upon the basis of this classification — judgments independent of the idiosyncrasies of the individual mind — essentially sum up the *aim and method of modern science* [ital. his] .... The classification of facts, the recognition of their sequence and relative significance is the function of science."[3]

Not only does Carlson reject non-experimental authority, but he also combines with his empirical scientific method a disjunction between knowledge and belief that can be turned to his embarrassment. In the article just quoted he continues, "The scientist tries to rid himself of all faiths and beliefs. He either knows or he does not know. If he knows, there is no room for faith or belief. If he does not know, he has no right to faith or belief."

He then illustrates his point by listing several Biblical miracles, some of the views of the Koran, the Vedas, the Book of Mormon, and the writings of Mary Baker Eddy; and then without fear of successful contradiction concludes, "a good deal of 'revealed' information about the nature of the world and the nature of man has proved entirely erroneous."

The extent to which science, according to Professor Carlson's experimentation, prohibits belief in the supernatural is most clearly stated a page or two later. "Many intelligent people ... retain a distillate of the supernatural in form of beliefs in a 'moral purpose' in the universe. And having injected human ethics into an obviously a-moral universe, they endow man with personal immortality.... Even this form

---

3. Third edition, p. 6 (The Macmillan Co., 1911). A contrary view is expressed by James B. Conant, *On Understanding Science*, pp. 6, 10, 14.

of the supernatural has no sanction in science or analyzed human needs, as I understand them."[4]

In the late nineteenth century a theological movement headed by Albrecht Ritschl tried to harmonize science and religion by a radical bifurcation of consciousness. Science was to deal with speculative truth, while religion was to concern itself with practical value-judgments. Since there was to be no truth in religion and no value in science, conflict could not arise. If this remarkable solution ever satisfied the liberal theologians, it never became the most popular view among scientists. Karl Pearson presumably speaks for all science when he says,[5] "The goal of science is clear — it is nothing short of the complete interpretation of the universe." And, "Science does much more than demand that it shall be left in undisturbed possession of what the theologian and metaphysician please to term its 'legitimate field.' It claims that the whole range of phenomena, mental as well as physical — the entire universe — is its field. It asserts that the scientific method is the sole gateway to the whole region of knowledge."

Reflection on these quotations raises a series of puzzling questions, some of which ought to be answered by the serious theologian and scientist alike. Clifford and Huxley, and anyone who opposes them, ought to make clear what is *sufficient* evidence. Is evidence sufficient only when it is logically demonstrative? Would Clifford and Huxley be satisfied with something less than demonstration, and if so how much less? More fundamental is the plain question, What is evidence? Comte and Pearson assume that facts and classifications can be empirically discovered. But can they? Comte was certain that the positive character of knowledge, now that it has passed beyond the theological and metaphysical stages, will never again change. But if Comte is the father of sociology, it is one of his own sons, Sorokin, who is sure that it will change again and again. Further, must we hold with Karl Pearson that the judgments

---

4. This denial of a cosmic purpose and of personal immortality, as an obvious conclusion of experimental science, seems to involve the same dismal view of human life that was found in Russell.

5. *Ibid.* pp. 14, 24.

of science are absolute? Will a judgment or fact, once for all discovered, never be abandoned in favor of a more up-to-date fact or judgment? Do scientists never revise their conclusions? And very much more to the point, is the scientific method the sole gateway to the whole region of knowledge? What experiment or what evidence is sufficient to prove that science is the sole gateway to all knowledge that is yet to be obtained? If there is a God, is it absolutely necessary that his existence be discovered by some infinitely sensitive Geiger counters? If moral distinctions and normative principles exist — in particular, Carlson's principle that a scientist has no right to believe anything — must such principles be discovered through a microscope? And finally, and very generally, what is scientific method? One must seriously question not merely the desirability but the possibility of rejecting *in toto* all non-observational and non-experimental authority in science. In other words, What is science?

Most of these questions, to be sure, do not seem to be very religious, and one may fear that they are irrelevant to a discussion of theism. Quite the contrary, the pertinence of scientific objections to the supernatural depends entirely on the nature of science and its limitations, if any.

Perhaps the easiest way to commence the discussion of this extraordinarily complicated subject is to dispose, first of all, of a popular notion that probably no longer commands wide acceptance. It is essentially Pearson's notion that science gives absolute judgments. The conclusions of science have often been regarded with an awe that takes them for final and infallible truth — science simply cannot be wrong. The history of science, however, shows that scientific method does not invariably arrive at the truth. For example, science is indebted to Gilbert for his experiments on magnetism. He used and had confidence in the scientific method. The ancient Stoics (and should we add the modern personalists?), who declare that the earth is a living being, he treats with scorn and derision; whereas true science can arrive at conclusions "not with mere probability, but with certainty."[6] Now, it were as foolish as false to deny that Gilbert was an important scientist; yet his procedure did not prevent him from asserting that it is the earth's magnetism, its verticity, that holds it in its rotational course. He also identified the earth's poles with the magnetic poles and dismissed the variation of the needle as due to some unknown obstacle. And one may even wonder whether his own ascription of a soul to the earth and his concept of an astral magnetic mind are so very far removed from the Stoic superstition he derides. No doubt excuses can be made for Gilbert, and his unfortunate remarks do not detract from his solid accomplishments. He lived at an early date; scientific methodology had not yet been adequately developed; and he was handicapped by the absurdities of medieval confusion. But is it entirely certain that scientific methodology is now adequate and that scientists are no longer handicapped by post-medieval confusion? To forestall the neglect of this consideration, a more recent example may be cited. Robert W. Woods began his volume on *Physical Optics* by describing the theory of the spectrum held before the time of Newton. It was thought at that time that the prism somehow manufactured the colors of the spectrum. Then Newton passed a beam of white light through a prism, produced the colors, passed the colors through another prism and got his beam of white light again. This experiment convinced him that the prism does not manufacture colors that previously did not exist, but separates colors that were actually merged in the white light. Wood writes, "Curiously enough this discovery, which we are taking as marking the beginning of our definite knowledge about light, is one which we shall demolish in the last chapter of this book, for our present idea regarding the action of the prism more nearly resembles the idea held previous to Newton's experiments: we now believe that the prism actually manu-

---

6. William Gilbert, *On the Loadstone and Magnetic Bodies* (1600), tr. by P. F. Mottelay, 1892. pp. 178, 180, 327, 328, 329, 333 (Edwards Brothers).

factures the colored light."[7] Scientific judgments therefore, far from being absolute, are, as Plato long ago knew, essentially tentative and stand in need of constant revision. Scientific procedure does not invariably grasp the truth; on the contrary it has a long record of accepting what is later thought to be false.

Facts, Laws, and Verification

But, it may be asserted, although the laws of science are tentative and are modified from time to time, becoming more accurate in the process, there are, as a basis for these approximations, certain absolute facts. After all, a fact is a fact, and no one can change it. The advantage science has over theology is that it sticks to the facts. Still, one must not go too fast. The practical mind that loves facts and distrusts theory should acquire some patience and pause a while over the theory of facts. There may at first be reluctance to face the question, What is fact? Yet, if facts are unyielding absolutes, it ought not to prove too difficult to show what a fact is. Let us try. Is it a fact that the earth is round? In the Middle Ages the common people thought it was flat. Since then, evidence has accumulated (considerable evidence was known to astronomers during the Middle Ages) and has been disseminated, until today everyone takes it as a fact that the earth is round. But strictly, is it the earth's roundness that is a fact, or is it the items of evidence that are facts on which the conclusion of the earth's roundness rests? For example, the shadow of the earth on the moon during a lunar eclipse has a round edge: perhaps this is a *fact,* and the roundness of the earth is a *theory.* Of course, it is not a fact that the earth is a sphere: it is flattened at the poles. But if it is not a fact that the earth is perfectly round (spherical), what is the fact? Is it a fact that the earth is an oblate spheroid? But this term embraces a variety of forms and proportions: which form exactly is the absolute unchangeable fact? Why not say simply that the earth has some shape or other? Surely this is a fact — though science does not pride itself on sticking to facts such as this.

---

7. Would Professor Carlson grant Wood the right to believe?

Above, it was said that the shadow of the earth in a lunar eclipse is a fact — on which the roundness of the earth is erected as a theory. But is even the shadow a fact? Is it not rather the fact that a certain darkness on the moon has a round edge, and is it not a theory that this darkness is the shadow of the earth?

This type of analysis seems to lead to the conclusion that all, or at least many, alleged facts are theories developed out of simpler items of perception. The problem naturally arises whether there is any fact that is not a theory. Is there anything seen directly as what it is? No doubt many people at Atlantic City on a fine summer's day have seen an airplane high in the air pursuing an even course; and as they have watched the plane so high and so small, it has flapped its wings and dived to get a fish. Was it a fact that it was an airplane, or was this a theory about a small object in the sky?[8] What is a fact?

There is one type of fact that seems to be preeminently scientific: it is the length of a line. When a scientist measures the boiling point of water, he measures a line — the length of mercury in a tube. When he measures the density of gold, he measures a line — the distance on a piece of steel between a scratch called zero and another scratch called, perhaps, nineteen. Similarly he measures another length to determine the amperes of an electric circuit. It may be that scientists never measure anything else than the lengths of lines; at least it is quite safe to say that no significant experiment can be completed without measuring a line. Therefore if science is to be understood, careful thought must be given to this exceedingly important step in experimentation. It has been shown that science is not a body of fixed truths, and if the length of a line turns out not to be a fact, the essential nature of science will have to be sought, not in its results, but in its methods. The experimental method, rather than the particular laws or

8. This analysis of the datum of sensation leads to most interesting and most delicate questions. Possibly nothing is *given* in sensation. *Cf.* Brand Blanshard, *The Nature of Thought*, Vol. I, pp. 1-159, (Allen and Unwin, 1939).

facts discovered, is the important thing. And to understand the experimental method, an analysis of the process of measuring a length is as instructive as it is for determining whether or not science deals with facts.

Fact or not, the length of a line, be it mercury in a tube or the distance between scratches on a dial, is most difficult to ascertain. To put a ruler against the line and say, "nineteen," would be altogether unscientific. The scientist does of course put a ruler of some sort to the line and does read off nineteen spaces, or whatever it may happen to be; but he never supposes that this is the fact he wants. After he measures the distance between the two scratches on his bar of steel, he measures it again. And strange as it may seem the length has changed. The lump of gold that a moment before weighed about nineteen units of the same volume of water now weighs less. When the scientist tries it a third time, the gold seems to have gained weight, that is, the line has become longer. The experiment is continued until the rigorous demands of science are satisfied, or the patience of the scientist is exhausted, and he finds himself with a list of numbers. Now it may be a fact (the empirical evidence seems to favor it) that the lump of gold, weighed these many times, is constantly changing; or the fact may be (not an impossibility) that the scientist's eyes blink so much that he cannot see the same length twice; or both of these may be facts. But instead of sticking to these facts, the scientist chooses to stick to the fact that he has a list of numbers.

These numbers he adds; the sum he divides by the number of readings; and this gives him an arithmetical average, 19.3 for example. This new value, 19.3, does not occur, we may well suppose, in the original list. That list contained 19.29, 19.28, 19.31, 19.32, but never a 19.30. But if this is the case, could the arithmetic mean be the 'real' length of the line, the fact itself? By what experimental procedure does one determine that the average is the sought-for fact and that none of the observed readings is? Or, further, would it not be justifiable for the scientist to choose the mode, or the median, instead of the arithmetic mean. Is it not a fact that the mode is the length — as much a fact at least as that the average is? Really, is it not more the fact, because the mode occurred several times in the list, while the mean has not occurred at all? Or, should we say that in this essential item of scientific procedure, science throws all the facts (observations) out the window and sticks to what is not a fact (the unobserved average)? Perhaps there is an aesthetic delight in averages that is not found in modes. Unless therefore some balance, some vernier, some scale shows our senses that averages are facts and that modes are not, can the scientist do anything but trust his aesthetic taste?

However, in any experiment that goes beyond a student's exercise, there is more to be considered. The scientist not only calculates the average, but he also takes the difference between each reading and the average, and calculates the average of these differences to construct a figure denoting variable error. The result of the previous example could be $19.3 \pm .01$. Suppose now that these repetitions of one measurement are a part of a much more complicated problem designed to determine a law of nature. The problem might be the determination of the law of gravity. As is known, the attraction of gravity, in the Newtonian theory, is directly proportional to the product of two masses and inversely proportional to the square of the distance between them. How could this law have been obtained by experimental procedures? It was not and could not have been obtained by measuring a series of lengths and (assuming unit masses) discovering that the value of the force equaled a fraction whose denominator was always the square of the distance. A length cannot be measured. If it could, the experimenter might have discovered that the force between the two masses, when they are a unit distance apart, was 100 units; he might then have measured the force when the two masses were two units apart and have discovered that it was 25 units; and a similar measurement at four units distance would have given the value of 6.25. The experimenter presumably would then have made a graph and indicated the values so obtained as points on the graph. Measuring four units on the x axis, he would have put a dot 6.25 units above it; and at two units on the x axis he would have put a dot 25 units above it; and so on. By plotting a curve through these points the experimenter would have *discovered* the law of gravity. But as has been seen, the length of a line cannot be measured. The values for the forces therefore will not be numbers like 6.25, but something like 6.25 $+$ .0043. And since the same difficulty inheres in measuring the distances, the scientist will not have unit distances but other values with variable errors. When these values are transferred to a graph, they cannot be represented by points. On the x axis the scientist will have to measure off two units more or less, and on the y axis, 6.25 more or less. It will be necessary to indicate these measurements, not by points, but by rectangular areas. But, as an elementary account of curves would show, through a series of areas, an infinite number of curves may be passed. To be sure, there is also an infinite number of curves that cannot be drawn through these particular areas, and therefore the experimental material definitely rules out an infinite number of equations; but this truth is irrelevant to the present argument. The important thing is that areas allow the possibility of an infinite number of curves; that is, measurements with vari-

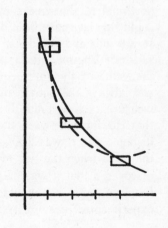

able errors allow an infinite number of natural laws. The particular law that the scientist announces to the world is not a *discovery* forced on him by so-called facts; it is rather a choice from among an infinity of laws all of which enjoy the same experimental basis. Thus it is seen that the falsity of science derives directly from its ideal of accuracy. It may be a fact that gold is heavier than water, but it is not a scientific fact; it may be a fact that the longer and the farther a body falls, the faster it goes, but Galileo was not interested in this type of fact. The scientist wants mathematical accuracy; and when he cannot discover it, he makes it. Since he chooses his law from among an infinite number of equally possible laws, the probability that he has chosen the "true" law is one over infinity, i.e. zero; or, in plain English, the scientist has no chance of hitting upon the "real" laws of nature. No one doubts that scientific laws are useful: by them the atomic bomb was invented. The point of all this argument is merely this: however *useful* scientific laws are, they cannot be *true*.[9] Or, at the very least, the point of all this argument is that scientific laws are not *discovered* but are *chosen*.

Perhaps both points should be maintained. Not only are scientific laws non-empirical, they must indeed be false. Take for example the law of the pendulum. It states that the period of the swing is proportional to the square root of the pendulum's length. But when the scientific presuppositions of this law are examined, it will be found that the pendulum so described must have its weight concentrated at a point, its string must be tensionless, and there must be no friction on its axis. Since obviously no such pendulum ever existed, it follows that the law of the pendulum describes imaginary pen-

9. *Cf.* Henri Poincaré, La Science et l'Hypothèse, pp. 189-190: "le but de [la théorie de la lumière] n'était pas de savoir s'il y a réelement un éther, s'il est ou non formé d'atomes, si ces atomes se meuvent dans tel ou tel sens; c'était de prévoir les phénomènes optiques . . . [mouvement et courant électrique sont] appellations [qui] n'étaient que des images substituées aux objects réels que la nature nous cachera éternellement. . . . Que tel phénomène périodique . . . soit réelement dû à la vibration de tel atome qui . . . se déplace veritablement dans tel ou tel sens, voilá ce qui n'est ni certain ni intéressant."

dulums and that real pendulums do not obey the law of physics. Note especially that the analysis does not separate pendulums under laboratory conditions from pendulums in living-room clocks, and does not conclude that in the laboratory, but not in the living-room, the laws of physics hold. The analysis shows that no physical pendulum, no matter how excellent the laboratory, satisfies the scientist's requirements. The scientist's world is (on pre-Heisenberg theory) perfectly mathematical, but the sense world is not.

Naturally a great many people, steeped in nineteenth century scientific traditions, react violently to the idea that science is all false. Did we not make the atom bomb, they say? Does not vaccination prevent smallpox? Cannot we predict the position of Jupiter and an eclipse of the sun? Verified prediction makes it forever ridiculous to attack science. This reaction is of course understandable, however irrational it may be. The argument has not "attacked" science at all; it has insisted that science is extremely useful — though by its own requirements it must be false. The aim nowhere has been to attack science; the aim is to show what science is.

How science can be useful though false is illustrated in a delightful textbook on inductive logic.[10] Milk fever, the illustration goes, until late in the nineteenth century, was a disease frequently fatal to cows. A veterinarian proposed the theory that it was caused by bacteria in the cow's udder. The cure therefore was to disinfect the cow, which the veterinarian proceded to do by injecting Lugol solution in each teat. The mortality under this treatment fell from a previous ninety percent to thirty. Does not this successful treatment prove that the bacteria were killed and that Lugol cured the disease? Unfortunately another veterinarian was caught without the Lugol solution one day, and he injected plain boiled water. The cow recovered. Had water killed the bacteria? What is worse, it was found later that air could be pumped into the

---

10. Harold A. Larrabee, *Reliable Knowledge*, p. 191. (Houghton Mifflin Co., 1945).

cows' udders with equally beneficial results. The original science was wrong, but it cured the cows none the less.

A closer examination of the logic of verification should be made. In the example above, the first veterinarian probably argued: If bacteria cause milk fever, Lugol solution will cure; the disinfectant does cure it; therefore I have verified the hypothesis that bacteria cause milk fever. This argument, as would be explained in a course of deductive logic, is a fallacy. Its invalidity may perhaps be more clearly seen in an artifical example: if a student doggedly works through Plato's Republic in Greek, he will know the Greek language; this student knows Greek; therefore he has read Plato's Republic. This is the fallacy of asserting the consequent, and it is invalid whenever used. But it is precisely this fallacy that is used in every case of verification. If the law of gravitation is true, a freely falling body will have a constant acceleration, and the eclipse will begin at 2:58:03 p. m.: but freely falling bodies do have a constant acceleration and the eclipse did begin at 2:58:03 p. m.; therefore the law of gravitation is true. Or, if the periodic table of atomic weights is true, a new element of such and such a weight must exist; this new element has now been discovered; therefore the periodic table is verified. And, if I eat roast turkey and plum pudding, I lose my appetite; I have lost my appetite; therefore we had roast turkey for dinner. All these arguments are equally invalid. But sometimes there is an adverse reaction if it is claimed that verification never proves the truth of a scientific law. Is it worse to "attack" science, or to "murder" logic?

Formation of Concepts

With these considerations in mind it is now time to outline the most serious limitations of science. Up to this point it has been assumed that the meaning of the word *length* was known, even though no one could measure a length. Now it must be asked, What does length mean? Does it have an unambiguous definition? Or, are several different things indiscriminately called length? In general, how are the concepts of physics to be formulated?[11] The difficulty now being approached arises from a source not hitherto mentioned. The impossibility of obtaining a fact in science, of discovering the length of a line, depended psychologically on the difference threshold. Because of the human inability to distinguish between two items not widely separated, it was necessary to repeat experiments, calculate averages and errors, and introduce a number of non-empirical factors before coming to a result. In addition to the difference threshold there are the upper and lower thresholds of sensation. There are sounds, at least there are air vibrations, so high that the human ear is not stimulated, although a dog may hear them. As one goes down the scale, there finally are vibrations so low in frequency that they are similarly inaudible. Or, one may cite lengths too short to be seen and lengths in the celestial galaxies too large to be seen. What is the scientific status of concepts that apply above and below the limits of sensation? Is the submicroscopic length a length in the same sense as a visible length is?

A serious examination of these matters has been made, no doubt by several scholars, but especially by the eminent physicist, P. W. Bridgman. It is worthwhile to make an extended series of quotations.[12]

"All these experiments are concerned with things so small as to be forever beyond the possibility of direct experience. . . . Thus we observe an emission line in a spectroscope and may infer an electron jumping from one energy level to another in an atom.

"The experimental facts are so utterly different from those of our ordinary experience that not only do we apparently have to give up generalizations from past experience as broad as the field equations of electro-dynamics, for instance, but

<hr/>

11. An answer to this question from an historical point of view is given in the extremely interesting and enlightening, but tantalizingly short book, *On Understanding Science* by James B. Conant, (Yale University Press, 1947).

12. P. W. Bridgman, *The Logic of Modern Physics,* pp. viii, ix, 5, 7, 21-22, 30, 32, 56-57, (The Macmillan Co., 1927).

it is even being questioned whether our ordinary forms of thought are applicable in the new domain; it is often suggested, for example, that the concepts of space and time break down.

"What do we mean by the length of an object? We evidently know what we mean by length if we can tell what the length of any and every object is, and for the physicist nothing more is required. To find the length of an object, we have to perform certain physical operations. The concept of length is therefore fixed when the operations by which length is measured are fixed: that is, the concept of length involves as much as and nothing more than the set of operations by which length is determined. In general, we mean by any concept nothing more than a set of operations; *the concept is synonymous with the corresponding set of operations.*

"The concepts can be defined only in the range of actual experiment, and are undefined and meaningless in regions untouched by experiment. It follows that strictly we cannot make statements at all about regions as yet untouched. . . .

"What is the possible meaning of the statement that the diameter of an electron is 10^{-13} cm.? Again, the only answer is found by examining the operations by which the number 10^{-13} was obtained. This number came by solving certain equations derived from the field equations of electrodynamics, into which certain numerical data obtained by experiment had been substituted. The concept of length has therefore now been so modified as to include that theory of electricity embodied in the field equations, and, most important, assumes the correctness of extending these equations from the dimentions in which they may be verified experimentally into a region in which their correctness is one of the most important and problematical of present day questions in physics. . . . As a matter or fact, the concept of length disappears as an independent thing and fuses in a complicated way with other concepts, all of which are themselves altered thereby. . . .

"It would doubtless conduce greatly to clarity of thought if the operational mode of thinking were adopted in all fields of inquiry as well as in the physical.

"Let anyone examine in operational terms any popular present day discussion of religious or moral questions to realize the magnitude of the reformation awaiting us.

"Consider now another construct, one of the most important of physics, that of the electric field. In the first place, an examination of the operations by which we determine the electric field at any point will show that it is a construct in that it is not a direct datum of experience. . . . The field is, then, clearly a construct. Next, from the formal point of view of mathematics, it is a good construct, because there is a one to one correspondence between the electric field and the electric charges in terms of which it is defined. . . . Now, nearly every physicist takes the next step, and ascribes physical reality to the electric field, in that he thinks that at every point of the field there is some real physical phenomenon taking place. . . . At first this view most naturally involved as a corollary the existence of a medium, but lately it has become the fashion to say that the medium does not exist, and that only the field is real. The reality of the field is self-consciously inculcated in our elementary teaching . . . and is considered the most fundamental concept of all modern electrical theory. Yet in spite of this, I believe[13] that a critical examination will show that the ascription of physical reality to the electric field is entirely without justification."

This series of quotations from Bridgman, set together instead of being distributed as several points, concludes some of the previous argument and prepares for the next particular. According to Bridgman's operationalism a scientific concept is defined by the experimental operations employed in obtaining a list of readings; and therefore the microscopic and telescopic lengths are conceptually different matters, with the result that it is only by confusion that we apply the name length to both. If this is so, and there is a respectable number of scientists who hold to this view of things, a great deal that passes under the title of scientific information is fundamentally misleading. To speak of the sun as ninety million miles

13. Will Professor Carlson permit Bridgman to believe?

distant from the earth, or of the star as some billions of miles distant, is to assume that lengths in inches, feet, and miles on the earth's surface are the same sort of distances that separate the stars. But since the operations used in measuring these two sets of "lengths" are different, it follows that there is no "distance" between the earth and the sun. Similarly, any other concept that has been used in connection with different operations is equally ambiguous and misleading. To carry this thought one step further, it may be added that the operations of science change from time to time, and when they change all the old concepts are discarded. If a new instrument should be invented for the measuring of stellar distances, the results would not be the "length" of previous experimentation. A new method of measuring means that something different is being measured, for "the concept is synonymous with the corresponding operations." And this substitution of concepts, even more than the original troubles in measuring a line, remove from science any absoluteness that Carlson and Clifford wish to find.[14]

The operational analysis of scientific procedure, while it effectively disposes of the naive scientific philosophy of the nineteenth century, faces difficulties of its own. Operationalism was formulated in an attempt to be more consistently experimental. The motive is clear-cut, and enjoys wide approval. But one result of this more consistent empiricism is, in the quotation above, the disappearance of any electric field that is physically real. And if Bridgman's method should be applied to other items, no doubt some of them would vanish too. The question comes, whether anything would remain in existence. According to the thrust of operationalism it would seem that only operations themselves could survive the annihilating analysis. And if this is so, a curious result ensues. Careful scientific procedure was originally invented for the purpose of overcoming the grossness of ordinary sensation. The unaided eye cannot make fine distinctions and therefore

14. *Cf.* Carroll C. Pratt, *The Logic of Modern Psychology*, pp. 62, 63, 67, 68, (The Macmillan Company, 1939).

delicate instruments had to be invented in order accurately to measure, say, a length. A length was supposed to be some sort of real attribute of a physical thing. Now length turns out to be just the operations themselves. And how can the scientist observe and define the operations? Will he depend on his unaided eyes to describe the instruments and the procedure, or will he invent other more delicate instruments to measure the operations, ad infinitum? There seems to be in all this a thoroughgoing epistemological relativism that makes the obtaining of truth impossible; and if scientific procedure cannot obtain truth, it can offer no absolute arguments against theism nor can it say truthfully that "the scientific method is the sole gateway to the whole region of knowledge."

Mechanical Model

The mention of theism, reminding us of our main theme, calls attention to another item in the quotations from Bridgman. In the history of the struggle between religion and science one of the chief weapons used against religion has been the mechanical image of nature. It has been held by irreligious philosophers and scientists from Democritus through La Place to their contemporary disciples that the world is composed of small, discrete particles, called atoms or point centers of force, which move according to the laws of mechanics; and that therefore there is no God. There could be no God because the term God means some sort of spiritual being not composed of atoms, and because a God would introduce purpose into what Carlson has called "an obviously a-moral universe."

Some replies to this materialistic or mechanistic view have been based on the assumption that regularity and machinery are better evidence of a divine machinist than the irregularities of chance or miracles are. That is, the reply holds that the mechanistic argument against God is a fallacy: the premises may be admitted without necessitating the conclusions. More recently, physicists, quite apart from any argument about theism, have adopted an indeterministic view of nature. The Heisenberg 'indeterminacy principle' rejects mechanism and substitutes random motions and statistical laws. Some theists have gladly accepted this as scientific proof, absolutely true, that nature is not mechanical. And if nature is not mechanical, there is room for God. But the whole matter is not very satisfactory. If the mechanistic argument against God is invalid, the indeterminist argument for God is not less so. If it is assumed that the universe can be *completely* explained by atoms in mechanical motion, God has been ruled out by assumption; on the other hand, if it is assumed that the universe can be *completely* explained by point centers of force in random motion, God is likewise ruled out by assumption. Presumably one could assume that God fashioned the mechanism as easily as one could assume that God can find a place in an indeterministic universe. The relation of these theories to theism is not best described by this line of argument.

A more pertinent and penetrating analysis of this new development in physics will lead to the conclusion that neither mechanism nor indeterminism has been proved. They are both assumptions.

Applicable to the mechanical image of nature and to any other image of nature as well are the following restrictions by Bridgman.[15]

"Diametrically opposed to the views above, there is another ideal of the explanatory process which is held by many physicists . . . namely, the endeavor to devise beyond the limits of present experiment a structure built of elements like some of those of our present experience, in the action of which we endeavor to find the explanation of phenomena in the present range. Now a program such as this, as a serious program for the final correlation of nature, is entirely opposed to the spirit of the considerations expounded here. . . . Yet this has been the attitude of many eminent physicists, for example, Faraday and Maxwell, in seeking to explain distant electrical action by the propagation through a medium of a mechanical push or pull, or by Hertz, who sought in all phe-

---

15. *Op. cit.* pp. 43 ff.

nomena the effect of concealed masses with ordinary mechanical inertia. . . . From a less serious point of view, however, it may be quite justified to make such a working hypothesis as that in the action of electrical forces may be discovered the same elements with which we are familiar in the everyday experiences of mechanics. For such a hypothesis often enables us to make partial correlations which suggest new experimental tests, and thus gives the stimulus to an extension of our experimental horizon. Many physicists recognize the tentative character of such attempted explanations, but others apparently take them more seriously, as for example Lord Kelvin in his continuous life-long attempts to find a mechanical explanation of all physical phenomena. This quotation from Kelvin is illuminating. 'I never satisfy myself until I can make a mechanical model of a thing. If I can make a mechanical model, I can understand it. As long as I cannot make a mechanical model all the way through, I cannot understand it' . . . . The instinctive demand for a mechanism is fortified by observation of the many important cases in which mechanisms have been discovered or invented. However, the significance of such successful attempts must be subjected to the most careful scrutiny. The matter has been discussed by Poincaré,[16] who showed that not only is it always possible to find a mechanistic explanation of any phenomenon (Hertz's program was a perfectly possible one), but there are always an infinite number of such explanations. This is very unsatisfactory. We want to be able to find the *real* mechanism. Now, an examination of specific proposed mechanisms will show that most mechanisms are more complicated than the simple physical phenomenon which they are invented to explain, in that they have more independently variable attributes than the phenomenon has been yet proved to have. . . . If, then, a mechanism is to be taken seriously as actually corresponding to reality, we must demand that it have no more degrees of freedom than the original phenomenon, and we must also be sure that the phenomenon has no undiscovered features. Phys-

16. Henri Poincaré, *La Science et l'Hypothèse.*

ical experience shows that such conditions are most difficult to meet, and indeed the probability is that they are impossible."

Mechanical models, however, have not been without their exponents, even in the face of these criticisms. The point that a mechanical model usually has more independently variable attributes than the phenomenon may be immediately dismissed. Classical mechanism has always postulated that the model must have as few variables as possible, and in Democritus these attributes were shape, position, and motion. Contemporary mechanists whatever they substitute for these attributes, are willing to insist that they be fewer or as few as are found in any phenomenon. The more serious problem that mechanism must face is the new indeterminacy. Has it been proved that nature is not mechanical? This question was carefully explored and answered negatively by Chester T. Ruddick.[17] And more recently C. West Churchman[18] has built on Ruddick's argument.

It would seem that Ruddick's excellent analysis shows well enough that physical indeterminacy is not forced on one by any experimental data: Heisenberg has not "proved" that the elements of nature are lawless. But on the other hand the mechanical image of nature is likewise unproved. Whether one wishes to accept a mechanical model or an indeterminism is a matter of choice. Churchman chooses mechanism because he believes that it is essential to the purpose of science. Not only does he discount Bridgman's skepticism as to natural images in general, but he labors to overcome all scientific relativism. On one page he seems to make the claim "adequately to refute the charge that relativism makes against any absolute answer to problems of science."[19] Two chapters later, after considerable detailed analysis, he writes, "We take this analysis to be based on the assumption that whatever may be the meaning of purpose [without which science cannot be understood], this meaning must be consistent with the physicist's aims, i.e.,

17. *On the Contingency of Natural Law*, in The Monist, July 1932.
18. *Theory of Experimental Inference,* (The Macmillan Company, 1948).
19. *Ibid.* p. 173.

it must not conflict with a physical interpretation of nature in accordance with deterministic laws."[20]

At this point one naturally asks, why must a physicist's aims be restricted to mechanical models? While Heisenberg may not have "proved" indeterminism, does it not remain a respectable scientific hypothesis? Could it not possibly be true? To such questions Churchman's answer seems to be that a scientist must assume an image that will *guarantee* answers to his problems.[21] Presumably Heisenberg's general views, even if they should turn out to be correct descriptions of nature, will make at least some questions unanswerable. And in this case, apparently, all scientific work might as well be abandoned.

Physics, History, and Ethics

There is a prior and much more important question: What is the purpose of science? Perhaps Bridgman might be inclined to list this with his other "Meaningless Questions," but Churchman, going far beyond the narrower scope of Bridgman's work, does not shrink from integrating science with a general view of society. A theory of science must explain the purpose of science; and since this purpose is a part of a more general purpose, the more restricted questions of physical experimentation must be answered in the light of the history of society. Churchman indeed is willing to wait for his answers until the general purposes common to all the societies of the ages, if such exist, are discovered.[22]

But do such exist? It is no doubt a mark of scientific patience to await the completion of the science of history, but until views of history are accepted, is anyone in position to state the limitations or the absence of limitations of scientific endeavor? If one person hopes that a future science of history will justify the mechanical image of nature so that answers to questions may be guaranteed, may not another person hope

20. *Ibid.* p. 193.
21. *Ibid.* p. 203.
22. *Ibid.* p. 252.

that all images of nature are artificial constructs, corresponding to nothing real, and that a science of history will not
alter this analysis?

Churchman, however, is very thorough. He sees that history requires ethical judgments. In constructing his science
of history, involving as it does certain definite proposals of
a political nature, "we wish to have no sympathy with a
program aimed to simplify our desires, or eliminate them."[23]
"To make a long story short and oversimplified, we suppose that it is possible by an examination of the histories of
societies with respect to their aims and conflicts, to determine
predominant purposes expressive of the aims of man, not as
viewed from one age or social group, but as viewed throughout all the changes of societies in their various historical
aspects. Such predominant purpose let us call 'historical.'
Let us then define the most general purpose, or ideal, to be the
satisfaction of any given historical purpose; or, in experimental terms, let us say that the measure of progress is the measure
of a random individual's power (probability of attainment)
with respect to the set of historical purposes. Examples of
such historical purposes would evidently be health, comfort,
security, and similar aims."

This statement is modified a little later on.[24] He says,
"The moral obligation of a community is not only to remove
exploitation, but also to increase without limit the probability
that any random individual will satisfy all his legitimate desires, i.e., all desires that are consistent with the general aims
of mankind."

It is in these last pages of the book that Churchman tries
to make good the word he spoke in his Preface.[25] "As the
essay will try to show, the presuppositions of inquiry become
far more complicated than early experimental science dreamed.
This is emphasized by the persistent claim of the essay that
the simplest question of fact in science requires for even an

23. *Ibid.* pp. 261, 262.
24. *Ibid.* p. 276.
25. *Ibid.* pp. vii-viii.

approximation, a judgment of value. This is a far stronger claim than even the contemporary pragmatic writers are willing to make for ethical theory. We are *not* merely claiming that ethical judgments can be included within the scope of science; this claim is by now well recognized by serious students of method. We are rather making the much stronger claim that the science of ethics (like all the principal branches of science) is basic[26] to the meaning of any question the experimental scientist raises. All the so-called 'facts' of science imply for their meaning a judgment of value."

These sound like the sentiments to which, by a radically different approach, the arguments of the present volume have come. Many of the sentences of the two books could be interchanged — but few of the paragraphs. Churchman and the present writer agree, it seems, that if there are any scientific facts, they are unattainable values with zero variable error; and that experimental results therefore do not necessitate the particular laws currently taught in physics texts. These laws are approximations,[27] the result of choices, and can never be true. Further, it is agreed, in opposition to the earlier empiricism, that physics requires some sort of a priori. Presumably Churchman reflects his own views and is not merely expounding Kant, when he writes,[28] "But space and time are not enough to permit us to construct an understandable world; or, rather, the conditions under which a space-time framework can be used by the experimenter should be made clearer. We need only consider how the experimenter differentiates objects in time. He does this by means of a timepiece which must be so constructed that changes occur in it at regular intervals; that is, the timepiece is constructed to obey some 'mechanical' law; without some such regularly operating mechanism to rely on, the experimenter would have no way of calculating time. Questions about time would still

---

26. On pp. 226, 233 it is denied that any science is basic: there is reciprocal influence and "spiral" development.

27. Churchman has an elaborate theory of stochastic limits, but it is doubtful that it affects the present argument.

28. *Ibid.* pp. 127, 129.

be meaningful, perhaps, if all clocks stopped, but such questions would be meaningless if there were no regularity in nature at all, for then there would be no way of determining the passage of time except by a mystical intuition of duration à la Bergson, an intuition that is meaningless for the experimental scientist since it is inexpressible. . . . The Kantian position is not easy to grasp; indeed it is all too often misinterpreted. Kant's demand or postulate that there exists a determinism in nature is not scientific wishful thinking. He does not mean to assert that a nondeterministic world would be a discouraging one for the scientist interested in formulating a description of nature. His demand is not one to be confirmed or refuted by examining the world of all possible experiences. Rather, for Kant *no* investigations can be made, *no* world of experience can exist, unless a regularity of nature is presupposed. There would be no laws of nature, no facts of nature (except the immediacies) unless we had already imposed on nature a certain form. It is not that the mind, in a Humean sense, 'unconsciously' puts regularity into the world; it is rather that the very possibility of mind and an observable world require as a necessary condition a natural determinism."

That some presuppositions are necessary seems to be a point of agreement, though it does not follow that there is agreement on the particular presuppositions. That there must be some sort of regularity in nature in order that even one question be answerable is very plausible; but it does not follow that this must be the regularity of a mechanical image. Churchman admits that "questions about time would still be meaningful, perhaps, if all clocks stopped"; and possibly he could be pressed to admit that no actual clock can be constructed to obey mechanical law perfectly. In this case it is not clear why a mechanical image of all nature must be presupposed. Something less might be sufficient. If, for example, every particle of matter or point center of force be presupposed to travel in an unbroken space-time path, could not some questions be answered without requiring the particles to obey the laws of mechanics?

Such thoughts lead to extremely interesting speculations, but the issue of a mechanical image is not so important to the acceptance or rejection of theism as many mechanists and many theists think. Although it is a widely held opinion that mechanism and theism are logically incompatible, this is so only if it is assumed that no question about the universe can be answered except in mechanical terms. But Churchman's analysis shows one method of harmonizing inviolable mechanism with significant teleology. No doubt Churchman's harmonization is unsatisfactory from a theistic point of view, but it suggests the possibility that theistic teleology may also be logically consistent with mechanism.

The major difficulties with this most excellent analysis of experimental inference lie in another direction. Since Churchman makes the laws of science dependent on ethical principles, one must examine his method of obtaining these principles. In general it may be said that Churchman rejects the "rationalistic" method: perhaps he would not go so far as to say that experiment is necessary to determine whether a self-contradictory position is true or not,[29] possibly logic is a non-experimental science, although the book is not too clear on this point; but at any rate, "To the empirical temperament, however, the purely formal can never be said to have meaning; for him, the questions asked must be translatable into a definite experience or set of experiences before it can be said to be meaningful. This is the fundamental viewpoint (though variant with the meaning of experience) of the classical positivism of Comte, of the modern logical positivists, and of the operationalists.... In general, the mind that inquires into nature, and finds such inquiry the only meaningful kind, seems forced to accept an experiential criterion of meaningfulness, and to regard many of the classical problems of science, of art, of ethics, and of religion, as meaningless, since apparently no

29. Bridgman, *The Nature of Physical Theory* (Princeton University Press, 1936), pp. 36-38, seems to do exactly this. He confuses the logical principal, x is either A or non-A with the empirical question, is x A? His elementary troubles in applying operational philosophy to logic should have led him to discard operationalism instead of discarding logic.

success could ever be made in showing how such questions can be put to the test of experience. Few can doubt the healthy impact that the positivist position has had upon modes of inquiry; it has sharply distinguished the schools of thought, and has raised a standard under which the proponents of experimental method can fight their battle against a reactionary movement. To return to a pre-positivistic viewpoint is to return to a pre-scientific viewpoint, to become as reactionary as an advocate of the indisputable power of the sovereign in the eyes of one with a democratic outlook."[30]

Later he says,[31] "The proposed measure of efficiency will not receive its validation through the fact that it may 'appeal' to the rationally minded individual, or seem to some to make the only possible sense out of the situation. Such appeals are rationalistic in their method, and by implication attempt to set up a nonexperimental criterion for the science of ethics. It is important therefore to indicate that the principles of the science of ethics which we are about to propose must eventually be subjected to an historical test to determine their validity." And the only difficulty he recognizes is the practical difficulty of accumulating enough experience to arrive at a general science of history.[32]

To this type of theory the preceding chapter on ethics attempted to reply. Basically it was that observation can at best describe what is and cannot decide what ought to be. The observation and description of what societies predominantly think is value, gives no basis for concluding that the items in question are values. If one reads between the lines, running the risk of misrepresenting Churchman's views, it would seem that the bottom of his argument is something as follows: over the centuries men have had many desires, and the more these desires are satisfied, the better; only experimental science can satisfy desires; desires that science cannot satisfy are

30. *Ibid*, pp. 214-215. The connection between science and democracy is interesting: does he imply that a sovereign democracy does not claim indisputable power?
31. *Ibid*. p. 252.
32. *Ibid*. p. 262.

illegitimate; therefore one is obliged to accept the experimental philosophy. In effect this seems to mean that even if God should exist and should be able to satisfy the desire for personal immortality, it would still be morally wrong to have such a desire because only God and not science could satisfy it; and it would still be meaningless to speak of God because spiritual communion and not scientific verification would prove his existence. Or, if Churchman would not express himself just so with reference to these theistic inferences, at least it can be maintained that his minor premise assumes the point at issue. He holds that only science can satisfy desires, and any desire that science cannot satisfy is illegitimate. But this is circular. He wishes to justify the experimentalist philosophy; he does so by asserting that only science can satisfy our desires; but when certain desires are mentioned which science cannot satisfy, he replies that such desires are illegitimate. And why are they illegitimate? Because they conflict with the experimentalist philosophy. At least I judge that this is what may be found between the lines. However that may be, Churchman insists on the moral obligation of a community to remove exploitation and on the need of man's cooperation with man in the conquest of nature. Many will agree with him; but what argument could he use with a person who believes that cooperation is slave-morality and that dictatorial irresponsibility is worth the price of less social productivity? Or, to take other values that he has mentioned, health and comfort, for example: what reason can he give for asserting these to be values? Does no reason need to be given? Or, is it sufficient to say that health is a necessary means to many other values? If this latter reply is made, the question must be repeated — what is the argument to justify these other values? To come to a very basic question, why should it be assumed that life is worth living? Health is no doubt a value, if the activities of life are values. But is life worth the trouble? It is true that most people desire to live; but from the proposition that all people except suicides desire to live, it does not follow that all people ought to preserve their lives. Perhaps the suicides are the wiser. Here are questions that the tenor of experimental philosophy does not seem able to answer, for whatever Churchman might say in answer to these objections, I fear that his answer would prove to be rationalistic. Or else irrational.[33]

Conclusion

Since the discussion of science has returned us to ethics, a phrase from the previous chapter will serve to introduce a conclusion. One of the theories there criticized depended on assuming a Reason spelled with a capital R. At the beginning of the present chapter too, Science was assumed with a capital S. It is this assumption that has been called in question. There is no Science to which final appeal can be made; there are only scientists and their various theories. It was easy to show that the Science of infallible law does not exist; it was not much more difficult to show that absolute facts do not exist; it may have been a little subtle to argue that the concepts of science change with the operations; and when the methods, as opposed to the results, of science are taken as the ultimately important matter, an attempt was made to show that scientists do not agree on the methods. Furthermore, all these methods depend on faith, choice, or, as Clifford would have to say, "insufficient evidence." No scientific or observational proof can be given for the uniformity of nature, and much less can experience demonstrate that "the scientific method is the sole gateway to the whole region of knowledge." On the contrary, a plausible analysis showed that science was incapable of arriving at any truth whatever. This may account for the delightful remark of Spengler[34] that "it may be asserted that the downright faith that Haeckel, for example, pins to the names atom, matter, energy, is not essentially different from the fetishism of Neanderthal Man."

---

33. *The Will to Believe,* by William James, can still be studied with profit. A. E. Taylor, *Does God Exist?* (The Macmillan Company, 1947) pp. 16, 30, also argues that a belief in science depends on nonscientific factors.

34. *Op. cit.* Vol. I, Chap. XI, p. 397, note 1.

Nothing therefore that comes out of observation, no matter with what scientific care the observations are made, can discredit the arguments of the previous chapters or motivate a choice against theism. Ethics and history do not depend on science, but science depends on them. A philosopher who was so thoroughly wrong that he was often right stated the exact truth when he said, "the moral (or immoral) purpose in every philosophy has constituted the true vital germ out of which the entire plant has always grown. Indeed to understand how the abstrusest metaphysical assertions of a philosopher have been arrived at, it is always well (and wise) to first ask oneself, 'What morality do they (or does he) aim at?' "[35]

---

35. Friedrich Nietzsche, *Beyond Good and Evil*, I, 6.

VI

RELIGION

CHAPTER VI

Religion

THE problems of history, politics, and ethics, so it has been argued, require for their solution certain theistic presuppositions. Naturalism or humanism, on the contrary, leads to inconsistency, despair, or suicide. But the fact that naturalism has proved intolerable does not of itself imply that the particular Christian presuppositions underlying the whole of the present volume are the only principles capable of supporting a satisfactory worldview. If theism is indeed necessary to the intelligibility of history, possibly Mohammedan theism or some other form would function as well as or even better than Christian theism. There has not been much argument so far to rule out such a possibility. Apparently the best general procedure for one who wishes to recommend Christian theism is to show that other forms of theism are inconsistent mixtures. If some of their propositions should be carried to their logical conclusions, naturalism and eventually skepticism would result; whereas if justice is to be done to possible interpretations of other of their assertions, Christianity would have to be assumed.

Since a discussion of Mohammedan theism and several other types, however theoretically necessary to a complete exposition, would not be of particular interest at this time and place, their omission requires a choice between two alternative procedures, each with its own danger. The first of these seems to be what the argument logically requires: an analysis of non-Christian theism in general — the formulation and criticism of factors common to Mohammedanism, Judaism, and all other non-Christian religions. But if this is attempted, the analyst may mistake an accident of theism for its common quality; or, if he envisages correctly the common quality of all theisms, the perfect generality may suffer from extreme vagueness or ambiguity; or still worse, just as in the traditional logic the concept Not-Man is unmanageable because it includes worms, stars, and airplanes, so the negative concept of non-Christian theism may prove devoid of significant common elements. The second alternative is to choose a single but typical form of modern religious thought. This procedure would sacrifice generality and leave the argument technically incomplete, but it would have the advantages of obvious pertinence, importance, and above all definiteness. It would also serve as a model and provide hints for a similar treatment of other types of non-Christian theism.

The selection of such a typical form of modern religious philosophy is largely arbitrary: the only limitation is that the theory be fairly well known and its author prominent. One must disclaim any intent to make invidious comparisons in such a choice, for any one of half a dozen contemporary writers might equally well be selected. With all the randomness, therefore, of an honest roulette wheel, the pointer spins around the list of eligibles and stops on the name of Edgar Sheffield Brightman. In his theory of a finite god he himself claims to present a common type of religious thought, exemplified anciently in Plato and more recently in David Hume, John Stuart Mill, William James, F. C. S. Schiller, H. G. Wells, Henri Bergson, William Pepperell Montague, Vergilius Ferm, Georgia Harkness, and others. While an analysis of this theory leaves other views untouched, surely the list of its advocates insures the importance of its consideration.

Method

The first and most crucial matter in any philosophy of religion, as indeed it is in all phases of philosophy, is the method chosen. A method poorly adapted to an investigation usually results in failure. It may start the train of thought off in the wrong direction, or it may prevent the consideration of certain alternatives by an implicit and unexamined assumption that they are false. Thus some of the contending views would be condemned in advance without a hearing. Brightman is explicit as to his method: "The keynote of the book is experience. . . . The facts of experience are summarized in the sciences. As a philosophy of religion, this book is an interpretation of science, but is not itself science. The science of religion gives the facts of everyday religious experience as they appear to the historian, the psychologist, and the sociologist. Philosophy in all its branches relies upon science and has no organized subject matter apart from the facts set forth by science."[1] Later on he states that the proper method of philosophical interpretation "starts with the empirical subject matter to be criticized, discovers its meaning and structure, and then relates it to other areas of experience and thought."[2]

Clearly these two quotations presuppose a view of science, of facts, and of the discovery of structure and meaning; but Brightman has not made it clear which view of scientific method he accepts: he briefly criticizes Bridgman and operationalism; undoubtedly he rejects the conclusions of Clifford, Pearson, and Carlson, but possibly he might retain some of their method. In another volume[3] he stresses the differences in method between one science and another, while at the same time he speaks of something common to all scientific method. Because of this incompleteness of exposition, some of the arguments of the previous chapter may not be applicable; but its main conclusions seem to undermine Brightman's position. For example, he approves of the objectivity of science "if man is to discover truth without prejudice";[4] and he definitely states that "physics must of course exclude facts irrelevant to it; physics must exclude all moral, religious, and metaphysical judgments from its experiments and laws."[5] This has been shown to be impossible, for the previous conclusion was not

---

1. Edgar Sheffield Brightman: *A Philosophy of Religion,* p. vii., (Prentice-Hall, Inc., 1940).
2. *Ibid.,* p. 116.
3. Edgar Sheffield Brightman, *Nature and Values,* pp. 100-102, (Abingdon-Cokebury Press, 1945).
4. *Ibid.,* p. 78.
5. *Ibid.,* p. 103.

that "philosophy in all its branches relies upon science and has no organized subject matter apart from the facts set forth by science," but rather that science in all its branches relies upon philosophy and that the method chosen determines the facts. If, however, this initial criticism seems too summary, the best procedure will be an attention to detail. Since experience is the keynote of Brightman's philosophy, the term should be carefully defined, for even Kant used it ambiguously; and John Dewey has extended its meaning until, as Brightman notes, the suggestion has been made to abolish its use. But it is better, if possible, to define it. Brightman tries to tell us just what it means to him. "Our experience consists of our entire conscious life. . . . All human knowledge begins, continues, and ends in experience." "Experience as used in this book is a word that refers to the immediate data of consciousness; whatever is present in consciousness is said to be experienced. The individual experiences his experience."[6]

With this definition Brightman immediately proposes to refute the apriorists who distinguish between experience and reason. Experience for them is not "whatever is present in consciousness" but consists of data given in sense, while reason consists of eternal principles not derived from these data. Four apples may be inferred from sense data, but the truth that two and two are four is an eternal, universal, and necessary truth. Faith in God for the apriorists is not like the inference that four apples exist, says Brightman, but it is like the truth that two and two are four, or, rather, like the axioms and postulates on which this truth depends. The rejection of the a priori view is of such importance that the risks of misinterpreting Brightman's argument should be minimized by direct quotation. "An empiricist would reply to an apriorist somewhat as follows: It is misleading, he would say, to declare that there is anything independent of experience. The case of the apriorist derives its force from the indubitable fact that there is a difference in importance between four apples and $2 + 2 = 4$. The empiricist insists, however, that the process

6. *A Philosophy of Religion*, pp. 1, 163.

of thinking that $2 + 2 = 4$ is as truly a conscious experience as is the process of observing four McIntosh Reds. The same is true of our thought regarding any axiom or postulate. The assertion that one part of experience is independent of all experience is logically contradictory. The trouble arises from using the word experience in a restricted meaning (as confined to sensations or like content) and then forgetting the restrictions. It is better to be a thoroughgoing empiricist and define experience as meaning all that is at any time present in consciousness. ... It is possible that some truths are universal and necessary; but this fact cannot be known prior to experiences of thinking and observing."[7]

The influence of Auguste Comte, William James, and their disciples, as they reacted against what seemed the mysterious legerdemain of Hegel's system, has made empiricism the predominant style in science, philosophy, and religion. There are styles in philosophy as there are in women's dress, and there may come a time when past styles will be resurrected. A student who has an historical sense and who knows to what extent social superstition presses on all of us should not consider too weighty any contention that apriorism is passé and empiricism is up-to-date. In fact a part of the reason for Brightman's insistence on empiricism is the resurgence of apriorism in the theology of Barth, Brunner, and like minded writers.

When one turns from styles, popularity, and first impressions to analysis and argument, empiricism may not have the best of it. In one sense it is of course futile to fuss about the choice of a definition; if a writer wishes to use the term experience as coextensive with consciousness, the reader's first responsibility is simply to remember the meaning of the author. But there is more than this involved. A motivation, which must be understood, lies behind the choice of a definition; and if its purpose is to refute opposing positions, one must judge as to its success.

---

7. *Ibid.*, pp. 2-4.

In another instance Brightman recognizes that important distinctions can, by redefinition, be passed over in silence, and that when a term is made all inclusive, it comes to mean nothing in particular. Naturalism uses this device to avoid discussion of religion, and Brightman objects to the prejudging of religious questions by defining nature as everything that exists. "Such a usage is debasing to the term, leaves the word supernatural without any discussable meaning, and makes it possible that all the old distinctions between nature and the supernatural, mind and matter, may be really distinctions within nature."[8] Does not Brightman's definition of experience leave the term a priori without any discussable meaning and so prejudge many questions?

Of course this is not to say that Brightman intended to treat apriorism inadequately. Probably the motivation behind Brightman's definition of experience lies in the widely admitted deficiencies of earlier empiricism, for he complains that "it is purely arbitrary to elevate sense experience to a preferred position while ignoring the fact that values are as truly present in consciousness as are sense data."[9] Now, sense data were thus elevated, perhaps illegitimately but not altogether arbitrarily, because it was thought that sensation was the test of objectivity. And this is true not only of early empiricism but of the apriorist Kant as well. Both schools held that unless appeal is made to sense experience, one may either be deluded by hallucinations or beguiled by the uncontrolled play of one's own fancy. Obviously Brightman believes that by redefining experience so as to include, not sensory material only, but the entire contents of consciousness, he can refute apriorism, improve on his empirical predecessors, and maintain objectivity as well. But whether he succeeds in any of these three aims is something to be examined.

---

8. *Nature and Values*, p. 76, *et passim.*
9. *A Philosophy of Religion*, p. 124.

First, the redefinition of experience and its accompanying explanation fail to convict the apriorists of self-contradiction. If experience be defined as "all that is at any time present in consciousness," it indubitably follows that "the process of thinking that $2 + 2 = 4$ is as truly a conscious experience as is the process of observing four McIntosh Reds." But this does not settle, it only obscures the question whether we learn, prove, or abstract $2 + 2 = 4$ from the visual experiences of seeing apples. Neither the critical Kant nor the rationalist Descartes before him ever denied that when we think arithmetic, we are thinking. Kant would be entirely ready to admit Brightman's contention that universal or a priori truths "cannot be known [temporally] prior to the experiences of thinking. . . ." Indeed Kant opens his *Critique of Pure Reason* by saying, "That all our knowledge begins with experience there can be no doubt. . . . But though all our knowledge begins with experience, it by no means follows that all arises out of [or, is founded on] experience." Kant therefore is not guilty of Brightman's easy contradiction "that one part of experience is independent of all experience." Kant is facing an epistemological problem. He wants to show how knowledge is possible, and in particular how necessary truths are possible. To do so he does not, as Brightman suggests, use the word experience in a restricted meaning and then forget the restriction. It could be Brightman rather who has erased the distinction and has forgotten that he erased it. What Brightman calls experience, Kant divides into reason and sense, or form and matter; no doubt we are conscious of both in combination; but Kant's point is that the "form" of knowledge is not based on, implied by, or abstracted from the sensory "matter." To erase the distinction between reason and sense, between the necessary and contingent, and say merely that we are conscious of both elements gives no help in solving Kant's problem. It is nothing but tautology to say that the process of thinking $2 + 2 = 4$ is a process of thinking. Kant aimed to assign to each of two distinct factors its exact function. "Thoughts without content are void," he says; and "intuitions without

conceptions are blind." To obscure this distinction and label
it all experience may change the name but it does not refute
the theory. There are many flaws in Kant, but when he says
that there are universal and necessary truths which transcend
sense data, he is not guilty of the logical contradiction with
which Brightman charges apriorism. Apriorism therefore
remains as a possible theory.

The second and third points are best considered together,
for whether or not Brightman improves on the earlier empiricism, he fails at last to provide protection against hallucinations or lesser fancies. It is true that Locke's analysis of
external experience into simple ideas of sensation cannot be
defended; and if positivistic tendencies have still further
minimized internal experience, it would naturally seem that
empiricism has unduly elevated sensation at the expense of
other items of consciousness. In this case a wider definition
of experience is a tempting expedient. But the expedient is
unsuccessful because there are deeper flaws in empiricism than
the one mentioned, flaws that are retained under the new definition. As Kant showed, the cause of empiricism's failure
was not its sensory definition of experience — Locke in fact
did not restrict experience to sensation — but the impossibility
of basing universality and necessity on momentary states of
consciousness. The propositions of mathematics and the basic
principles of physics are allegedly true at all times and in all
cases. Such truths cannot be established on experience, not
because the experiences are sensory, but because they are momentary particulars. Sensation failed to arrive at universality,
not because it was sensation, but because it was contingent.
Therefore Brightman's wider definition of experience does not
avoid the difficulty. If a sensation is a fleeting temporal event,
a non-sensory state of consciousness is equally so. And from
such, universal propositions cannot be obtained. This means
that objectivity is left without foundation. If there are no
a priori forms identical in all learning minds, the contents of
of experience will be so personally subjective that it will be
difficult to escape solipsism. Just as one man's toothache is

not another's, and as one person's taste for olives is not another's distaste, so one individual's idea of two, cause, logic, God, or even stone, might have no common element with another's. The true, the good, and the beautiful would at the same time be the false, the evil, and the ugly.

But since this line of criticism is so comprehensive that its development must run into the following chapter, and since Brightman is by no means unaware of these difficulties, one must have patience to follow the argument step by step. If the redefinition of experience is insufficient to refute apriorism, still this failure is equally insufficient to refute empiricism. It will be necessary to see how things work out. Can Brightman surmount the difficulties? Can he do so consistently with his own principles? Or are there logical gaps between his premises and his conclusions?

Value

Although the wider definitions of experience did not succeed in meeting the apriorist position head-on and could not substantiate its charge of logical contradiction, yet empiricism might still be found acceptable if it could justify necessity and universality. And it is this that Brightman attempts to do in his theory of value.

Above, Brightman was quoted as saying that it was arbitrary to give preference to sense experience while ignoring the other items, particularly the values, that are just as truly present in consciousness. It is not so accurate to say that previous philosophers ignored these values as that they placed a different interpretation upon them, for what Brightman means by values is incontrovertibly contained in consciousness. The definition is important: "Value means whatever is actually liked, prized, esteemed, desired, approved, or enjoyed by anyone at any time. . . . Good is synonymous with value."[10]

From this definition of good and value it follows that if I esteem or approve the practice of prayer, prayer is good; it also follows that if I desire or enjoy whiskey, whiskey is good.

---

10. *Ibid.*, p. 88.

Earlier (p. 12) he said that experience contains many statements about better and worse, such as, it is better to live than to die, better to be honest than dishonest, better to listen to a symphony than to a dance orchestra. Let it be so: there are people who pray and people who drink whiskey, there are people who enjoy symphonies and people who do not. It is quite clear that the existence in experience of values in the sense of whatever anyone likes is neither disputable nor important. The crux of the matter is to pass, if possible, from the several conscious states of liking prayer, whiskey, or dance orchestras, things which should be called apparent values, to a statement that one of these things is a real or actual value. In the English language the word value is not uniformly restricted to the fact that somebody happens to like something; often, perhaps usually, it carries the connotation of something that is really valuable, of something that everybody ought to like even though most people do not. Because of this connotation the critic must be unusually alert to determine whether an argument beginning with Brightman's definition of value concludes with value in its usual sense of actual value. The word is loaded and slippery. Of course "experience" contains the statement, It is better to live than to die; but experience also contains the statement, It is better to die than live. Experience also frequently contains the statement, It is better to be dishonest than honest. The important question is not, What does experience contain? but, Which statement is true?

Brightman faces this crucial test. First he defines an ideal: "An ideal is a general concept of a type of experience which we value." When we doubt, as sometimes we do, whether we approve our own feelings of the moment, we ask, " 'Do we regard the value as expressive of our mature judgment?' What we do in such circumstances is to consult our ideals and use them to judge our values."[11] This seems to mean that we consult our general concept of what we like and use it to judge what we like. If our value of the moment contradicts our general concept, "then either we have made an error in

---

11. *Ibid.,* p. 90, 91.

valuing [i.e. we do not really like what we like at the moment]
or we have made an error in defining" [i.e. our general concept
of experiences which we value is not the concept of what we
actually value].

This perplexing situation is amended somewhat by slightly
more explicit directions. In answering the logical positivists
who deny the distinction between values and true values,
Brightman says, "Verification is a process of relating experiences and of building up a coherent rational system of thought
and experience,"[12] by emphasizing either logical analysis, practical consequences, or the coherence of the whole of experience.
"When value-claims are consistent and coherent with each other
and with the other facts of experience, then the claims are
verified; and such value claims are *true* values."[13]

Is this method of verification satisfactory? Can one pass
from value-claims to true values in the way Brightman indicates? The first step of the process of verification is to choose
values that are consistent with each other. But this direction
is useless for the purpose because it can be carried out in
opposite ways. One set of values, like gambling and whiskey,
may be self-consistent, and a second set, like prayer and
church attendance or miserliness and solitude, may also be
self-consistent; but the two or three sets may be entirely incompatible as sets. The process of verification outlined will
direct us not to combine gambling and miserliness, but it is
of no help in choosing one of the combinations.

Similarly, it is useless to tell us to choose the value or the
set of values that is consistent with the other facts of experience.
The idea of a coherence of the whole of experience, which plays
such a prominent part in Brightman's thinking, is not only
difficult to apply, but also vague in meaning. Logical consistency can be clearly defined, but Brightman insists that coherence is more than consistency. This is a point to be
remembered when the opposition between reason and revelation is later discussed, for the vagueness and inapplicability
found here are repeated there. To go beyond the logical con-

---

12. *Ibid.*, p. 92.
13. *Ibid.*, p. 93.

sistency of propositions and place the choice of values on the ground of consistency with the other facts of experience is unsatisfactory because any fact of experience is consistent with any other fact of experience for the simple reason that both occur. A desire to live is consistent with experience, and so is the desire to commit suicide. The life of Stalin is just as consistent with all the facts of experience as is the life of Mr. Milquetoast. No doubt "the fact that religious values exist and have existed throughout history is one of the most certain facts known to man";[14] but it is just as certain that the values of drunkenness and despotism exist and have existed throughout history. Brightman seems to have failed to find an empirical bridge between value-claims, i.e., the fact that I like something, and true or real values, i.e., what everybody ought to like.

However, when it is said that Brightman fails to connect values with true values, he can verbally object to the conclusion, for he has given a special definition of "true" value. As previously he attempted to dispose of apriorism by a new definition of experience, here too he proposes a definition of "true" that obscures the problem. "A true value, then, is what we still value after the testing of our empirical values by rational norms (rational meaning logically consistent and coherent), and after the tests of analysis, practical consequences, and coherent wholeness have been applied to the experience."[15] It may be granted without argument that from value this sort of "true" value may be obtained; that is, from the fact that I like several things now and continue to have experiences, it will result that at a later date I shall still like something or other. But this is unsatisfactory because men in all ages, Caesar, Thomas Aquinas, Napoleon, Pasteur, and Professor Brightman himself, have analyzed, have calculated practical consequences, and have looked for coherent wholeness, with the result that each one has chosen as "true" value types of experience that another one would call evil.

---

14. *Ibid.*, p. 105.
15. *Ibid.*, p. 93.

Looking through several of Brightman's volumes in which he discusses value, I receive the impression that one of the basic flaws in his arguments is the tacit though possibly unrecognized assumption that really after all everybody agrees as to what is good and evil. There seems to be no serious attempt to refute those who repudiate as evil the things Brightman thinks are good. In Plato's *Gorgias,* it may be remembered, Socrates was able to refute Polus because Polus made "shameful" admissions in deference to common respectable opinion; but Callicles was open and frank and said what he really thought. Socrates commended him because his frankness made his statements more consistent than those of Polus, and hence made him, Callicles, a more worthy opponent. Even so, one suspects that Callicles was refuted only because the author Plato slipped some "shameful" admissions into Callicles' replies. Similarly, so it seems to me, Brightman relies on the unwillingness of his opponent openly to repudiate the respectable ideals of sweetness and light, and for this reason the opposing position is not squarely met. His identification of specific goods or norms particularly highlights the gap between his empirical premises and his ethical and religious conclusions. For example, Brightman obviously approves the four freedoms, but his interpretation of them would not win universal acceptance. Take the freedom of religion. Christ said, "No man cometh unto the Father but by me." But Brightman says, "When the creed of any one faith implies or expresses the belief that each faith is the one and only way to worship God, how can believers in such a faith honestly grant freedom to other faiths without a certain condescension incompatible with respect for personality?"[16] Does this suggest that a government run on Brightman's principles would deny religious freedom to Christ, or merely that Christ was guilty of immoral condescension? In the same vein he says, "Whatever differences there may be in creed, religious men and women should be one in heart."[17] But it is precisely the creeds

16. *Nature and Values,* p. 75.
17. *Ibid.,* p. 166.

of a Shintoist or Stalinist militarist and of a Quaker pacifist that prevent them from being one in heart. Disparagement of creed minimizes conviction and the value of truth for the guidance of life, and it reduces religion to a nonintellectual emotion. Again he says, "God is man's fellow sufferer. He dies every Good Friday but rises every Easter."[18] Those who accept the Bible think that a single dying, once for all, is sufficient. Brightman also emphasizes the norms of reason and love, *logos-agape,* or reasonable love. He seems to be exceedingly sure of them. But when he insists on the value of love *agape,* does he mean what, say, Brunner means by *agape*?[19] One cannot be sure of the meaning intended by a simple use of the Greek term. What normative propositions does *agape* lay down? What actions does it require? Or is it an amorphous feeling that somehow is good in itself? Similarly worship is said to be an international and universal value.[20] But is the worship of idols, or of a finite god, a value? A true value? These considerations suggest that insofar as Brightman's ideals are not vague, they are sufficiently repellent to some people to stand in need of empirical evidence; they ought not without argument to be assumed as universally obligatory, for clearly there is a wide logical gap between Brightman's premise that all people have likes and dislikes and his conclusion that all people ought to value precisely these particulars.

By his definition of "true" value, therefore, Brightman evades the real problem, for "true" value is not *true* value. Brightman has not shown that I ought to like what I like, much less that everybody ought to like what I like. Yet only this will satisfy the requirements of ethical theory. And Brightman recognizes that these are the requirements, for he connects value with the notion of "should" (i.e., ought?), and says, "A value not only contains the assertion 'I like prayer,' but as an overtone, 'you all ought to like it.' "[21] But

---

18. *Ibid.*, p. 159.
19. Emil Brunner, *The Divine-Human Encounter,* pp. 90-91, (The Westminster Press, 1943).
20. *Nature and Values,* p. 87.
21. *A Philosophy of Religion,* pp. 11, 92.

none of Brightman's empirical premises logically implies universal obligations, or any obligation at all.

In another volume Brightman makes a more determined attempt to face this decisive issue. He defines a value as whatever is liked, and a true value as whatever is liked in the light of our whole experience. Then coming to obligation, he writes, "On our view obligation is binding because it is self-imposed, or, as Kant would say, autonomous. Obligation does not arise from the mere command of a foreign power like society or even God Himself; we are bound to do what we recognize that we ought to do; and the obligation is binding, inescapable, because we have imposed it on ourselves. We cannot evade the jurisdiction of laws that we ourselves have made."[22]

Some of this is more assertion than argument. It is equally easy to assert that obligation arises solely because of the mere command of God. And an obligation based on the command of God seems more binding than the jurisdiction of self-imposed laws. Why cannot we evade the jurisdiction of laws that we ourselves have made? After all, if I make a rule or law to govern my conduct, and at a later date discover that the law is inconvenient, why can I not amend or repeal the law? It will not do to say, as Brightman does, merely that morality is rational, and that a man who violates obligation violates reason. What is needed, if Brightman is to make his point, is some method of showing the specific obligation of devotion to human welfare that figures in his argument. But this essential factor, Brightman completely omits. With Kant, Brightman asserts that morality has the prerogative of legislating for religion; that most men agree (and we may ignore those who disagree?) that less of faith or reason is involved in acknowledging an obligation than in believing in God; that many men who have been unable to accept the belief in God have nevertheless (inconsistently?) been loyal to obligation; and that morality is logically prior to religion, for

---

22. *Religious Values*, pp. 15, 51-61 (The Abingdon Press, 1925).

a man must acknowledge goodness before he can acknowledge God.

To sum up: These Kantian elements, though now labeled empirical, are still open to the objections detailed in the chapter on ethics. Unless more cogent reasons are brought to light, plausibility remains with the earlier conclusions that theology is logically prior to ethics, that God's commands constitute moral obligation, that a denial of God's sovereignty consistently implies a repudiation of some of the values Brightman wishes to maintain, that man is not autonomous, and that the definition of goodness requires a prior knowledge of God. In addition to these previous conclusions it has now been shown that Brightman's improved empiricism does not logically arrive at objectivity and universality. There is no rational process that leads from an individual's likes and dislikes, no matter how combined in sets or repeatedly "verified" in his experience, to the conclusion that he *ought* to like what he does or to the wider conclusion that everybody ought to like the same things. This, it would seem, is not an auspicious beginning for a philosophy of religion.

Is God Essential to Religion?

"The idea of God is uniquely essential to religion."[23] Such a statement can be understood only if the terms God and religion are defined. The attempt to define religion is notoriously futile. One might think that the many authors who have written books on religion or the philosophy of religion should know what they are discussing, but, as Brightman notes, J. H. Leuba in *A Psychological Study of Religion* gives a bewildering list of contradictory definitions. William James says,[24] "Religion ... shall mean for us the feelings, acts, and experiences of individual men in their solitude, so far as they apprehend themselves to stand in relation to whatever they may consider divine." Note the inclusion of the phrase "in

23. *A Philosophy of Religion*, p. 133.
24. *Varieties of Religious Experience*, p. 31, (Longmans, Green and Co., 1902).

their solitude." W. K. Wright means something quite different by the term religion. He says, "Religion is the endeavor to secure the conservation of socially recognized values."[25] Brightman follows Wright in emphasizing the conservation of values and then combines the social emphasis of Wright with a slight recognition of the individual. His definition is, "Religion is concerned about experiences which are regarded of supreme value; devotion toward a power or powers believed to originate, increase, and conserve these values; and some suitable expression of this concern and devotion, whether through symbolic rites or through other individual and social conduct."[26]

The difficulty inherent in the attempt to define religion arises from the fact that there are many mutually contradictory religions; they may all be wrong, but not more than one can be true. Or, to cast the matter in Brightman's phraseology, there are many mutually incompatible experiences which different people regard of supreme value. Now, if a definition is framed to express the common character of all religions, either the result is so vague as to be virtually meaningless or, worse, it may be found that there is no common quality. On the other hand, if a definition is framed to do justice to real values and the true religion, all the false religions would object to its non-empirical and prejudiced character. There is a further difficulty with the empirical attempt to find a common quality in all religions. In the work of Emile Durkheim the difficulty is quite evident, though Brightman's development obscures it. Durkheim tests a number of suggested definitions by applying them to historical religions,[27] and thus claims to discover what is common to them all. If, for example, a particular factor, such as the doctrine of the Trinity, is not found in Mohammedanism, then it cannot be included in the general definition of religion. One of the important factors so tested is the belief in God. Is this essential to religion? Is this common to all religions? It will be noted that Brightman has

---

25. *A Student's Philosophy of Religion*, p. 47, (The Macmillan Co., 1924).
26. *Op. cit.*, p. 17.
27. *Les Formes Elémentaires de la Vie Religieuse, Livre I*, Chap. V.

said "the idea of God is uniquely essential to religion."[28]   But
Durkheim shows that Buddhism has no belief in God and that
therefore this belief is not a factor to be included in a general
definition.   Brightman himself, in spite of the sentence quoted,
seems to agree, for he also writes "It has often been said, for
instance, that a value experience is religious if it has God as
its object.   But this definition is confronted by the existence of
atheistic religions like Hinayana Buddhism, modern religious
humanism, and Communism."[29]

What the empirical method fails to observe is its own circularity.   The problem is to find the common element in all
religions in order to form a definition of religion.   Suppose
the problem were to find the common element in all snarks
in order to form a definition of snark in general.   The empirical
method would require an examination of snarks; but this examination could proceed only if it were first known what a
snark was.   If the Bellman or the Barrister could recognize a
Snark when he saw one, he might seek it with thimbles and
care, and upon examination determine whether the characteristics of Boojums are essential to all Snarks.   But an ordinary
mortal would not know enough to use a thimble, and with all
his care would not know a snark if he met one.   That is, the
empirical examination can take place only after the definition is
accepted.   Durkheim has rejected the belief in God as essential
to religion because Buddhism does not have that belief.   But
how can one know whether Buddhism is a religion or not?
If it is known that the idea of God is essential to religion, it
follows that Buddhism is not a religion; but no examination
of Buddhism will tell whether religion requires the idea of
God.   Communism certainly and possibly even humanism, as
Brightman notes, may in an acceptable colloquial sense be
called religions because religion may mean whatever principles
a person accepts as the guide of his life.   Similarly the term
God can sometimes be stretched, as when the Bible refers to

---

28. If by *uniquely* essential Brightman means that the idea of God is the
only element common to all religions, he should meet Durkheim's argument that a church and a bifurcated universe are common.

29. *Op cit.*, p. 103.

some people whose god is their belly. And if the term God is stretched to the limit, it follows of necessity that the idea of God is essential to religion. The humanist's god in that case would be the belief that there is no God. But if God is used in a more definite sense, and particularly if God is used in the most definite sense of Almighty Creator, then not all religions contain the idea of God, and Brightman's religion is one that does not.

Inasmuch, therefore, as Brightman asserts that the idea of God is uniquely essential to religion, one must ask what he means by the term God. He writes, "God, in all the discussions of this book, means primarily the Source and Continuer of Values, and the problem of belief in God is the problem of finding a definition of the axiogenetic and axiosoteric aspects of reality. . . ."[30] Earlier he had asserted, "The statement, 'God is the creator of the universe,' or 'the source of all being,' is an irreligious statement, if it means that whatever may be thought of as the source of all being is therefore to be regarded as God."[31] And again,[32] "God is worshipped solely as a source of value."

The problem therefore is to prove the existence of a Source of Values, or, better, since values may depend on man or physical nature, to determine whether there exists a personal, superhuman Source of Values. How can God be known?

Can God Be Known?

Brightman examines six proposed ways of knowing God. For the present purpose it will be sufficient to consider the second of these six: revelation. Having just finished an interesting critique of mysticism, Brightman begins his review of revelation by contrasting the mystic emphasis on the immanence of God with the transcendence of God as held by Calvinists, Barthians, Mohammedans, Christian Scientists, and some Catholics. His discussion, however, applies more directly to the Barthians than it does to the Calvinists and some

---

30. *Op. cit.,* p. 209.
31. *Op. cit.,* p. 135.
32. *Op. cit.,* p. 230, *cf.* pp. 134, 198, 302.

others. The Calvinists and the Catholics assert both the immanence and the transcendence of God, and they quote from the Bible to the effect that "in Him we live and move and have our being."[33] But Brightman seems to have in mind a non-immanent transcendent God that is not characteristic of Christianity. This is made clear by his use of the Barthian phrase "totally other." For the Calvinist and the Catholic, God is not totally other: there is a resemblance. Calvin[34] expounds the doctrine of the image of God in man and makes many references to the Scriptures. It will be possible, nonetheless, to disregard the Barthian particularities that Brightman has directly in view, and discover his criticism of revelation as held by a Calvinist or Catholic. A Christian might accept as fair enough Brightman's description of this position, namely that "man by his own powers can never discover or experience God. God . . . would remain forever unknown, or forever only an unverified guess, an entity whose plans and nature were hidden from us, unless he revealed himself."[35]

The accompanying phraseology, however, needs some modification. When Brightman says that believers in revelation "distrust the powers of human reason," the honorific connotations of the term reason create an initial prejudice. Some discrimination is required. Although a distrust of reason in one sense may be the equivalent of insanity, a distrust of reason in another sense may be entirely rational. Reason has different meanings, and also there are different types of distrust. For example, both the Catholic and the Calvinist would object to Brightman's unqualified statement, but their objections would be based on different grounds.

The Catholic, as is clear from the vigorous development of Neoscholasticism, trusts reason, in a certain area, as implicitly as or even more than the modern philosopher. The principles of cosmology, including the proof of the existence of God, can be elaborated on the basis of sensation and abstraction

---

33. Acts 17:28. Cf. Psa. 139:7-12; Jer. 23:23-24; *et passim.*
34. *Institutes* I, xv. 3.
35. *Op. cit.,* p. 172.

and are demonstratively certain. God, however, possesses information that cannot be abstracted from the natural world. For example, since creation is the common act of the Trinity and does not involve any of the personal distinctions, an examination of the world will prove the existence of God, but it will not reveal that this God exists in three persons. For man to have this and other divine information God must tell him. To the Catholic this unlimited trust in reason within a limited area with the corresponding distrust beyond those limits, is no more unreasonable than that a man should trust his strength to lift a hundred pounds but find himself unable to lift five hundred.

The Calvinists would also, but from another point of view, wish to guard the expression of trust or distrust in reason. Although in the main they have been particularly interested in theology and have not worked out a detailed system of philosophy comparable with Neoscholasticism, they more or less closely follow the general Augustinian tradition that places much less faith in reason than Thomism does. Contrary to the Catholic limited distrust in reason, the Protestant theologians, though some may have wavered, usually repudiate natural theology and assert that the traditional proofs of God's existence are not logically or "mathematically" demonstrative. Calvinism indeed may be said to place no faith at all in reason, in the sense that man would know nothing whatever about God, unless God had revealed himself. This distrust in or incompetency of reason is not irrational, if God exists. If God is a person interested in human beings, it would be unreasonable to deny that he could reveal himself. It would also be likely that he might have information which man could not obtain apart from a special revelation. And particularly if God is omnipotent, it would necessarily follow that man could know nothing of him unless he wished man to. In Calvinism revelation is not confined to the Bible, for God has set his glory upon the heavens and has written his law on man's heart. Unfortunately, however, sin has so vitiated human powers that man can read neither the heavens nor his own heart aright. Because of this inability a verbal revelation, now written in the Bible, is necessary if man is to be informed of the possibility and the method of escaping the penalty of sin. Since there is nothing inherently or logically impossible in such an arrangement, any argument against revelation must take care to escape the judgment of William James: "A rule of thinking which would absolutely prevent me from acknowledging certain kinds of truth if those kinds of truth were really there, would be an irrational rule."[36] Many discussions of the possibility of revelation have violated this dictum.

More important than distinguishing between the Catholic and Calvinistic types of distrust is the necessity to specify the meanings of the term reason, for God, religion, and value are not the only terms to be defined. In the seventeenth century Descartes, Spinoza, and Leibniz made reason the apriori and only source of truth by contrasting it with sensation. This contrast and this meaning of reason is irrelevant here because in religious discussions the contrast is between reason and revelation, and the term reason may, depending on the author's epistemology, include sensation. Another meaning of reason, frequent in general conversation, refers to the forms of logic. A valid syllogism is in accord with reason, and a fallacy is irrational. When opposition is being made to revelation, reason ought not to bear this ordinary logical meaning because revelation is entirely compatible with the deduction of necessary conclusions from revealed information. The textbooks of Systematic Theology are full of reasoning. Even Tertullian reasoned. It would be difficult to show that any revelational theologian distrusted reason in this sense. Possibly the Barthian theory of paradox, involving — if one may trust precarious deductions from the rather difficult language of that prominent author — the notion that God's mind is self-contradictory and that He is unable to solve the problems of the world because they are inherently insoluble, would reject reason even in this logical sense. But Barthianism, though

---

36. *The Will to Believe*, X.

influential at the present time, is not typical, at least in these implications, of the historical forms of revelational theology.

Reason may have still another meaning, which Brightman expresses more clearly in his earlier volume. Reason "is the body of most general principles used by the mind in organizing experience and arriving at judgments accepted as true . . . Revelation is not the most general body of principles used by the mind. Revelation must be tested by reasonableness, not reasonableness by revelation . . . it is not a criterion of truth but presupposes a criterion by which it is judged."[37] The later book presumably presents the same view; at least it says, "Accordingly, reason — concrete and inclusively empirical, not merely abstract and formal — is the supreme source of religious insight, the supreme way of knowing about God, whether He is, or whether He is not."[38]

To trace out the implications of these statements is an interesting and difficult task. In the first place there are certain epistemological presuppositions that will require some treatment in the following chapter. But even here it should be noted that Brightman contrasts a concrete and inclusively empirical reason with a reason that is merely formal. Logical consistency would be merely formal, and the coherence of the whole would perhaps illustrate the concrete and empirical.[39] Now, a contrast between form and matter is sometimes a convenience hard to avoid; but if it is taken to be more than a momentary convenience for a certain level of discussion and is asserted as an ultimate distinction, the result seems to be some form of logical positivism. It brings back to mind Churchman's arguments against what he called rationalism and his statement that "the purely formal can have no meaning."[40] But at various places in the present volume it has been intimated that logic, instead of being merely formal, is an integral part of reality. Something purely formal would be entirely arbitrary; it could be used or rejected at will; it

37. *Religious Values*, pp. 21, 22.
38. *A Philosophy of Religion*, p. 192.
39. *Ibid.*, p. 192, "Consistency does not demand coherence."
40. (See p. 224).

could be replaced by another form equally useful; but this is not true of the laws of logic. They cannot be replaced. To whatever extent Brightman's theory of religion depends on such a distinction between the formal and the concrete, to that extent it has an unacceptable epistemological foundation.

It is by no means clear what this extent is, for, in the second place, the reason that Brightman needs for his theory of religion, the reason he contrasts with revelation, the concrete and empirical reason, is left undefined; and it is difficult to discuss with assurance what is not clearly presented. Some general statements are made about it — it is the supreme way of knowing about God — but what it is, is not said. It is not an activity of the mind such as may be contrasted with the activity of sensing, but, on the contrary, it is a set of principles that could be written down on paper. And as has been said, these principles are not the laws of contradiction, excluded middle, and any other formal laws there may be. If Brightman has anywhere listed these most general propositions used by the mind in organizing experience, I have overlooked it. In his *Nature and Values*[41] he offers a definition of reason in nine norms; but these seem to be formal logical principles rather than the empirical propositions of concrete reason. But whatever they are, they are the supreme source of religious insight, and not religious alone, for they are used by the mind in organizing experience and arriving at (any) judgments accepted as true. They are therefore the supreme source of all truth.

This appeal to certain original propositions as the supreme source of all truth seems strange in an empiricist. It is the tone and language of Spinoza or Plato. In other places also Brightman speaks of the Rational Given and the realm of Platonic Ideas.[42] Brightman recognizes that this language will seem strange but he declares that the paradox rests on a mis-

---

41. P. 106.
42. *Ibid.*, p. 337; cf. Journal of Bible and Religion, XVIII, 1, Jan. 1950, *A Personalistic Philosophy of History,* p. 8.

apprehension.[43] He then explains the three stages of arriving at truth. The first stage is to gather all the facts. The second stage is the construction of hypotheses both regarding methods and meanings. The third stage is the verification or the falsification of the hypotheses by determining whether or not the hypotheses include all the data and organize them coherently.[44] The work of thought, he continues, is never done. "Yet it is the faith of religion that in all the changes that may come, certain constants of value will abide. This faith can never be asserted on philosophical grounds as dogma, but it may be entertained as a working hypothesis used in the discovery and testing of truth about the Continuer of Value in the universe." These hypotheses "are therefore not certain, but they are heuristic. Such at least is the faith on which progress in science rests, and it is not incoherent to suppose that a similar faith is valid in the realm of religious knowledge."

These last sentences have the true empirical ring, but one may begin to wonder what has happened to "reason," not the forms of logic but the set of propositions that is the supreme source of truth. Let no objection be made to a faith or hope that some constants of value will eternally abide; the difficult question is, Which? If concrete and empirical reason consists simply in empty generalities, such as the abiding of some value or other, it does not seem that reason is so terribly important; but if reason is concrete and empirical, if the propositions that compose it are specific and definite, then on Brightman's showing has not reason become uncertain and heuristic? And has or has not Brightman contradicted himself when on the one hand he allows that new experiences are always emerging and that "as long as men are men . . . alternative hypotheses . . . will always be possible,"[45] and on the other hand he asserts

---

43. *Ibid.*, pp. 192-194.

44. This shows that Brightman's empiricism is not limited to defining experience as all that consciousness contains, by which easy definition he hoped to remove apriorism from consideration, but involves a view of fact and experiment, though vaguely stated, to which some of the arguments of the previous chapter apply.

45. *Ibid.*, p. 194.

a faith that some constants of value will never change? It seems to me that if there is no contradiction, there is at least a confusion. The Rational Given and all that can legitimately lay claim to Platonic immutability on Brightman's position proves to be nothing else than the "merely" formal laws of logic. In this sense of the word reason we have principles that can organize all experience. But, then, it seems, the trust so rightly placed in logic is sometimes transferred illicitly, for the purpose of making it a supreme source of truth superior to anything God could reveal, to norms, ideals, or empirical principles that are here consistently recognized as heuristic.

If this criticism is so far valid, the definition of reason and the relation of reason to revelation must be seen in a new light. A paraphrase of Brightman's phraseology, pointing up the difficulties, will help. Reason is a set of general heuristic principles that the mind uses today and tomorrow replaces with a different set. Since an alternative principle is always possible, any criterion of truth or value is only temporary. Prayer as a "true" value may be approved by the current source of truth, and whiskey as a "true" value may be approved by tomorrow's criterion; and more strictly within the sphere of revelation, today's criterion may approve the Bible, tomorrow's will justify the Koran, and the next week's or last week's may be incompatible with any revelation at all. Revelation of course must be tested by reasonableness, not reasonableness by revelation, for "reason" is the supreme source of religious insight.

This paraphrase is not intended as sarcasm, though the language is pointed. Two remarks may help to show that these are correct implications from Brightman's statements. First, the situation that Brightman describes is not that of a man who is simply unsure which principles are true; it is not the case of a man who is conscious of ignorance and who is searching for the truth. Beyond this simple condition of ignorance the empiricist as described is convinced that the "true" value of today and the principle of reason he now uses may and probably must be false tomorrow. He knows that his principles are heuristic and that he cannot have the truth. This would be discouraging. Then, in the second place, — an inference from the first remark, — it is not a situation in which a principle may be discovered and retained. If the first theorem learned is a permanent acquisition, ignorance of all the others does not undermine a hope of progress; but when one must revise the set of propositions that one has taken as the test of all truth, the result would seem to be a skepticism in which moral decision has become impossible.

But set these considerations aside: there is another difficulty. Even though the charge of skepticism is not pressed, Brightman has given no argument to justify his assertion that a set of revealed truths cannot be used by the mind to organize experience. Surely this is an overstatement in view of the Christian philosophers in past centuries who assuredly organized their worldviews on the basis of the doctrines of the Trinity and Creation. Brightman has stated "Revelation is not the most general body of principles used by the mind." Of some minds this is true. But why cannot revealed propositions be the criterion of truth? Is not Brightman's statement equivalent to the unsupported assertion that God could not possibly reveal such propositions? And if it is equivalent, it must be said that the assertion is not an empirical discovery based on facts, observation, or experience; it is an apriori assumption that begs the question and that falls under the stricture of William James' irrational rule.

One of Brightman's paragraphs may be taken as an attempt to face this difficulty. "It would be fatal," he says "to rational [heuristic?] integrity to grant that the mind should trust the Divine Spirit to guide it to accept the right revelation in the absence of reasons or evidence; for then there would be no way of telling the voice of God from the voice of the devil."[46]

Of course, if there is no Divine Spirit, it is useless to ask whether we should trust him. Some opposition to revelation settles the matter by the prior denial of theism in general. But for the present purpose it is assumed not only that theism is

---

46. *Ibid.*, pp. 174-175.

a possible view but that God really exists. If the Spirit of God speaks, how can one tell his voice from that of the devil in the absence of reasons or evidence? At issue is whether Brightman's objection to revelation is consistent with the existence of God. On the assumption that there is a God, and more particularly on the assumption that God exists as described in the Bible, what "evidence" could he give to man that he was God? And the answer to this question must not again be an irrational rule that would prevent the acceptance of a truth, if that truth were really there. Otherwise the conclusions already arrived at stand.

How then could God show to a man that it was God speaking? Suppose God should say, "I will make of thee a great nation . . . and I will bless them that bless thee and curse him that curseth thee." Would God call the devil and ask Abraham to believe the devil's corroborative statements? Is the devil's word good evidence of God's veracity? It would not seem so. Nor is the solution to be found in God's appealing to another man in order to convince the doubter. Aside from the fact that this other man is no more of an authority than the devil, the main question reappears unanswered in his case also. What reason can this man have to conclude that God is making a revelation to him? It is inherent in the very nature of the case that the best witness to God's existence and revelation is God himself. There can be no higher source of truth. God may, to be sure, furnish "evidences" to man. He may send an earthquake, a fire, or a still small voice; he may work spectacular miracles, or as in the cases of Isaiah and Peter he may produce inwardly an awful consciousness of sin, so that the recipient of the revelation is compelled to cry out, "Woe is me! for I am undone; because I am a man of unclean lips." But whether it be an external spectacle or an inward "horror of great darkness," all of this is God's witnessing to himself.

If the evidence that Brightman demands are such matters as these, his contention has little weight. But he seems to have a different type of evidence in mind. After all, to say that God must give evidence by revealing himself is tautological. The particular evidences mentioned are themselves revelation in a sense; and surely Brightman not only would reject the idea of a revelation being its own evidence, he also explicitly rejects the testimony of the Spirit, and he bases his rejection of this testimony on the indisputable though peculiar fact that it has alienated John Dewey.[47]

Accordingly, Brightman must be understood as requiring some independent evidence of revelation. He demands "reasons" other than theophanies and other than the propositions God reveals, for "revelation must be tested by reasonableness, not reasonableness by revelation." This reasonableness or these reasons must therefore be something superior to and independent of the revelation to be tested; doubtless they are the concrete and empirical reason discussed above. Now, aside from the fact that this form of reason was left vague and undefined, does not the whole procedure return us to the rule deplored by William James? If there is a God, the Calvinists may possibly be right in saying that the knowledge of God is fundamental and by it one must judge worldviews and their details. But Brightman requires as evidence for Calvinism a type of reason that would prohibit God from revealing the basic truths that organize experience. That is, if one agrees to abide by Brightman's test, one could never substantiate such a revelation, even if there should be one.

The situation is similar to the issue between Aristotle and Sophism relative to demonstration. If everything is to be demonstrated, the demonstration turns out to be either circular or an infinite regress. Both are unsatisfactory. Therefore some things cannot be demonstrated. These are first principles which themselves are the basis or beginning of argument; and if they are the beginning, they cannot have been previously argued. To require a proof of a first principle is to misunderstand the whole procedure. Brightman in effect has argued: the Calvinists begin with God and revelation; they should be made to prove their first principle; since they cannot do so, it follows that Calvinism must be rejected, that experience,

---

47. *Ibid.*, p. 173.

chiefly of value, be made basic, and that God and his revelation are not the body of principles for the organization of experience. But this is a *petitio principii* and a basic misunderstanding.

What Is God?

The discussion now moves to the central topic of the existence and nature of God. The existence of God is a matter that Brightman settles quite easily. He notes that atheists usually repudiate the existence of a certain type of God or they oppose the policies of certain believers in God, and yet they grant "that there must be some superhuman Continuer and Source of Value. . . . Thus the atheism most commonly met with is but a family quarrel in the religious household about the source and continuation of value; it is not fundamentally irreligious. Truly irreligious atheism is to be found only where there is complete skepticism about any value in life. He who believes that there is nothing worthwhile is the thoroughgoing atheist."[48]

This statement seems to be both untrue and logically inconclusive. It seems to be untrue because there are atheists who assert the existence of values without admitting any superhuman Source and Continuer of Values. To argue as if all were agreed on some sort of Superhuman Source is unwarranted. For example, Samuel Butler in *The Way of All Flesh* approves the values of wealth and sexual pleasure and repudiates the values of church attendance. Theodore Dreiser also. But does this make them theists and enroll them in a family religious quarrel? Brightman refers to those value-blind individuals who perceive no difference in value between Edgar Guest and Shakespeare, between Irving Berlin and Wagner, or St. Bartholomew's Eve and the Sermon on the Mount. Perhaps there are people who are actually value-blind and who perceive no difference between Guest and Shakespeare, between baseball and chess, and between pleasure and pain. With these people Brightman says it is hardly worthwhile to argue. It is, however, extremely worthwhile, necessary, in

---

48. *Ibid.*, p. 202.

fact, to argue with those persons who clearly perceive differences in value and who prefer Guest above Shakespeare and St. Bartholomew's Eve above the Sermon on the Mount. All such people admit the existence of values, but not all of them grant the existence of a Superhuman Source of Value. Brightman asserts that only value-blind individuals are atheists, and thereby he implies that "dogs and sorcerers and whoremongers and murderers and idolaters and whosoever loveth and maketh a lie" are truly religious theists because they have their values, their likes and dislikes.

This brings the argument back to a problem that has already appeared under various guises. It is the question of definition. In this case the question is, What is God? Brightman writes,[49] "God, in all the discussions of this book, means primarily the Source and Continuer of Values." In this sentence the word 'superhuman' is omitted and it naturally follows that everyone who distinguishes values, everyone who likes something, is a believer in God. But the question remains open whether "God" is oneself, a Sistine Madonna, or Samuel Butler's prostitutes, Or, whether, perhaps, "God" is *God*.

The first thought that might occur to one is that there are several sources of value, such as chess and Shakespeare. Brightman therefore very appropriately begins his argument by trying to show that the Source of Value is one. He relies first of all on the unity of natural law. Value, likes, and preferences occur in a universe of law. "Natural law constitutes one system; the goal of one single equation to epitomize the entire physical universe is perhaps not so fantastically unattainable as it seems."[50]

It is inconvenient and unnecessary to discuss the view of science reflected in this sentence. A single, universal equation might seem to be an overoptimistic goal; but if it should be possible, and if "the interaction of all parts of the universe seems to be a necessary postulate if science is to be true or if 'matter' and 'mind' (whatever 'matter' and 'mind' may be)

49. *Ibid.*, p. 209; *cf.* pp. 198, 202.
50. *Ibid.*, p. 205.

are to affect one another,"[51] one may wonder whether Brightman has made impossible the freedom of choice he uses later. But at any rate, let us make no objection to some sort of unity of natural law, even though it is not the mechanical unity of an equation.

A merely natural uniformity, however, would not greatly advance the argument. If the physical forces of the universe are hostile to human ideals, or even if they are neutral, Brightman's conclusions would be unfounded. For one thing, he must prove or assume that tendencies within the realm of the scientifically observable, tendencies which in a neutral naturalism help to produce human values, are not properly called God. Admitting, indeed insisting that such tendencies exist, Brightman believes that metaphysical naturalists have failed because they have left "axiogenetic processes uninterpreted, unrelated to the rest of existence, as flowers blooming mysteriously in a hostile soil."[52]

Following the tradition of personalistic idealism, Brightman would prefer to say that nature is a part of God rather than that God is a part of nature. The objects and processes that occur in space — and these may be called nature — are only a part of conscious experience. In addition to the experience of spatial factors, consciousness includes time, ideals, love, logical implication, personal identity, morality, and worship. Brightman therefore concludes that "the spatial aspect of God is a vast, yet subordinate area of the divine being."[53]

This step at first seems to have changed "God" from the Source of Values to an All that Spinoza would be willing to call Nature. Brightman, however, takes pains to argue that God is not All. Chiefly, he relies on the contention that pantheism cannot explain the evil in the world. If God were All, then God would have to include all the ignorance and crime of human beings; but God cannot include as a part of himself any person who errs or sins; and further some forms of pan-

---

51. *Ibid.*, p. 206.
52. *Ibid.*, p. 216.
53. *Ibid.*, p. 218.

theism make freedom impossible by the determinism of the
whole; therefore God is not All.

The crux of this argument is found in the minor premise,
viz., God cannot include sinful persons; and Brightman gives
no reasons to support this premise except the bare statement
that a good God just cannot do this. Miss Calkins, another
personalist, has argued in detail to show how an ommiscient
Absolute can both be good and include error and evil. Brightman does not face her arguments.[54]

The difficulty is aggravated by the use of the term *include*.
Before asking whether God includes ignorance and crime,
one should ask what is meant by God's including anything.
The Bible states quite generally, "In Him we live, and move,
and have our being." The Christian view therefore must be
that God "includes" everybody. Does Brightman mean that
God is not conscious of a crime or of a criminal? This is
perhaps what he means, and the point will come up again; but
if so, it is not evident that "for God to include [have knowledge
of a particular act of] moral evil would make the divine an
incoherent chaos and would destroy distinctions between good
and evil."[55]

Developing his personalistic philosophy and coming to a
more positive answer to the question, What is God? Brightman
tries to justify the position that the Source of Values is a person. All empirical data are conscious experiences. All
physical forces are known only insofar as they produce conscious experiences. The universe provides evidence of law
and order, and also of biological and psychological purpose.
The history and the sociology of religion culminating in an
ideal of universal benevolence add to these prior factors and
together make the hypothesis of a personal God more inclusive
and coherent than the hypothesis of impersonalistic naturalism.
Since this is a matter of hypothesis, postulation, or presupposition, Brightman may presumably be interpreted as rejecting

54. Mary Whiton Calkins, *The Persistent Problems of Philosophy*, 5th ed.,
pp. 455-479, (The Macmillan Company, 1929).
55. *Op. cit.*, p. 220.

the traditional theistic proofs as fallacious. To this extent his procedure and that of the present volume are in accord. The chapters on history, politics, and ethics attempted to show how the presupposition of a personal God introduced coherence, truth, and sanity into those studies, and how impersonalistic naturalism led to chaos. In contrast the differences are these. The original opposition to apriorism was based on a verbalism; and if in other places empiricism comes to be observation and discovery, it runs afoul of the analysis of science, law, and fact. There is no objection to postulating some types of natural uniformity to explain the observed evidences of law and order in the physical universe; but there is no evidence on which to postulate a harmony of all human values, ideals, and purposes; on the contrary, so far as evidence goes, the goods and purposes of men seem to be in irreconcilable conflict. Then too there is agreement that consistency is a test of truth, and in some philosophical writings consistency and coherence are synonyms; but insofar as Brightman's category of coherence is not mere formal consistency, it is so poorly defined as to be useless and even meaningless. And finally the disagreement will extend to show that Brightman's hypothesis is either self-contradictory or not so inclusive as another hypothesis, and that it fails to explain or solve the problems for which it was accepted. As this attempt is made it will soon appear that a major disagreement relates to the nature of God, for the question, What is God? has not yet been fully answered.

Good and Evil

The difficulties concerning the nature of God focus in the question of good and evil. This age-old enigma has inclined some thinkers to deny the existence of God and to posit a neutral naturalism. Brightman cleverly disposes of this attitude by remarking that "It combines the marvels of Melchizedek with those of Topsy; without father or mother in the entire universe good and evil 'just growed.' "[56] But clever though the remark may be, the justification of theism depends on

---

56. *Op. cit.*, p. 272.

elaborating a consistent account of good and evil: without consistency theism would have to bow to naturalism.

Brightman approaches the subject by distinguishing between intrinsic and instrumental goods. Optimism he then defines as the view that the world contains nothing but intrinsic goods and perfect instruments for their attainment, while pessimism holds that nothing exists but intrinsic evils and their corresponding perfect instruments. He concludes this section by the assertion, "It is hardly necessary to do more than to state these views in order to create the presumption that they are both unreal, and that both rest on a torturing of the actual facts."[57] But whatever the initial impression may be, surely Schopenhauer would conceive this to be a too summary dismissal of pessimism, and the main contention in the following pages will be that optimism, when freed from several fallacious inferences and misunderstandings that made possible the shallow caricature of Voltaire's *Candide,* is the preferable hypothesis.

In developing his theory of good and evil for the purpose of avoiding a neutral naturalism, Brightman has occasional difficulty in deciding whether a particular value is intrinsic or instrumental, but he seems never to hesitate in distinguishing good from evil. "The simplest form of good or value is always a desire striving for fulfillment."[58] But Plato, arguing against Callicles in the *Gorgias,* as well as Schopenhauer, takes desire to be evil. There follows a dialectic of desire in which Brightman tries to discover the most desirable objects. He rises from the desire for the mere possession of physical things to their use, but as mere activity is not valuable, there must be desire for other persons in a social relation. But to be satisfying, the social activity must conform to ideals, and ideals are not only super-individual but also supersocial. True value therefore is an objective union of ideal and personality. And a Supreme Person affords a coherent account of the objectivity

---

57. *Op. cit.,* p. 243.
58. *Op. cit.,* p. 252.

of ideals implied by value experience.[59]   Although Brightman
seems to have forgotten that his previous definition of ideals
— general concepts of what we like — furnishes no ground for
supposing that ideals are objective, he admits that this dialectic
of desire is not an altogether satisfactory argument for the
existence of a Supreme Person.   Yet the incompleteness of the
argument, he maintains, is no reason for rejecting the belief
in that Person.   Perhaps an examination of evil — we have
considered only good so far — will remove some of the incompleteness.

Sometimes moral evil is explained as a result of human
freedom.   There is some truth in this, he says.   That an artisan
can construct a machine out of materials at hand without
knowing its future history, Brightman takes as empirical
assurance of God's creating mankind with a free will.[60]   But
there is much evil, indeed much moral evil that cannot be
explained by free will.   Another proffered explanation is that
evil and particularly non-moral evil is a punishment for moral
evil.   While logically possible, this view is repugnant to the
ethical sense of modern idealists, and even criminologists no
longer believe in punishment.   Apparently there is unimpeach-
able empirical evidence somewhere that God never punished
anybody and that idealists and criminologists have a trustworthy ethical sense.[61]   There are also other explanations of
evil, such as: evil is disciplinary; evil is incomplete good;
evil is a needed contrast to good to avoid monotony; and so on.
But they are all unsatisfactory.   What is needed, and what the

---

59. *Cf. op. cit.*, pp. 253-257.

60. Note the implication that God does not know the future.

61. *Op. cit.* p. 261. The question, "Does perfect love punish?" in its context gives the the impression that God never punishes anyone, and this seems
to be what the argument requires. The impression is only slightly weakened by the remark that the unjust distribution of non-moral evils makes
it impossible to suppose that punishment affords an explanation of more
than a very few evils. Brightman states that Jesus rejected this crude
theory of punishment in John 9:3. Jesus no doubt rejected the connection
between some non-moral evils and certain particular sins. But as for rejecting the idea of punishment, what does the Sermon on the Mount mean in
Matt. 7:21-23, 27?

empirical phenomena of good and evil point to, is the theory of a finite god.

Absolute Theism

If neutral naturalism cannot explain the existence of good and evil, of ideals, values, likes, and dislikes, one must examine the theistic position. Or, rather, one must choose between two theistic[62] positions: absolutism and finitism.

"Theistic absolutism,"[63] not to be confused with Hegelian pantheistic absolutism, "is the view that the will of God faces no conditions within the divine experience which that will did not create, or at least approve, whereas theistic finitism is the opposing view, namely that the will of God does face conditions within divine experience which that will neither created nor approves."

In view of these definitions it is strange that Brightman instead of seeing the source of theistic absolutism in the first verse of the Bible says that the root of theistic absolutism is to be found in Aristotle. Not only does the Hebrew concept of God antedate Aristotle — witness Isaiah 45:6-7, "I am the Lord, and there is none else. I form the light and create darkness: I make peace and create evil: I the Lord do all these things"; — but also Brightman can make a theistic absolutist out of Aristotle only by a very narrow construction of his definition of absolutism. Aristotle's First Mover may be called absolute, that is, the Unmoved Mover may be said to have no experience that he did not create or approve, only because he creates nothing at all and is ignorant of what he does not approve. Aristotle writes, "Are there not some things about which it is incredible that it should think?"[64] It would

---

62. Brightman has his own definition of theism. What Christian theologians usually call theism, Brightman terms deism, neglecting the distinction between eighteenth century Deism and Christianity. This seems to be because Brightman thinks that Christianity teaches a non-immanent transcendent God, as does Barth, instead of an immanent-transcendent God, as does Calvin.

63. *Op. cit.*, p. 282.

64. *Metaphysics*, 1074 b. 25.

seem therefore that the Aristotelian God is, shall we say, only one third as absolute as the Hebrew God.

The argument for finitism is advanced by noting, as Brightman does in several places, that even the absolutely absolute God of the Scriptures has one necessary limitation. He cannot do the impossible. Brightman seems to approve of Knudson's analysis that this restriction on God's power is traceable to limitations within the structure of reality,[65] rather than to the logical conditions of self-contradiction. "Neither absolutist nor finitist," he says, "supposes that the laws of reason were created by an arbitrary fiat of will; reason is an eternal and uncreated attribute of God, not dependent on his will." To this attempted weakening of absolutism, the thoroughgoing theist might reply in the first instance that God can indeed do anything even though he cannot make a three sided square or a stone too heavy for him to lift. This, however, is no limitation on his power because a three sided square is *nothing*. God's power would be limited only if there were *something* he could not do. Or, in other words, when one proposes to set such a problem for God, one has not set a problem at all because the words are meaningless.

There is to be sure a more profound problem in the relation between God's will and the law of contradiction. No doubt reason may be called an eternal attribute of God, and as such it is uncreated. It does not follow, however, that the laws of reason are independent of the will of God or in any way limit his power. The laws of reason may be taken as descriptive of the activity of God's will, and hence dependent on it though not created as the world has been created. This involves a view of God's will, nature, and being that must be referred to later. But in any case Brightman must be adjudged mistaken when he asserts that "neither absolutist nor finitist would doubt that God limited himself when he created beings with a power of choice."[66] Consistent absolutists, like John Calvin and Jonathan Edwards, deny that God has limited

65. *Op. cit.*, pp. 285, 303.
66. *Op. cit.*, p. 303.

himself in any way. He can still do anything; in particular he can and does control the choices of created wills. "He doeth according to his will in the army of heaven, and among the inhabitants of the earth: and none can stay his hand."[67] If Brightman had invariably presented the absolute position in its full consistency. it would have been more difficult for him to arrive at his conclusions.

The limitations on God with respect to logic were used, mistakenly as has been shown, to stress the similarities between finitism and absolutism. Other considerations furnish sharp contrasts. The Christian conception of God is to be rejected, argues Brightman, because it is based on an appeal to ignorance. "Absolutism entails the admission that we cannot explain the surd evils. . . . But if the absolutist believes that we truly are ignorant, what right has he to assert at the same time that we have knowledge?"[68] One may ask in reply how Brightman knows there are surd evils? This is one of the points at issue, and he seems to have no consistent argument to support this position. Yet without the assumption of surd evils, there is no reason to reject absolutism. But the chief difficulty in the argument comes from its ambiguous language. When it is admitted that the absolutist cannot explain a particular evil, which Brightman assumes to be a surd evil, it does not mean that absolutism has failed to explain all evil. It means merely that one man cannot explain in detail this one evil. This one man, however, even while he admits his ignorance of this detailed explanation, still may know a general explanation. There is nothing inconsistent in being ignorant of one matter, for example the exact course of a particular river, and knowing quite well that all rivers flow from high ground to low. Brightman's premise correctly states the ignorance of a particular, but his conclusion requires an ignorance of something else, and therefore his argument is fallacious.

This paragraph in Brightman also illustrates a constant difficulty. If the issues of religion are to be discussed, an

---

67. Dan. 4:35; *cf.* Psalm 135:6.
68. *Op. cit.,* pp. 309, 310.

author must choose between addressing himself to absolutism in general or to a particular form of absolutism; he must discuss the common element in all forms of theism or non-theism, or he must select a single form of theism. The present chapter has selected Brightman as an outstanding example of one type of thought and has deliberately set aside all other forms of religion. For this reason the conclusion to which this volume comes will not be completely justified. Brightman, on the other hand, has chosen to discuss absolutism in general rather than to limit himself to one particular form. As an ideal this is highly commendable, but it has its own peculiar danger — a danger all too evident in the present paragraph. There may be forms of absolutism to which Brightman's argument applies in full force. But there are other forms to which it does not apply at all. It does not apply to Christianity. Absolutism with its Hegelian connotations is not the term that a Christian would normally apply to Christianity, but unless it is assumed that Brightman means so to classify it, there is no generality to his argument. He must therefore be so understood. But then it follows that he has failed to seize the common element in all absolutism and has unwittingly centered attention on an accident. If he wishes to give a completely general argument against all absolutism, he ought not to disregard its most consistent and most conspicuous form.

Of course Brightman does not always disregard Christianity. In the next paragraph he urges as an objection to absolutism that it ascribes surd evils to the divine will. "Martin Luther was frank enough on this score."[69] And so was John Calvin. And this was the faith of all the Presbyterian and Reformed churches,[70] regardless of how they may have deteriorated since the time of their early purity and vigor. In opposition to

---

69. *Op. cit.*, p. 310.
70. *Cf.* Westminster Confession of Faith, Article III. Edwin A. Burt, *Types of Religious Philosophy*, (Harper and Brothers, 1939), p. 458, note 3, unsympathetic though usually accurate, says, "There is, of course, much in fundamentalist theory that intimates a far more genial conception of God than this. But the aspects of the theory above discussed are essential to it . . . Were they removed from fundamentalism, it would no longer be fundamentalism."

Martin Luther, Brightman cites Francis Bacon, though even Brightman cannot conceal from himself that Bacon is hardly a religious authority equal to Martin Luther. Surely a thinker who stresses religious experience ought to value the experience of the leaders of the Protestant Reformation above that of a scoundrel. What approaches an argument against absolutism in this paragraph is the consideration that this principle of the Reformation "would serve to account for any kind of world whatever. Since it would apply to any possible world apriori, it has no special use in accounting for the particular features of our world, whether good or evil."[71]

But this is not strictly accurate. The principle would not apply in a world such as Leibniz describes, or for that matter in a world such as Brightman describes — if these are "possible" worlds. It does apply of course to all the evils of the world described in the Bible, though admittedly it is not a detailed explanation of any one evil. But this is no objection to the theory. The law of gravitation applies to the motions of every pair of bodies, but the general formula $G = \dfrac{m_1 \, m_2}{d^2}$ is not a detailed explanation of the final strike-out of the world series. A general position is not disproved by its generality. And an ignorance of the exact masses and distances involved in pitching a baseball is not a sufficient refutation of the law of gravitation.

Brightman next brings against the Christian position another objection which to many people seems to have more force than the preceding. Since absolute theism holds that all apparent evils are really good, one might with equal plausibility argue that the apparent goods are really evil. If an event, like an earthquake or habitual drunkenness, by every empirical standard judged to be evil, is in fact a good, then why may not terra firma and sobriety be considered real evils? In other words absolutism leads to complete skepticism with respect to values. But once more this argument conceals some ambiguities. The chapter on ethics attempted to show that it was empiricism, not theism, which led to skepticism. Theism

71. *Op. cit.*, p. 311.

makes the sharpest possible distinction between good and evil, right and wrong. But the distinctions are not the ones Brightman assumes for his argument. An earthquake in itself is neither good nor evil; only as it effects a human being is it one or the other. And when it affects several human beings, it may be both good and evil. Brightman seems to think that an event which is a real evil cannot also be a real good. But of all the events and doctrines that comprise Christianity, the most prominent contradicts Brightman's argument. The crucifixion of Christ — was it good or evil? To Judas and the Pharisees it was a crime productive only of evil and of the greatest of evils. To the disciples on the other hand it was productive of the greatest of goods. Brightman apparently bases his argument on the false proposition that what is good for one man must be good for all. And this proposition in turn is probably based on an idea of the spiritual unity of the human race that Christianity repudiates. In the chapter on History St. Augustine's *City of God* was used as a clear statement of the Christian position: the human race is broken into two mutually exclusive cities; their motives, aims, principles, and destinies are different; and accordingly it is with perfect consistency and without entailing the moral skepticism Brightman fears that the same event may be judged to be both good and evil.

One further argument against absolutism must be examined before going on to the positive exposition of finitism. Absolutism, Brightman asserts, cuts the nerve of moral endeavor. Since the world is already perfect, it is useless to try to improve it. Since every evil is really a good, there is no evil to eliminate. "Fortunately," however, the Calvinists, to repeat a well worn observation, "have labored for their God just as though all were not predestined and as though they were free."[72] Their conduct, it may be generously granted, conflicts with their theory. But those who use this threadbare theme are never generous enough to consider whether there is the slightest possibility that the Calvinists are consistent. It seems to

---

72. *Op. cit.*, p. 312.

go without saying that they must be inconsistent, and to grant them this blindness is to compliment them. But could not the Calvinists have labored for their God, not as though they were not predestined to do so, but because they were predestined to do so? Could they not have striven, not because they were free to do otherwise, but because they were foreordained to do as they did? After all Calvin was not exactly an imbecile; in fact he acquired a reputation for logic; why then gratuitously impute inconsistency to him with condescending generosity? Further, there is ambiguity in the complaint that since the world is perfect and evils are really good, there is no point in trying to make it better. The world at a given moment is perfect in the sense that its condition is exactly what is required to produce the condition of the next moment. The course of history perfectly develops according to plan. And no other conditions could with such perfect efficiency work out that plan. On the other hand this perfect world is not perfect in the sense of having its history finished. Events remain to be accomplished. The consistent absolutist does not try to make the world conform more perfectly or more efficiently to God's plan of history, but he acts to forward the course of history. Christ walked the Via Dolorosa, not because the road itself was the perfected end, but because it was an indispensable means to that end. And with this understanding it may even be said that the absolutist strives to eliminate evils, evils that in some reference are also goods. Saul's persecution of the Christians was both evil and good, in different respects and to different persons; yet Christ met him on the road to Damascus and eliminated that evil. It had served its purpose, and history was then ready to proceed without it.

It would seem therefore that Brightman's arguments against absolute theism are ambiguous, irrelevant, or in some way fallacious. He has failed to demonstrate any inconsistency in the Christian position. But since, nonetheless, he discards absolutism, the next step is the exposition of finitism.

A Finite God

Theistic finitism "holds that the eternal will of God faces given conditions which that will did not create. . . . All theistic finitists agree that there is something in the universe not created by God and not a result of voluntary divine self-limitation, which God finds as either obstacle or instrument to His will."[73]

This position is supported by the arguments and facts which were destructive of absolutism: it is an inspiration to moral endeavor; it maintains the distinction between good and evil; the evils are not ascribed to the will of God; and it is not based on ignorance but on an interpretation of actual experience.

Aside from these points which refute absolutism, there is additional positive evidence. Biological evolution with a struggle for existence that makes nature red in tooth and claw is not an entirely wasteful process. The earlier stages of evolution show organisms fit to survive for only a short period of time, but the later stages include the human organism that is equipped to survive for a much longer time. This argument, clearly, is reminiscent of the theory of progress; and how assurance of humanity's continuance can be based on anything but hope and ignorance is not evident, for the lower forms of life have already survived longer than the human race, and the evidence that man will survive a still longer period is missing. When it is said that as far as we can see into the past and as far as we can see into the future, a good purpose is "the dominant never ultimately thwarted factor"[74] the limits of empiricism have been transcended. Brightman argues that a creative rational will at work within limitations not of its own making would produce a world such as this, and that therefore a finite god is a reasonable hypothesis. It may be true that a rational limited will might produce a wasteful nature red in tooth and claw, if its power were small and its limitations great. If there were such a being, one ought to pity

73. *Op. cit.,* pp. 313, 314.
74. *Op. cit.,* p. 318.

it. But when Brightman continues and asserts that it is "a spirit never conquered by the difficulties," he is projecting a future that could be assured only by Omnipotence.

Brightman has rejected the apriori optimism according to which everything is controlled by a flawless plan; he favors a meliorism in which by some hit and miss procedure things are slowly improving; but apparently he does not hold that meliorism as much as optimism presupposes Omnipotence. He seems to be distrustful of power. "Goodness," he says, "is more fundamental than power."[75] This is an important statement and it should be defended with detailed reasoning; yet Brightman passes over it in eleven lines with mere assertions, such as, "there is nothing worthy of worship in power as such." But though these apriori assertions, without argument or empirical evidence, are consistent with Brightman's view of the nature of God as the Source of Values, they are inconsistent with his empirical method. Yet it is precisely in this apriori assumption that Brightman finds the essence of religion. "After all," he says, "the object of religious worship is a perfect ideal rather than a perfect power. ... The limiting of the ideal by theistic absolutism is more irreligious than the limiting of power by theistic finitism."[76] If this is true, then Martin Luther was a most irreligious man. And almost as irreligious are all those who pray, "Almighty God, the Father of our Lord Jesus Christ. .." or who recite, "I believe in God, the Father Almighty." A perusal of the Prayer Book would discover a considerable amount of irreligion; that is, empirical evidence would be found of a religion that is at fundamental variance with the religion of Professor Brightman. Its ideals would not be his ideals; nor would its God be his god.

It is interesting to note how empiricists allow their own apriori assumptions to color their "facts" and "discoveries." Brightman is not the only one whose results contradict his announced method. It is a common failing precisely because there can be no results without apriori factors. For example,

75. *Op. cit.*, p. 319.
76. *Op. cit.*, p. 326.

an empirical psychologist attempts by the use of a questionnaire to determine the religious development of his students. The students are asked to assign one of five degrees of importance to each of fifty factors, and the summation of their answers will be an empirical measure of their religiosity. Four of the factors are these: Feeling of close communion with nature; a feeling of the sublime; a feeling of the mystery of existence; awe in the presence of nature's beauty and grandeur. Aside from the fact that these four factors stress "feeling" and would seem to prejudge the question whether religion is mainly intellectual or emotional, it is clear that these four factors reveal a predilection for nature worship and discriminate against other religions. The same questionnaire contains these additional factors: feeling of personal adequacy; feeling potentialities of moral greatness; feeling of personal worth; appreciation of man's potentialities for moral greatness. A Christian, convinced of his sin and misery, knowing his need of God's unmerited favor and strength, and considering pride and spiritual self-reliance as evils to be avoided, would mark all these factors zero, and would so fail to raise his score. That is, the greater his religious development, the less his score would be. What the questionnaire actually does is to define the investigator's notion of religion and to test students for conformity to that religion. Other students, who may be thoroughly devoted to another religion, are simply classed as undeveloped.

Because empiricism cannot avoid apriori prejudgments, Brightman is neither empirical nor accurate when he refers above to "the limiting of the ideal by theistic absolutism." Theistic absolutism does not limit the ideal: it has a different ideal. All through, Brightman has surreptitiously introduced his own values into the argument; he has not squarely faced the possibility of values inconsistent with his whether they be the ideals of Stalin or of theistic absolutism. And having thus prejudged the question, he naturally concludes that a large section of religion is irreligious. Let every man defend his own religion; let him in the interests of clarity and honesty show that his religion is not another religion; but if religion is supposed to be the generic common quality of all religions, an empiricist should not call one of them irreligious. It would be better to deny that religions have a common quality.

Brightman of course wants to maintain a belief in a finite good god; but why cannot his arguments conclude with equal logic in favor of a finite evil god? The empirical method is as satisfactory for one as for the other. This world, so far as empiricism describes its past and refrains from unempirical prophecies, is just the type of world that would result from the activity of a finite evil god who does his best to make things unpleasant, but, being of limited intelligence and power, has not quite succeeded. He is unconquered by difficulty, however, and as far as we can see into the future we may be sure that he will continue to do worse and worse. Given a baffling mixture of good and evil, it is no more logical to believe in a little god than in a little devil.

Not only must finitism face these insuperable objections that are peculiar to it, but it also aggravates difficulties that are usually raised against absolutism. A frequent, perhaps the most popular of all objections to absolutism, and one that Brightman repeatedly urges, is that absolutism fails to absolve God of responsibility for creating the evils in the world. The reply to this objection that is found in Isaiah 45 and Romans 9, developed by Calvin and argued in detail by Jonathan Edwards, receives little or no attention from Brightman. But he cannot hide from himself that the same objection will be raised against his own view. The question is, has he a better answer than Jonathan Edwards? God knew, that is, Brightman's finite god knew that man would suffer from surd evils, and yet he created him. Brightman is willing to face this paradox, the problem of evil, because avoidance of it can be bought only by refusing to face the problem of good. He is convinced that naturalism can explain neither good nor evil, and so is forced to assume a divine power. Accordingly the reality of the physical universe is located wholly within the conscious experience of God. Energy and force are the finite god's will controlling and directing this experience. All events in physical nature are events within this god. But man's personality is not a part of god or a rearrangement of matter. Man is a creation, but he is created under given conditions by which the will of god is limited both by rational and non-rational factors. Now the difference between absolutism and finitism is this: in absolutism God created voluntarily and omnipotently and hence uses evils as instrumental goods; but in finitism god sees that the evils are unjustifiable, and yet he creates other persons. If god did not create other persons, he would forfeit all the values of society. And this, no doubt, would be too much for him to endure. "Yet it is one thing to say that creation is justified in spite of surd evils entailed by the given and quite another thing to say ... that the finite God regarded the unavoidable evils as justified by the total outcome."[77] Just what the difference between these two statements is, Brightman does not explain.

And he further complicates the situation when he says, "He judges them [the evils] to be unjustifiable as well as unavoidable."[78] Why are evils unavoidable? If God is supreme and sovereign, he would be under no compulsion, and no created factor would be unavoidable; but with a finite god, the conditions are different. The compulsion that Brightman seems to lay upon his god is the compulsion of boredom. This finite god is the Continuer and Source of Value; if he did not create, he would "forfeit all the values in a social universe;" and therefore it would seem, though Brightman does not say so, that the finite god's happiness or goodness depends on the existence of human beings.

A criticism and a comparison may be made here. First, the criticism. Even if this god does not create or ordain evils, he creates persons, a given number, of such and such capabilities. Therefore the actual amount of goodness in the universe depends, presumably, on the divine will. Had this finite will created more persons, there would have been more value

---

77. *Op. cit.*, p. 334.
78. *Op. cit.*, p. 334.

than there is.   Here is an arbitrary divine choice, which in principle is similar to the Calvinism that Brightman is trying to escape; it differs in being more diluted and less consistent. Apparently the only way of avoiding this inconsistency or incompleteness would be to assert that the finite god has created all creatable persons. The maximum has been achieved. But Brightman gives no hint of availing himself of this doubtful expedient.   Second, a comparison, already begun.   God Almighty suffers from no compulsion of boredom.   He enjoys the "social values" of the Trinity of Persons; and his goodness does not depend on human beings.   He elects and foreordains whatsoever comes to pass.   Do not these points show that Jonathan Edwards was more self-consistent than his present day New England successor?   Or to use another term, is not faith in Almighty God more "open-eyed"[79] than faith in a weak divinity?

Brightman's faith is less rational and open-eyed because of a far deeper anomaly than has yet been mentioned.   It relates to the source of evil.   If the source of evil, of unavoidable evil, is not the divine will, what is it?   The answer is that God faces a recalcitrant Given.   This Given includes not only the uncreated laws of reason, the uncreated processes of nonrational consciousness, and the forms of space and time, but also "whatever in God is the source of surd evil."[80]   The source of surd evil is therefore in God himself, but while "it is eternal within the experience of God and hence had no other origin than God's eternal being," yet "it is not a product of will or created activity." The Given in God is unwilled, non-voluntary consciousness; God is not limited by anything external to himself.   "Strictly we should speak of a God whose will is finite rather than a finite God, for even the finite God is absolute in the sense of being the ultimate source of all creation."

The concession to Calvinism in this last phrase almost justifies writing the word God with a capital letter; but the view

---

79. *Op. cit.*, p. 334.
80. *Op. cit.*, p. 337.

of the Given introduces a puzzling duality. God seems to be a will plus a Given. The exact relation between them is not clear. Brightman does not define will, nor does he further describe the Given. Perhaps he might object to this terminology, but it would seem that the Given is the "nature" or "essence" of God, or at least a part of God's nature, and the will is something else. At any rate God is not will. The will of God is good — Brightman has never ceased to reiterate it; but if so, it must follow that the nature of God (should one say, God himself?) is evil. The Given, that is, the essence of God, "with its purposeless process"[81] constitutes so great an obstacle to divine willing that "the utmost endeavors of God lead to a blind alley and temporary defeat." God therefore is at war with himself; it must be himself for there is no other source of evil; he is not limited by anything external to Himself. Let God's will be good; God's nature or character is evil, and the totality of these two parts of God, his will plus his essence, forms a schizophrenic personality. God must be insane.

Because of God's insanity the meliorism of Brightman's system to which he is very much attached not only lacks all empirical basis, as was said before, but becomes incredible. He assures us that God's "consciousness is an eternally active will which eternally finds and controls the Given within every moment of his eternal experience." And[82] "God's control means that no defeat or frustration is final; that the will of God, partially thwarted by obstacles in the chaotic Given, finds new avenues of advance, and forever moves on in the cosmic creation of new values." But on what is this assurance based? Is it any more plausible than that a victim of dementia praecox can cure himself? Brightman produces no reason to believe that the blind alleys, the defeats, and frustrations to which God has been reduced in the past will not continue and increase forever. And meliorism is all the more improbable because God is not faced with some external limitation that perhaps with effort

81. *Op. cit.*, p. 338.
82. *Op. cit.*, pp. 336, 338.

he could overcome: his limitation is an inner limitation, he is fighting against his own character, nature, or essence, and not until his will eradicates his essence can success be assured. To succeed, God must commit suicide. But until the day that God commits suicide, mankind, ever perfectible never perfected, will continue to walk God's blind alleys and false starts in a regularity that resembles the fate of Tantalus and Sisyphus.

On one basis and on one basis alone is it possible to have good hope for the future, and that basis is Almighty God. Anything limiting God, whether it be something external or an internal given chaos, makes the future uncertain. Any conclusion based on mere empirical observation makes the future both uncertain and dismal. But if the apparent evils, which are real evils to the people of the earthly city, are deliberately chosen means to the production of good for the people of the City of God, then it is possible to look at both the past and the future with equanimity, and with logical consistency.

Brightman has attempted to find a middle position between Biblical Christianity and atheistic naturalism. The result, as it seems to be with all such compromises, is incoherence.

VII

EPISTEMOLOGY

CHAPTER VII

Epistemology

T HROUGHOUT the chapters of this volume certain presuppositions relative to the possibility, the nature, and the methods of knowledge, have appeared beneath an historical, scientific, or religious surface. This type of inquiry, epistemology as it is called, must now be brought into sharper focus, for it is the crucial point in philosophy. Whether a political assertion be made, or whether the subject be botany, aesthetics, or Latin grammar, one may always ask, either seriously or in derision, How do you know? Even systems of philosophy, like Neoscholaticism, which make metaphysics and being rather than epistemology and knowing the logical basis of their theory, must still meet the most serious objections to their views in the field of epistemology. The question, How do you know? may seem simple enough; but the answer virtually controls the whole system of philosophy.

Not everyone agrees in so emphasizing the importance of the theory of knowledge. Will Durant in *The Story of Philosophy* expresses his belief that "epistemology has kidnapped modern philosophy, and well-nigh ruined it." This expression, in conjunction with the subtitle of the book, *The Lives and Opinions of the Greater Philosophers,* may explain why he devotes fifty-eight pages to Voltaire, who can hardly qualify as a Greater Philosopher, and only eight pages to Hegel. Such a lack of balance is evidence that a refusal to face the question, How do you know? determines the outcome as completely as any positive answer. Durant's repudiation of epistemology doubtless orginates with John Dewey. This voluminous writer has consistently disparaged epistemology because, according to Blanshard,[1] a careful study of the problems of knowledge almost inevitably leads to an idealistic or dualistic metaphysics which would be inconsistent with Dewey's naturalism.

Skepticism

In the order of exposition the first answer to the question, How do we know? is the negative reply that we do not know. Knowledge is impossible. This is a conclusion to which various thinkers have come for several different reasons.

First, some people have adopted this reply because of exhaustion. The subtlety and slipperiness of epistemological paradoxes easily produce despair. In the history of philosophy this first occurred as a reaction to the baffling arguments of Zeno the Eleatic. If the tortoise is given a head start, Achilles cannot overtake him because everytime Achilles arrives at the point where the tortoise was, the tortoise is no longer there — he has had a fraction of a second to go on just a bit. And at every moment of the flight of an arrow its extremities are coincident with two points in space; but to be coincident with two points is to be at rest; therefore at every moment of the alleged flight, the arrow is at rest. The difficulties of solving these enigmas were so great that the last of the Pre-socratics gave up and accepted the conclusion that knowledge is impossible.

Second, some people have adopted skepticism because of more positive evidence. Common opinion credits sensation with furnishing information about the world. But dreams and illusions, while they last, are as vivid and as real to us as are sensory images. If we pinch ourselves to make sure that we are awake, we are reminded that we might be dreaming that we are pinching ourselves. It is therefore impossible to tell when we are dreaming and when we are awake. Furthermore, two supposedly real objects can produce identical sensory ex-

---

1. *The Nature of Thought*, Vol. 1, p. 369. (George Allen and Unwin, 1939).

perience, as happens when we see twins. And more commonly
one object may produce various sensory images. Which of
these images adequately represents the object cannot be known.
We cannot compare the objects with each image in turn, for
our only contact with the object is through the images. And
again, it is said that dogs are color blind; it is also said that
dogs have a keener sense of smell and hearing than human
beings. If then dogs possibly have better hearing, what evidence is there to prevent us from supposing that they have
better sight also? Possibly the world has no color and the
dogs see it correctly; we human beings have color hallucinations. These hallucinations may be so impressive that it would
be necessary to conclude that we are insane. Is there any
proof that we are not? And Descartes lays on a crushing
blow: for all we know, since we do not know anything yet,
there may be an omnipotent demon whose great delight it is
to be constantly deceiving us. He is so powerful that he makes
us think that two and two are four, when as a matter of actual
fact two and two are five. And if this be so, obviously knowledge is impossible.

In the third place there are some views which, though still
properly called skeptical, are so developed in detail that they
could possibly be classified under the next section of relativism.
In antiquity Protagoras is the outstanding example. He begins
by observing that a cool breeze is stimulating to a man in
good health, but the same breeze is cold and disagreeable to a
man with a fever. This wind therefore is both pleasant and
unpleasant. Each man tells the truth when he applies his own
predicate to the wind. Apparently truth is easy to obtain, for
no one can be mistaken; each man is the measure of all things
and all things are as they appear to be. But then Protagoras
points out that the wind is stimulating only in relation to one
man, and the wind is disagreeable only to the other man.
If there were no men, and if we should consider the wind
just as it is in itself, it would be neither stimulating nor disagreeable; neither cool nor cold; neither strong nor gentle; in
fact the wind alone by itself would be nothing. It exists only

in relation to someone.   Truth therefore is impossible to obtain, for no predicate attaches to anything in itself.   There is
no cool wind, there is no wind, except as a product of two
opposing factors.   The sensory motions of one person in conjunction with external motions produce a collision or an event
that may be called an exhilarating wind.   But even if it were
possible to know that the external motions were the same,
the collision of these motions with another person would
produce a different wind.   And this other person may be the
"same" person at another time.   For example, Socrates in
health is one person, and when wine touches his tongue, there
is a sensation of sweetness.   But Socrates sick is another person, and when wine touches this different tongue, a sensation
of bitterness appears.   All sensations stand on the same footing.
No one is truer than another; no one is more false than another;
they are merely different.   Hence everyone may say, my sensations are true because they are mine; and I am the sole judge
of my own sensations.   All judgments are true; no one can
possibly think falsely; for man is the measure of all things.

In modern times David Hume held to a very similar position.
He begins by remarking that although man is a rational being
and draws his proper food and nourishment from science, the
bounds of human understanding are so narrow that little satisfaction can be hoped for in this particular.   No doubt the skeptics admit the certainty of present impressions; and Hume
makes much of a distinction between *impressions* that are live-
ly and vivid and *ideas* that are pale and weak; yet Hume is as
vague as Protagoras concerning the origin of these impressions.   Then too Hume, unlike Protagoras, hides the implication that memory so-called is merely another present state of
consciousness.   In this and in some other respects Hume at
times seems to be a little removed from skepticism.   But the
troublesome difficulty is to find some evidence that assures us
of any real existence or matter of fact beyond the present testimony of our senses or the records of our memory.   Such evidence
would have to depend on what is thought to be the necessary
connection between a cause and its effect.   If one ask a man

why he believes that his friend is in France, argues Hume, he would give as a reason some present fact, such as a letter received from the friend. But were there no causal connection between the letter and the friend's whereabouts, the inference that he is in France would be entirely precarious. Hume then analyzes the notion of causation. The knowledge of this relation cannot have been attained by any reasonings apriori. Let an object, for example a powder of unknown chemical composition, be presented to a man of ever so strong natural reason and abilities; if that object be entirely new to him, he will not be able, by the most accurate examination of its sensible qualities, to discover any of its causes or effects. These can be learned only by experience. After many experiences we become accustomed to the fact that the use of this powder, baking powder or arsenic as the case may be, is followed by certain events called effects. But though we become so accustomed, we still fail to see any reason for such a conjunction, we still fail to see any necessary connection between these powders and their several effects. Why the one can be used in food and why the other is poison remain as mysterious as ever. We perceive that an event called an effect follows another event called a cause, but we do not perceive that one event causes a later event. Neither reason nor experience justified the idea of causality or necessary connection. The ultimate springs of natural operations are totally shut up from human curiosity and inquiry. The most perfect philosophy of the natural kind, says Hume, only staves off our ignorance a little longer; as perhaps the most perfect philosophy of the metaphysical kind serves only to discover larger portions of it.

Hume does not exactly glory in his ignorance but rather attempts to make room for probability. This must be discussed later. However, if his analysis of causality as merely sequence in time be accepted, and if a knowledge of matters of fact beyond the present testimony of our senses depends on a law of cause and effect, it follows that nothing besides our momentary impressions and fleeting ideas can be known. And once more each man is the measure of his own condition.

Perhaps not even man is the measure of his condition. The skepticism of Hume and Protagoras does not stop with man's ignorance of an objective world; but even while claiming certainty for present impressions the two philosophers annihilate the self that might have the impressions. The notion of an abiding self that has or perceives the impressions and that, being identical with yesterday's self, may remember the past, Hume regards as a groundless fancy. Only impressions exist. Just as he left obscure what these impressions were impressions of, so also he fails to find anything that is impressed. I may venture to affirm, Hume writes, that a person is nothing but a bundle or collection of different perceptions, which succeed each other with an inconceivable rapidity, and are in perpetual flux and movement. This bundle is never destroyed all at once during our lives; parts vanish and other parts appear; and in this sense the "same" bundle continues its existence. But although the bundle is the same bundle, the absence of any string to tie the parts together would seem to permit us to call any list of impressions a self or person. What are colloquially called Johnny's toothache and the dentist's annoyance at having to treat a small boy could be called a bundle. And while this bundle might not remain together as long as some other collections, it seems to meet every qualification for a transitory Humean self.

The illustration Plato used to point up a similar flaw in Protagoras was the wooden horse of Troy. If there is no unitary self that can compare disparate sensations and produce conceptual judgments, the bundle of sensations or senses could be tied together only by some sort of wooden horse. Each man in the horse represents a sense or an impression; but though each man of the illustration was a real Greek soldier, the wooden horse or bundle of impressions could not be a living, thinking person. It could not be said to know.

Hume obviously tries to avoid the more repugnant extremes of skepticism, and just as obviously, it would seem, he fails. More often than not he uses the expressions of colloquial language and common sense; he states his dissatisfaction with some of his conclusions and even repudiated his early *Treatise of Human Nature;* but when he omitted from his later work some of his earlier conclusions, he offered no constructive substitute to take their place. Insofar therefore as Hume makes any distinctive contribution to the history of philosophy, he must be considered a skeptic.[2]

Perhaps the ancients took their philosophy more seriously than the moderns do. The Cynics, the Epicureans, the Stoics, when they came to their conclusions, lived by them. Whether Hume's reluctance to accord full value to skepticism is itself a skeptical attitude toward all philosophic argument, or whether it is a dogmatic suspicion that skepticism is false may be debated. Pyrrho in antiquity did not adopt such an ambiguous position. For him knowledge was impossible and nothing made any difference. One day he stepped back quickly as a four horse chariot swung around the corner at a reckless speed. One of his students chided him on his lack of consistency: he should not have stepped out of the way, for it made no difference. Pyrrho had the skeptical reply. "That is why I stepped back," he said, "for it makes no difference."

Is there an answer to skepticism? William James said, No, neither moral skepticism nor intellectual skepticism can be refuted by logic. This, however, has not been the attitude of most dogmatists — the philosophers who believe truth is obtainable — and one could do worse than to examine Plato's and Aristotle's attempts at a logical refutation.

Plato pointed out that Protagoras' skepticism was expressed in two ways. Sometimes he said that man is the measure and

2. The eminent Norman Kemp Smith, in his *The Philosophy of David Hume,* pp. 79ff, 443ff, 497ff., *et passim* (Macmillan and Co., Ltd., 1941) tries to defend Hume from the charge of skepticism. He rejects the traditional interpretation of Hume as expressed by T. H. Green, Selby-Bigge, the Mills, Leslie Stephen, *et al.,* which assumes that Hume's thought is a logical development from the principles of Locke and Berkeley. N. K. Smith has shown other influences at work, especially that of Francis Hutcheson; but I remain unconvinced of the main thesis. At best Smith shows that Hume was inconsistent and frequently failed to relate the several parts of his own system. To me the main thrust of Hume's writings is found in the skeptical implications of empiricism. *Cf.* James Seth, *English Philosophers,* pp. 150, 156, 168, (J. M. Dent & Sons, Ltd., 1912).

that everyone is right. The wind is truly exhilarating; the wind is truly disagreeable. But if everybody is right in whatever he thinks, then Plato is right when he believes that Protagoras is wrong. Or, on the other hand, if the wind itself is nothing and everybody is wrong, then Protagoras too is wrong.

Aristotle said much the same thing in different language. Logic, he argued, is based on the laws of contradiction and excluded middle: object x cannot be both y and not-y; and object x must be either y or not-y. Now, any given word must signify one thing, or a finite number of things, or an infinite number of things. If the word has a finite number of meanings, then it would be possible to invent a name for each meaning, so that all words would have a single meaning. But if each word has an infinite number of meanings, reasoning and conversation have become impossible because not to have one meaning is to have no meaning. But if a word has a meaning the object cannot be both man and not-man. If the skeptic attempt to avoid this argument, he might do so by saying nothing. In this case, however, there is no skeptical theory awaiting refutation. Or, he might accuse Aristotle of begging the question by using the law of contradiction. But, then, if he says this, he has said something, and has himself admitted the force of logic.

St. Augustine also argues against skepticism. The skeptical Academy was still of recent memory in Augustine's day, and besides, his own anguished search for truth and early disappointment were too poignant an experience to be passed over in silence. He had once held with others that one cannot certainly know anything, and that probability is sufficient for the activity of life. With his conversion to Christianity he came to hold that one cannot fail to know the truth.

In the first place, probability without knowledge cannot be a guide for a moral life. If it were, a man might commit a most criminal act, but if he thought it was probably good he could not be blamed. And in any case, probability cannot be had unless one has truth first. The skeptics refer to propositions as false, doubtful, or probable; but these terms would have no meaning unless there is some truth. A false proposition is the contradictory of a true proposition. If one say a proposition is doubtful, one must recognize the possibility of its being true. And the probable or plausible is what resembles the truth. From all this it follows that unless a man knows the truth, he cannot know what is probable. Accordingly, if truth is not known, there is no reason for acting in one way rather than another. Life has become meaningless.

In the next place, logical forms are certain. The disjunction, either I am awake or I am asleep, is true without doubt; and similarly the implication, if there are no more than four elements, there are not five.

The skeptics, ancient and modern, do not seem to have paid sufficient attention to logic. They are likely to reply to the disjunction and implication above, that they contain no real information, or that they are trivial, or that they are merely formal. The adverb *merely* is a term of disparagement. Formal or not, the laws of logic are certainly true, and as Plato implied and as Aristotle explicitly said, a skeptic cannot propound his skepticism without using them. It is this that makes skepticism self-contradictory, and indicates that William James may have been mistaken when he said that skepticism cannot be refuted by logic.

But Augustine goes even further. He argues for the existence of trustworthy intellectual intuitions. Early in Kant's *Critique of Pure Reason* and repeatedly in the long middle section after the deduction of the categories, Kant relies, for many of his conclusions, on the denial of intellectual intuition. Augustine claims an intellectual intuition of his own existence. He is always able to embarrass his skeptical opponent by asking him if he knows he exists. He must exist to doubt, even to doubt his own existence. There can be no doubt, no illusions, no skepticism, unless one exists. From here Augustine goes on to construct what may loosely be called a Christian Platonism; for the moment, however, the conclusion is that skepticism has been refuted. And if a philosophy of any other name can be shown to be a disguised skepticism, it too must be rejected.

Relativism

In contrast with the ancients, like Pyrrho, who were open and unashamed in their skepticism, or like Kratylus who more consistently refused to talk and expressed his philosophy by a wave of the hand, the modern writers have more often adopted an epistemological relativism that obscures the underlying difficulties. Not always the immediate concern, epistemological principles are hidden beneath a facade of history, politics, or religion.

In the chapter on History this was first met with in the theory of progress, which was formulated as the law of history. The human race was pictured as improving, particularly in respect to liberty, justice, and equality. These and other aspects of a good society were criteria by which to judge the degree of progress. Then because liberty and justice seemed to be too static, these criteria were dropped and the goodness of a society was identified with the progress itself. And finally, to generalize the theory, it was stated that everything must progress, including the criteria themselves. But if this is so then progress as a criterion must progress into something else, with the result that if progress is the law of history, it must soon be repudiated as antiquated. Or, to divest the argument of its historical application and to consider its epistemological status, it could be compared with the view of Protagoras. Protagoras said, all statements are false. The theory of progress holds that all theories become false. From which it follows that if progress is now the truth, it will soon not be. Perhaps it is already false.

A second instance of relativism was referred to, if not well explained, in the chapter on Politics.[3] As a basis for, or he might say as a result of his study of history, Spengler has a relativistic epistemology. He was quoted as saying that there is no *man*, there are only *men;* and that political theories are threadbare school-exercises. Behind these allusions is a philosophy that shares certain characteristics of the views of

---

3. Pp. 105, 133; cf. p. 145.

Goethe, Nietzsche, and Bergson. Science, logic, and mathematics are deprecated on the ground that they cannot grasp the vital processes of life. As a microtome, in cutting a section, arrests the life process, so reason fixes and kills. The real thing that we wanted to study is no longer there; only its corpse remains. Similarly history is a living process that is not amenable to reason or logic. And philosophy, as a cultural activity, is an element of the historical situation. It moves; it lives; it changes. It has no everlasting or unalterable objectiveness; it gives us no eternal truths. Kant thought that he was stating universal and 'necessary principles; but, argues Spengler, his principles are necessary only for western thought. He failed to see the relativity of his own ideas; he failed to see that his philosophy was an expression of a particular culture. Like Aristotle, he believed in a universal human nature, a sort of Platonic Idea of Man. If there were such a thing as Man, it might be possible to discover the universal laws of thought; it might also be possible to discover the universal laws of morality. In this case philosophy could prescribe moral obligation for all men everywhere. Liberty and justice would be eternal principles. Military might would not make right. But there is no Man, there are only men.[4] Men, their philosophy, their concepts are the products of their culture. The western concept of freedom, or of property, or of a republic are not the concepts that the ancients had. There is no correlation between the two meanings. The Pyrrhonists were skeptical because of individual characteristics; we are skeptical because we see that philosophy is organic with the age. Not even mathematical concepts, such as number, are the same for two cultures. There is no universal mathematics. For example, the Greeks had only whole, positive numbers, while we have imaginary numbers and various number systems. History therefore should not be construed as a linear development; we are not the successors but simply the adorers of antiquity.

-----

4. *Op. cit.*, Vol. 1, pp. 21, 23, 24.

Whether or not western society will inevitably collapse is not the present matter for discussion. One may hold the most pessimistic views of our twentieth century civilization without subscribing to Spengler's philosophy, and it is the philosophy or more exactly the epistemology, not the historical prediction, that is of immediate interest. As a substitute for reason, logic, mathematics, and systems like those of Newton or Kant, Spengler uses a non-rational intuition or mystic vision like Plotinus, Dante, and Bruno did. This intuition provides the basic categories, such as Becoming and the Become, and History and Nature. These replace the rational and therefore inadequate principles of space and causality. But exactly at this point the same difficulty reappears. Relativism is always contradicting itself. Spengler ostensibly wants a view of history that applies to all past cultures. He aims at a comparative morphology and at general laws of cyclical development. But if his theory is true, and if the categories and intellectual equipment a man uses are products of and relative to his own culture, then the categories of Becoming and the Become, products of Spengler's civilization, apply just as little to ancient societies as the contemporary concept of number does. If a statement is true only within a given culture, and if there are no eternal truths or unalterable objectivity, and if rational theories are only threadbare school-exercises, Spengler's theory itself is only a temporary phenomenon. It cannot therefore be the law of history because if it is true, it is false.

Another instance of relativism, also in the chapter on Politics but more directly applicable to moral standards, was T. V. Smith's assumption that what Americans think is moral *is* moral. In this connection were quoted the lines from Oliver Wendell Holmes "truth was the majority vote of the nation that could lick all the others," and, "I am so skeptical as to our knowledge about the goodness and badness of laws that I have no practical criticism except what the crowd wants." This means that everybody is right, or if the principle is taken to apply not to individuals but only to nations or societies, then every society is right. Again a paraphrase of Plato's reply to Protagoras may be used: if the Communists think the Americans are evil, and if every society is right in what it thinks, then the Russians are right in thinking that American standards are evil. American standards therefore are both good and evil. But if a standard is called both good and evil *simpliciter,* or if a statement of that standard is said to be both true and false, the words good and evil, true and false, have no meaning. That is, T. V. Smith's theory, if it is true, is meaningless. A relativist might attempt to reply that moral standards are not good and evil *simpliciter.* Protagoras might have said that a statement is not both true and false without qualification. The statement is true to or for one man, and false to or for another; Plato omitted the all important relativity, and asserted *simpliciter* what Protagoras had asserted only with qualifications. This standard defense of relativism, however, does not withstand analysis. Protagoras may begin by saying that the wind is exhilarating to one man, but he intends his relativism to be true not only to and for himself, but for everyone. Relativism is always asserted absolutely. If it were not intended to apply generally, it would have no claim to philosophic importance. But if it is asserted universally, then its assertion contradicts what is being asserted. An absolutistic relativism is a self-contradiction. If it is true, it is false.

The same criticism holds of Hans Kelsen's theory of democracy. The theory of absolute truth is a basis of totalitarianism, he said; and therefore democracy must be based on relativism. "What is right today may be wrong tomorrow." As was pointed out, Kelsen asserts philosophic relativism as a philosophically absolute truth. If he is correct, he is mistaken.

Perhaps the most interesting of contemporary forms of relativism is found in recent religious theory. Barth and particularly Brunner make assertions that can hardly fail to lead to skepticism. The trouble is not, as Brightman says, that they use an apriori and desert empiricism, but rather that they relate the truth in God's mind to the contents of man's mind in such a way as to leave man without truth. In their reaction to the superficiality, and one might say the secularism, of the liberal modernistic theology, they remind professing Christians of essential but well-nigh forgotten themes, but at the same time they develop a theory of knowledge that would undermine not only Christianity but their own philosophy as well. Brunner's approach to the problem of religion, is not epistemological, but ontological; he is not primarily interested in "philosophy" but in religion. However, it is no less true of religious writings than it is of political and scientific theory that they presuppose an epistemology. And if the epistemology is unacceptable, the religion is equally so.

Brunner begins by stressing the point that religious faith centers in God. God is a person and not a proposition; and therefore faith is a personal relationship. As a natural consequence he insists on revelation. And more or less similarly to an argument in the preceding chapter Brunner recognizes that revelation's ultimate ground of validation cannot be a set of independent categories by which, according to Brightman, the mind organizes experience, but must be God himself. With this stress on a personal relation to God, Brunner consistently recognizes the break in this personal relation as a serious factor in life and thought. In contrast to modern liberal theology, which underestimated and sometimes denied the reality, extent, and power of sin, Brunner calls attention to its noetic as well as to its more overt effects. The confusion, blindness, and error due to sin is the more obvious and frequent as the subject matter is closer to God. Physics is less affected than anthropology, which in turn is less affected than theology. In this last subject, since it deals directly with God, sin causes the greatest amount of error, and the corrective function of faith is most needed. Up to this point there is nothing epistemologically objectionable. A sound epistemology cannot demand omniscience or complete freedom from error: its aim is not to show that all men or any man knows everything, but that some men can know something.

Here, however, ambiguity begins to creep in. Brunner not only says that there is more error due to sin in theology but also that in mathematics and logic there is no error at all.[5] This is the beginning of a confusion that runs through Brunner's thought and that of his followers. The concept of sin and its effect on mental activity is in keeping with Brunner's insistence on a personal center of religion; and to eliminate the concept of sin from Christian teaching would be to reduce it to incoherence; but when it is said that error is more obvious in theology than in mathematics, the reference point is not so much the academic subject-matter as it is the mental activity of the thinker. Subject-matter as such, let us say truth, is not affected by sin precisely because sin is personal. And because sin is personal men make mistakes in logic as well as in theology; not only in other volumes, but in logic textbooks also formal fallacies have unintentionally occurred. Logic, the law of contradiction, is not affected by sin. Even if everyone constantly violated the laws of logic, they would not be less true than if everyone constantly observed them. Or, to use another example, no matter how many errors in subtraction can be found on the stubs of our check-books, mathematics itself is unaffected. If therefore the reference is the mental activity, Brunner is incorrect in saying that no errors occur in logic; but if the reference is to subject-matter, sin has as little effect on theological propositions as it has on mathematics. The distinction between the psychological activity of thinking, as a unique event in time and subject to the multifarious conditions of different persons, and the propositions of logic or theology, which are true at all times and for all people, is a distinction that should not be difficult

---

5. *Offenbarung und Vernunft*, p. 378, (Zwingli-Verlag, Zurich, 1941). "Je näher etwas bei jenem Zentrum der Existenz liegt, wo es um das Ganze, das heisst aber um das Gottesverhältnis und das Sein der Person geht, desto grösser ist die Störung der Vernunfterkentnis durch die Sünde; je weiter ab etwas von diesem Zentrum liegt, desto weniger macht sich die Störungsfaktor geltend, desto geringer also wird der Unterschied zwischen gläubigem und ungläubigem Erkennen. Er wird maximal sein in der Theologie, minimal in den exakten Wissenschaften, und Null im Bereich des Formalen."

to make.   But apparently the complexities of religious discussion make it hard to remember.

Brunner, influenced by Kierkegaard, says that the thinker goes beyond abstract thought to the realm of the personal, where he is no longer a neutral observer, himself unchanged by the truth he thinks, but is himself affected in the very center of his being.   This may well be true.   That a man is changed by the truth (or falsehood) he thinks need not be questioned; but why a man cannot be changed by "abstract" truth and has to pass beyond it to another and ill-defined sphere is by no means clear.   If the arguments of the chapter on Science, and other passages, are convincing, man is at no time a neutral observer, and hence the distinction between two spheres and therefore the passage from one to the other cannot be maintained.

Brunner has proposed this personal sphere in the interests of his religious faith.   Within it God and man meet, and this meeting or encounter is truth.   He repeatedly[6] contrasts the traditional or philosophical distinction (Gegensatz) between subject and object with the new distinction between subject and subject.   Thus the truth of faith (Glaubenswahrheit) must be distinguished from the truth of reason (Vernunftwahrheit), or Du-Wahrheit from Es-Wahrheit.   Now, if this meant simply that faith, in addition to an acceptance of propositions that can be written down, involves a personal relationship, a trust, reliance, dependence, or confidence as older theologians called it, Brunner would be saying nothing new. In this case he would be in accord with Reformation theology except for having replaced the more familiar terms of faith and trust by the word truth adorned with some cumbrous German adjectives.   But that it is not simply a case of different terminology, that he is not repeating Reformation thought, and that his theory is not only a theory of faith but of truth as well, is seen in the relation he posits between these two kinds of truth.   Abstract, verbal, propositional truth is described as a pointer (Hinweis) to the personal truth.   And

6. *Wahrheit als Begegnung,* (Fruche-Verlag, Berlin, 1938).

some abstract truths point more directly than others — theology is a more direct pointer than mathematics. But even the words of Scripture, those passages in the Bible that Brunner accepts as witnesses to Christ (John 14:6, Rom. 3:21-31, but not Rom. 16), are only pointers. Words, all words, have merely instrumental significance. This does not mean, what is commonly recognized, that words are instruments or symbols for expressing thoughts. The letters, t, w, o, or the Arabic 2, are not the number itself; they are the visual or audible symbols used to refer to the intellectual concept. But Brunner goes beyond this banality. The conceptual content itself, as well as the verbal form, is not the real thing. The concept is only a frame, a receptacle, a means.[7] Not only are propositions merely pointers to the truth — perhaps one could escape skepticism while saying that true sentences point the way to God; but for Brunner a pointer is not necessarily true: even a false proposition is a pointer, for God is free from the limitations of abstract truth and can speak his "truth" through false statements.[8]

Brunner protests that this does not involve theological relativism. It is not a matter of indifference what one preaches or believes. Mohammedanism is not just as good for them as Christianity is for us; for there is a "sacramental" union between the words of Paul and the word of God that does not exist between the words of Mohammed and the word of God. God, to be sure, is free to reveal himself in false as well as in true sentences, but we, as worshippers of God, are

7. *Wahrheit als Begegnung*, p. 82, "Heir wird es unmissverständlich deutlich, dass das, was Gott uns geben will, in Worten nicht eigentlich, sondern nur hinweisend gegeben werden kann .... Darum weil er selbst (Jesus) das Wort Gottes ist, haben alle Worte bloss instrumentale Bedeutung. Nicht nur das sprachliche Wortgefäss, sondern auch sein begrifflicher Inhalt ist nicht die Sache selbst, sondern dessen Fassung, Gefäss, und Mittel."

8. *Ibid.* p. 88, "Ja, wir müssen noch weiter gehen und sagen: Gott kann, wenn er will, einem Menschen sogar durch falsche Lehre sein Wort sagen, und dementsprechend in einem falschen 'Credo-credo' das rechte Echo seines Wortes finden. Das ist kein Freibrief für unsorgfältige Lehre und Predigt oder theologischen Relativismus; denn wir bleiben an seine geschichtliche Offenbarung sowie an das Zeignis von ihre gebunden und damit auch an jenes Prinzip der Beziehungsnähe und die in ihm liegende Unterscheidung reiner und unreiner Lehre."

obligated to believe exactly what God says and to proclaim the Gospel faithfully in all its glorious falsity. Such an obligation to exactitude in false doctrine doubtless absolves Brunner's theory of the accusation of *theological* relativism; but it seems to insure a verdict of epistemological relativism. Any sacramental union that distinguishes the words of Paul from the words of Mohammed is of little importance if the words of Paul, by whom God's revelation has come, are, or, at least, may be false. An obligation to preach and believe falsehood would make truth immoral; and a God whose word is untrue is an admirable basis for skepticism.[9]

Empiricism

Of English origin a most determined attempt to avoid skepticism, an attempt that was discussed at length in the chapters on Science and on Religion, is found in the philosophy of empiricism. From the time of Roger Bacon and William of Ockham the British thinkers have favored a reliance on sensation and hard facts. During the seventeenth century when the continent was influenced toward rationalism by Descartes and Spinoza, who aimed to deduce all knowledge by logic alone without appeal to experience, Thomas Hobbes, however much the English disliked his politics and ethics, stood squarely in the English tradition of experimental methods. After Hobbes, an early forerunner of eighteenth century thought and the fountain head of most subsequent British philosophy, John Locke (1632-1704) formulated the principle of empiricism in his *Essay Concerning Human Understanding*. He wrote, "Whence has [the mind] all the materials of reason and knowledge? To this I answer in one word, from experience; in that all knowledge is founded, and

---

9. Cf. *Philosophie und Offenbarung*, p. 33: ". . . die Gotteserkenntnis, die wir durch Offenbarung haben, ist erst Als-Ob Erkenntnis. Die Erkenntnis. die nicht Als-Ob ist, heisst: Schauen von Angesicht zu Angesicht . . . Dieses Als-Ob hat aber nichts von Ungewissheit, von Hypothese an sich, denn es ist ein gottliches verbürgtes Als-Ob." And is this divine guarantee itself an As-If document?

from that it ultimately derives itself."[10] He argued at length
against the theory of innate ideas, which to him seemed to
be the basis and the basic flaw of rationalism, and accordingly
spoke of the mind as a sheet of white paper, void of all
characters, without any ideas, on which experience and
experience alone writes its lessons. The simplest ideas, out of
which all more complicated knowledge is produced, are, first,
ideas of sensation such as yellow, white, heat, cold, bitter,
sweet, and all those which we call sensible qualities, and second
ideas of reflection or inner experience, arising from the operation of our minds as it is employed with the first set, such as
perception, thinking, doubting, reasoning, willing, and all the
different actings of our own minds. With these two sets of
ideas to work on, the mind may compound sweet, white, and
cubical shape into a mode or thing and call it a lump of sugar.
Or it can form abstract ideas by considering all particular
lumps of sugar, and granulated, powdered, and brown sugar
too, and arrive at the abstract idea of sugar. Ideas of relation
also may be produced by comparison. The most abstract idea
that the mind produces is the idea of substance. Since simple
ideas like yellow and cold cannot exist alone by themselves,
for no one has ever perceived yellow walking down the street
unchaperoned, we accustom ourselves to suppose some substratum wherein the simple ideas subsist.[11] The substratum
of the ideas of sensation may be called matter; and as the
argument has the same force with respect to the ideas of
reflection, for neither does willing exist by itself in utter solitude, there must also be the idea of spiritual substance. Locke
recognizes some difficulty with these final results of abstraction.
If knowledge is based on experience alone, the experience of
yellow and of willing are self explanatory; but if we discard
or put to one side the sensory ideas of yellow, hard, and the
like, and abstract and fasten upon a remainder, this substratum
will have been divested of every experiential aspect.   Substance therefore is only a supposition of we know not what

10. Book II, Chap. 1, Paragraph 2.
11. *Ibid.*, II xxiii, 1.

support of such qualities. It is something unknown and unknowable. "By the complex idea of extended, figured, colored, and all other sensible qualities, which is all we know of it, we are as far from the idea of the substance of body, as if we knew nothing at all."[12]

Locke in his exposition of empiricism has used the term idea in a sense strange to the preceding rationalism and to much of previous philosophy. In the Platonic and Augustinian tradition, and even in Aristotelian scholasticism, the emphasis fell upon concepts, definitions, or intellectual objects. For Locke these Platonic Ideas do not exist, and the term idea comes to mean an image. Though there may be some difficulty in imagining or having an image of an act of will, this sort of internal experience is pictured after the analogy of the sensory images of white, yellow, and bitter. Images are the building blocks of knowledge; and however complicated their combinations may be, knowledge consists of images.

Berkeley begins the first chapter of his brilliant work by designating "the objects of human knowledge. It is evident to anyone who takes a survey of the objects of human knowledge, that they are either *ideas* actually (1) imprinted on the senses, or else such as are (2) perceived by attending to the passions and operations of the mind, or lastly, ideas (3) formed by help of memory and imagination. . . ."[13] Since Locke's abstract ideas do not fall under any of these three divisions, he was mistaken in thinking that there are any. Abstract ideas are meaningless words. There is nothing mysterious about a particular impression of yellow or the later memory image. But the abstract idea of color is an absurdity. What is common to yellow, red, white, and violet is certainly not yellow, red, white, or violet. That abstract idea of color therefore has no determinate color; there is nothing colored about it; and this is the equivalent of saying that color is not color. Or, what sort of thing is the abstract idea of man? A visible, particular man is either black, white, or

---

12. *Ibid.*, II, xxiii, 16.
13. *Principles of Human Knowledge.*

yellow, Abstract man could have only abstract color; he would have no particular stature or weight; he would have no sensory quality. Now, says Berkeley "I can imagine a man with two heads, or the upper parts of a man joined to the body of a horse. I can consider the hand, the eye, the nose, each by itself abstracted or separated from the rest of the body. But then whatever hand or eye I imagine, it must have some particular shape or color . . . I cannot by any effort of thought conceive the abstract idea above described."[14]

The implication of this is that if the abstract idea of man is an absurdity, all the more absurd is the idea of matter or material substance. Obviously our thoughts, passions, and ideas cannot exist without the mind; nor can combinations of sensations exist without the mind. But combinations of sensations are the sensible objects themselves. Mountains, trees, and rivers are things we perceive by sense, and what do we perceive besides our own ideas or sensations; and is it not plainly repugnant that any one of these or any combination of them should exist unperceived?

Berkeley was quite sure that there must exist a mind to have these impressions. A mountain is something perceived, and a perception can exist only in a mind. But Hume was acute enough to see the next step. If material substance is an absurdity because it is an abstract idea, so too is the spiritual substance or the mind. Experience consists entirely of images, impressions, and their resulting combinations. No one has experienced a Self. What common opinion calls a person is simply a bundle of images. And this, as was argued above, results in skepticism. If all knowledge is based on experience, we may conclude, there is no knowledge.

A few defenders of empiricism have tried to make use of later psychological studies. The attack has centered on Locke's simple ideas as the building blocks of knowledge. Gestalt psychology seems to have shown fairly well that the simple images of yellow and white are not seen so easily as more complex patterns. For example, whether a short horizontal

---

14. *Ibid.,* Introduction, x.

line is straight, curved up, or down, cannot so accurately be determined by looking at the line alone as it can if the line is in a circle with other horizontal and vertical lines so that it represents the mouth of a face. In this way the production of knowledge out of simple ideas, or the combination of simple ideas so as to make things, is brought into question, and it is concluded that we see things as wholes first, and only afterward analyze them into parts.

All this may be so, but it is a poor defense of empiricism. The trouble lies deeper. If knowledge is a result of sensory experience, or even of internal experience if after Hume there can be any *internal* experience, how could the ideas of space and time be obtained? Time has never been impressed on the senses so that we might have an image of it. If anyone thinks he has an image of time, let him describe its color, its shape, and smell. But more profoundly Kant argues, "The idea of time does not originate in our senses, but is presupposed by them. For sensory impressions can be represented as simultaneous or successive only through the idea of time. Succession does not produce the concept of time, but presupposes it."[15] Similarly, with respect to space Kant argues that the idea of space is not abstracted from external sensations, for I cannot conceive anything external to me except by representing it as in a place where I am not. Therefore external perceptions do not originate but presuppose the idea of space.

Space and time, for Kant, give the basis for mathematics — for geometry and arithmetic respectively. And the truths of mathematics are examples of truths that cannot be derived from experience. Teachers of small children may think that 'two and two are four' is taught by playing with marbles. Does not the teacher show the pupil how two marbles and two marbles make four marbles? Roll them together into a corner and see that there are four marbles. Then, after this is done with different colored marbles, and different sized marbles, and with pencils and erasers, the child generalizes or abstracts from his experience that truth that two and two are four. However,

---

15. *Inaugural Dissertation*, 14.

this explanation of the learning process seems to be unsatisfactory. In the first place, the child would have to recognize one marble before he could count two of them. Where did the concept of a unit come from? From the marble also? But would not the pupil have to have the concept of a unit before he recognized a marble as one? If he did not know one, he could not count one. He has to know the numbers in order to count. And in the second place, this consideration holds for four as well as for one. He must know four before he can count four marbles. Perhaps this can more clearly be seen if large numbers are used. Let the teacher try to teach the young child that 356 marbles and 791 marbles are 1147 marbles. Everyone has heard children say their numbers: one, two, three, four, seven, sixteen, five, twenty-one, sintillion. The young child who so counts cannot learn the example by counting marbles because he cannot count numbers. He can count marbles only after he can count numbers. And since numbers are not marbles or anything else sensory, it follows that arithmetic is not abstracted from experience. So much for mathematics.

Hume's analysis of causality also points up essentially the same difficulty in empiricism. While Hume treated the subject more or less in isolation, Kant saw that a general principle was involved. Physics as well as mathematics requires necessary and universal judgments, and these are impossible on an empirical basis. All images, sensations, or experiences are unique occurrences. Whether it be Locke's simple idea of yellow or whether it be a complicated whole of Gestalt psychology, the image is temporally conditioned. It is a mental event that occurs at just one moment in time. It never occurred before and it will never occur again. Hume wondered whether it could have any connection with a previous or a future event. If in one instance the experience of swallowing arsenic is followed by the unfortunate experience of poisoning, can it be logically inferred that a second case of swallowing arsenic will be followed by poisoning? Obviously a universal and necessary law to the effect that arsenic always results in poisoning cannot be validly established on one case or on a hundred cases. No doubt we are accustomed to this sequence of events just as we expect the sun to rise in the east tomorrow; but there is no logic by which we may begin with a few experiences of the past and arrive at a judgment about the future. Granted a wider experience than anyone has ever had, one might possibly be justified in concluding that natural law has been uniform in the past, but no amount of experience can ever show that nature will continue in the same way. If all knowledge is based on experience, no statement can validly be made about the future, for experience is always past. Even if it were possible to learn by experiment that two and two have always been four and that the sun has always risen in the east, there would be no conclusive reason for supposing that these things would be the same tomorrow. But not only does this principle of universality and necessity prevent an empirical knowledge of the future; it applies to the past as well. Since no one can have experienced every case, empiricism cannot consistently assert that the sun has always risen in the east, that two and two have always been four, or, to use one of Kant's examples, that all bodies are heavy. Similarly, no experience necessitates the conclusion that every change requires a cause.

More important still, the validity of syllogistic reasoning can never be based on experience. The laws of logic may well be called more important than the propositions of mathematics and physics because logic underlies them both. In all our conversation and writing the forms of logic are indispensable: without them discussion on every subject would cease. But if empiricism cannot establish the truth that two and two will always be four, neither can it assert that the conclusion of Barbara always and necessarily follows from the premises. Empiricism therefore is conclusively shown to be skeptical because the law of contradiction cannot be abstracted or obtained from temporally conditioned particulars. And without the law of contradiction it is impossible to say anything meaningful. Scientists like Pearson, Carlson, or Bridgman,

and liberal theologians like Brightman may produce complicated and persuasive systems of thought, but if they claim to
be empiricists their systems contradict their epistemological
principles, for if all knowledge is based on experience, there
is no knowledge.

Without any retraction of this conclusion, which is intended
to be a complete and final refutation of all empiricisms, our
understanding of the subject will be extended by an examination of a form of the theory that owes nothing to John Locke.
Toward the end of the Middle Ages Thomas Aquinas convinced European thinkers of a Christianized interpretation of
Aristotelianism; and the twentieth century has seen Neoscholasticism spring into prominence by reason of its official adoption by the Roman Catholic church.   Aristotle and Thomas
taught that knowledge begins in sensory experience and that
the mind through its ability to abstract may rise not only to
concepts and knowledge of natural laws but even to the
existence of God.   The previous objection to empiricism, that
one cannot abstract from experience a necessity and universality that is not there, will not be repeated; but criticism will
be directed against a device that seems to betray a· Thomistic
uneasiness as to the sufficiency of the empirical method.   It is
the theory of analogy.

The notion of analogy begins quite simply and innocently
in Aristotle.   He notes that when we call a book a medical
book and when we call an instrument a medical instrument,
and when we call a man a medical man, the predicate medical
does not bear exactly the same sense in the three instances.
The term is not equivocal, as is the case when we call Argos
the dog of Ulysses and when we call Sirius the dog in the
sky; but on the other hand the term is not strictly univocal.
It is analogical.

This simple distinction was elaborated by the Scholastics
and the Neoscholastics into a complicated theory, in which, it
would seem, the original situation no longer serves as a solid
basis.   The motivation and intricacies of the theory are seen
most clearly in the arguments for the existence of God and our

knowledge of him.   God, according to the Thomists, is an absolutely simple being; but a simple, eternal, and immaterial being cannot constitute an object proportionate to our human understanding.   Simplicity and eternity are not factors in our world of experience, and therefore we have no positive concept of them.   To say that God is eternal means nothing more than that God is not temporal.   What eternity positively means remains unknown to the human mind.   What man has in this instance may be called negative knowledge.

Similarly, when we call God wise and when we call a man wise, the term does not bear the same sense.   God's wisdom is not distinct from his essence or his being; but the wisdom of man is.   In general, there is no affirmation whatever that can be made of God and of man in the same sense.   The reason for this impossibility is not only that the predicates do not bear the same meaning in both cases, but that, far more radically, the copula *is* bears two different senses.   In God essence and existence are identical: what God is and that God is are the same.   In every case other than God this is not so.   Accordingly when we say God exists and when we say man or dog exists, the term *exist* does not mean the same thing.   Therefore no term, not even the copula, can be used univocally of God and man.

Now, if the only alternative to univocal predication were equivocal predication, knowledge of God derived by abstraction from experience would be patently impossible.   When words are used equivocally there is no definite relationship between the meanings, and knowledge of God would be in a state similar to a knowledge of Sirius that would be based on an experience of Ulysses' dog.   To avoid this fatal difficulty the Thomists are forced to find some intermediate between univocal and equivocal predication, and they appeal to analogy.   Between Argos and Sirius there is no resemblance, but in the case of God, man resembles God, they say, though God does not resemble man.[16]   This resemblance permits us to attach

16. Etienne Gilson, *The Philosophy of St. Thomas Aquinas,* pp. 109-110, (Herder, 1937).

some meaning to the statement God is, so that we are neither in complete ignorance, nor limited to negative knowledge, but have an analogical if not a univocal knowledge. Thus empiricism in its Thomistic form attempts to escape the limits of experience.

There seems to be a very serious objection to this theory of analogy. Aristotle's original analogies cause no difficulty. The term medical, whether applied to a man, a book, or an instrument, is presumably derived from experience. In all three cases there is a relationship to the science of medicine. And for this reason there is a univocal basis for the analogy. The term medical might univocally be defined as "having to do with the science of medicine"; and in this univocal sense the man, the book, and the instrument are all medical. Similarly all the analogies of common speech have a univocal basis. The paddle of a canoe is analogous to the paddles of a paddle-wheel steam boat; it may even be said to be analogous to a screw propeller. It is so because there is an area of common or univocal meaning. The paddle and the screw propeller are both devices for using power to make boats move through the water. The Neoscholastics list and classify different types of analogy; some are more complicated than the preceding. For example, it might be said that the mind is to the soul as the eye is to the body. Here there is an analogy, possibly between the mind and the eye, or possibly between two relationships. But no matter how complicated, or what type of analogy, an examination must discover some univocal element. The two terms must be like each other in some respect. If there were no likeness or similarity of any sort, there could be no analogy. And the point of likeness can be designated by a simple univocal term or phrase. The Thomists admit the likeness or resemblance in analogy; they deny the univocal basis. They transfer analogy from the status of a literary embellishment or pedagogical aid to that of a serious epistemological method. But this removes every real distinction between analogy and equivocation.

It follows therefore that the Thomistic proofs of the existence of God are invalid on two counts. First there are the previous empirical difficulties with causality, abstraction, and logic; but now there is this second. Even if no other fallacy were to be found in the arguments, and if we should arrive validly at the conclusion, God exists, this existence at which we have arrived would not be God's existence. Syllogisms and valid arguments require their terms to be used univocally. If this has been done, the "analogical" and actual existence of God has not been obtained. All through the argument the term *exist* or *is* has been used in a human or temporal sense; and if the argument is valid, the term in the conclusion must also have the same temporal sense. But in this sense of the word exist, God does not exist. Once more, empiricism has failed.

Apriorism

If the arguments of the last few paragraphs are sound, along with the considerations on empiricism that occurred in several of the earlier chapters, a satisfactory theory of epistemology must be some sort of apriorism with or without intellectual intuition. The notion that a blank mind can learn must be repudiated.

Of all the modern philosophers it is Immanuel Kant who is naturally thought of first as a representative of apriori theory. For him experience gives us a rather indefinite, even chaotic manifold of sensation, and the mind arranges, or imposes unity on, this manifold by the application of innate categories so that knowledge results. All items of knowledge are judgments or predications. A term, such as triangle, by itself cannot be either true or false. But if one say the triangle is an isosceles triangle, or the triangle is a four sided figure, one has said something either true or false. All judgments are classifications. This triangle is classified under the species of isosceles triangle, or, falsely, under the class of four sided figures. Two terms therefore, the subject and the predicate, are brought together. Thus the mind imposes unity on experience by judging or classifying. Since judgments or propositions are the products of the mind's unifying activity, the several types of judgment are witnesses to several functions of unity. These are the categories, the non-empirical contribution of the mind to knowledge — the prerequisites of learning. They are not based on or derived from experience, but rather the possibility of meaningful experience depends on them.

To one who has been impressed by the universal and necessary factors in knowledge, in particular the law of contradiction and the validity of implication, and who sees clearly the epistemological skepticism and ontological nihilism implied in empirical philosophy, this apriori view is inescapable. And yet when one comes to work out the details, there is danger of emulating Kant's many self-contradictions. At any rate, Kant's categories cannot be accepted as they are. For indefensible reasons Kant set down twelve types of judgment and thereby obtained twelve categories. But while a great many, almost all, scholars would agree in dropping from the list the singular, infinite, problematical, and apodeictical forms of judgment, there might not be the same unanimity in keeping the other seven: universal, particular, affirmative, negative, categorical, hypothetical, and disjunctive. Since, for example, any one of the latter three may be expressed in either of the other two forms, perhaps someone might wish to drop two of them from the list of the elemental types of judgment. This is a technical matter of the axiomatization of logic, and the result could well be the replacement of this list by a set of still simpler forms. If it be argued that several sets of axioms are equally possible and equally arbitrary, investigation will have to discover either that there is a common core in them all or that they are merely different expressions of the same meaning. It seems indubitable that one of the irreducible and indispensable forms will be "x is included in x"; but the identification of the remainder of the list of categories must await a growing unanimity in the results of symbolic logic.

The mention of Kant as the most outstanding modern exponent of an apriori theory of epistemology does not imply that his Critical philosophy can serve in a Christian world view. Part of the reason is to be found in a most interesting paragraph (pp. B. 167-168) at the end of the transcendental deduction of the categories. After asserting that there are only two ways in which a necessary harmony of experience with the conceptions of its objects can be cogitated, *viz.*: either experience makes these conceptions possible or the conceptions make the experience possible, Kant attempts to dispose of an alleged third view. This middle way holds that the categories are neither innate (selbstgedachte) and first apriori principles of cognition, nor derived from experience, but are merely subjective aptitudes for thought implanted in us contemporaneously with our existence, which were so ordered and disposed by our Creator that their exercise perfectly harmonizes with the laws of nature which regulate experience.

To this view Kant offers a lesser and a more serious objection. The first is that on this hypothesis it is left indeterminate how far one could drive the presupposition of predetermined aptitudes to future judgments. This briefly expressed objection may mean that the number of such aptitudes could be increased without limit; or that no end can be seen of the application of a particular aptitude, so that any false judgment could be defended on the basis of a preestablished harmony. Kant treats this objection lightly, perhaps because he senses that it applies to his own system too. Kant has precariously increased the number of categories to twelve, and the list could be increased indefinitely unless it should prove possible to arrive at a definitive list of the basic types of judgment. But if there is a way to limit the number of categories, why may we not hope to limit the list of aptitudes? And on the other interpretation of the objection, though an aptitude might be invoked in favor of a mistaken opinion, the category of causality could equally well be used to defend a false connection between a given event and an alleged cause. If Kant by any means can answer these objections for his own position, it is not at all clear that similar means are unavailable for this middle way.

The more serious objection to the preformation system is that it removes all necessity from the categories and returns us to skepticism. The concept of causality, for example, which expresses the necessity of a result under a presupposed condition, would be false if it depended only on an innate, optional, subjective necessity to connect certain empirical representations according to such a rule of relation. I could not say, argues Kant, that the effect is connected with the cause in the object, i.e., necessarily, but only that I am so constituted as to be unable to think otherwise.

Here Kant proposes a serious difficulty. However, it seems once again that the difficulty attaches to his own view as well. For him as well as for this preformation theory, the human mind thinks as it does because it cannot think otherwise. Alice in Wonderland by dint of hard practice was finally able to believe as many as six contradictions before breakfast. But Kant, living before the secret had been discovered, was unable to do so. He used the categories in his thinking because his mind was so constituted. If this is skepticism, then Kant too is a skeptic.

Further in answer to Kant's objection, but quite apart from the question whether or not he faithfully represented the view of some particular philosopher, it seems that he slightly slanted his description of the preformation theory toward skepticism by introducing into it certain unessential factors. For example, if in fact the Creator has implanted these aptitudes, or categories, in our minds, Kant must be mistaken in denying that they would be innate (selbstgedachte) and first apriori principles of cognition. What could more truly be innate than such implanted aptitudes? It must also be a mistake to describe them as optional (beliebigen). Surely if we are so constituted as to be unable to think otherwise, there is little optional in it.

Moreover, it is Kant's refusal to adopt the preformation theory or an equivalent that lands him in the major predicament of his Critique. In his view the uninformed sense data are entirely incoherent. Order is introduced into them by the mind alone, and what the real world might be like, or what the *Ding an sich* actually is, remains unknowable. The whole Postkantian development from Jacobi to Hegel convicts Kant of skepticism. Contrariwise, a preformation system, though it may face difficulties, need not count skepticism as one of them. The laws of nature, by hypothesis, are not merely the result of the subjective aptitudes of an individual's thought or of the thought of the race. They are objective with an objectivity that transcends Kant's.

Kant might continue to object that no one should be allowed to have his cake and his penny too. The categories are either derived from experience or they are innate. By this decisive disjunction, so Kant might argue, the preformation theory is proved to be unfair to organized philosophy. However, preformationism does not repudiate the disjunction as just stated: the categories are indeed innate, but in addition God has fashioned both the mind and the world so that they harmonize. And some such scheme must be accepted if the Kantian apriori is no less skeptical than empiricism. That the cake and penny illustration is inapplicable may be seen by asking the question, Does the law of contradiction hold in thought or does it hold with things? The objector would have to choose one and reject the other. But is it not more plausible to say that the law of contradiction applies both to thought and to things? Even a Ding-an-sich, unknowable if it is, cannot also be a Not-Ding-an-sich.

Another point to which Kant does not pay sufficient attention is the fact that all men have the same categories. Kant explains this phenomenon by making his apriori system the prerequisite to any learning by experience. Time, space, and the categories are inherent in the meaning of experimental knowledge. If all men learn, they must have the categories, not because they are men, but because they have learned. Perhaps there are some men who neither learn nor have the categories. And there might be angels or animals that have the categories, provided always that they learn by experience. This explanation of the uniformity of the categories among men does not seem to be altogether sufficient.

Emile Durkheim proposes an additional explanation. For him the categories are social products. They cannot be merely individual aptitudes, for if they were, the resulting subjectivism would be clearly skeptical. Accordingly, to provide an objectivity that goes beyond the individual, Durkheim suggests his social theory. Our notions of space or time derive from the position in which our ancestors pitched their tents and from the routine occurrence of religious festivals. So thoroughly have these notions been drilled into society that the individual is entirely unable to think otherwise. For the individual they are actually apriori, but for society they are the result of long experience. And Durkheim might be willing to admit that various societies have evolved different sets of categories. American Indians, for example, may believe in a finite, circular space, while other civilizations have different patterns.

This ingenious theory seems to rest on some remarkable assumptions. If the categories, the now necessary concepts of thought, are social products, there must have been a time when those concepts were not necessary. Primitive man therefore might have argued and learned by some principle inconsistent with the law of contradiction. He might have been not only lacking the disjunctive form of judgment, but in possession of a law of non-excluded middle. Then because of the supposed survival value of Aristotelian logic, or for all we know because of the aggressiveness, bigotry, and brutality of those original Peripatetics, the exponents of other logical systems were killed off or driven into the bush and jungle. And the result is that logical necessity is socialized biological necessity.

If this consideration does not make Durkheim's position unacceptable, one may add that socially compelled manners of thought give no guarantee of the nature of the world. The laws of sociology (and since Durkheim is primarily interested in sociology, this point should concern him most of all)have little chance of being true because the process Durkheim used in formulating them is on his own showing no more than a social convention. If Durkheim's account of apriori concepts is true, then Durkheim's sociology is false. And if the sociology is false, the epistemology based on it is false likewise.

Durkheim makes it clear that he adopts this view not only to avoid individual subjectivism, but also to avoid a belief in God. There is no experimental technique, he argues, to prove the existence of a Supreme Reason, and therefore it is not a scientific hypothesis. By so stating his objection to theism, Durkheim in effect assumes the point at issue. He assumes a particular view of science that has now been tried and found wanting; and he assumes that God would be a conclusion to be proved on the basis of assumptions, discoveries, techniques, or first principles that are more ultimate than God. Since, however, by the term God we mean the ultimate explanation of all things, and not merely Brightman's source of values, Durkheim has set an impossible condition.

The "proof" of God's existence, which is not at all a logical demonstration, results from showing that consistency is maintained by viewing all things as dependent on God. In the present instance, what hypothesis provides a ground for the common possession of the categories as adequately as Christian theism does? Though the existence and nature of God is insusceptible of formal demonstration, yet if Christian theism is true, there is no mystery in the fact that all human minds use the same categories, and there is no suspicion that the objective world or some Ding-an-sich escapes their necessary connections. Skepticism is ruled out and truth becomes possible.

A Theistic World

In addition to the argument concerning apriori categories to make learning possible, another condition is requisite that would be difficult to defend except on a theistic basis. Obviously if skepticism is to be repudiated and if knowledge is a reality, truth must exist. In ancient Greece Parmenides was the first to state it, and Plato repeated it: if a man knows, he must know something: to know nothing is not to know.

Knowledge therefore requires an existing object, and that object is truth — truth that always has and always will exist.

Contrary to ancient and medieval philosophy, the pragmatists and instrumentalists of contemporary times have tried to defend a "truth" that may be true today but was false yesterday and will be false tomorrow. They would quite agree that science is tentative; a scientific law is "true" so long as it works; but progress insures its replacement by another "truth." Very able, and, I would say, completely destructive criticisms of instrumentalism have been made, and their common theme seems to be that instrumentalism is self-contradictory. If truth changes, then the popular instrumentalism that is accepted as true today will be false tomorrow. As Thomism was true in the thirteenth century; so instrumentalism is true in the twentieth century; and within fifty years instrumentalism, in virtue of its own epistemology, will be false. But it is to be doubted whether John Dewey would appreciate the imminent passing of his experimentalism. As was said before, these relativistic theories tacitly assume their own absolutism. This or that hypothesis may be tentatively accepted for a limited purpose; but if all statements without exception are tentative, significant speech has become impossible. It follows then that truth must be unchangeable. What is true today always has been and always will be true. Any apparent exception, such as, It is raining today, is an elementary matter of ambiguity. Two and two are four; every event has a cause; and even, Columbus discovered America, are eternal and immutable truths. To speak of truth as changing is a misuse of language and a violation of logic.

The idealistic philosophers have argued plausibly that truth is also mental or spiritual. Without a mind truth could not exist. The object of knowledge is a proposition, a meaning, a significance; it is a thought. And this is necessary if communication is to be possible. If a truth, a proposition, or a thought were some physical motion in the brain, no two persons could have the same thought. A physical motion is a fleeting event numerically distinct from every other. Two persons cannot have the same motion, nor can one person have it twice. If this is what thought were, memory and communication would both be impossible. The reply might be made that although the motions are numerically distinct, they are generally similar; therefore today I have the motion, Columbus discovered America, and tomorrow I have another one like it. This reply, however, is faulty. Suppose for the sake of argument that two motions can be similar: a baseball pitcher can throw a curve and later a second curve like it; and one cortical quiver could be like a second. But how could anyone tell that the two motions were similar? On the behavioristic theory the motion or thought of similarity would have to be a third motion. And surely similarity is not similar to Columbus. Why could not a fourth motion, the motion or notion of inconsistency connect the past and present thoughts of Columbus? Or, more to the point, how could any motion connect two other motions that no longer exist? When the second motion occurs, the first thought of Columbus is gone. In its absence how can the second be compared with it and pronounced similar? If only we could remember it! But memory, the making present of the past, is impossible on a physical theory. The first motion as a physical event in time and space is completely and irretrievably gone. It may as a cause initiate a second motion, but it itself no longer exists; and to say that a nonexistent motion is similar to an existing motion is hardly more intelligible than to say they are the same. It is a peculiarity of mind and not of body that the past can be made present. Accordingly, if one may think the same thought twice, truth must be mental or spiritual. Not only does it defy time; it defies space as well, for if communication is to be possible, the identical truth must be in two minds at once. If, in opposition, anyone wishes to deny that an immaterial idea can exist in two minds at once, his denial must be conceived to exist in his own mind only; and since it has not registered in any other mind, it does not occur to us to refute it.

With considerations such as these Augustine was able to explain the learning and the teaching process. The teacher in the classroom does not give his students ideas. The ideas or truths are discovered by the student in his own mind; and as he contemplates the truth within, he judges whether the teacher has taught the truth. But though the truth is discovered within the mind, it is not a product of the student. Truth is not individual, but universal; truth did not begin when we were born, it has always existed.

Is all this any more than the assertion that there is an eternal, immutable Mind, a Supreme Reason, a personal, living God? The truths or propositions that may be known are the thoughts of God, the eternal thought of God. And insofar as man knows anything he is in contact with God's mind. Since, further, God's mind is God, we may legitimately borrow the figurative language, if not the precise meaning, of the mystics and say, we have a vision of God.

This involves a view of the world radically different from that of popular science. In science the mechanical model has been a seductive ideal. The world was conceived as consisting fundamentally of hard little pellets whose motions were described by the laws of mechanics. Sufficient argument has been given to show that there is no experimental data sufficient to compel acceptance of this model. Perhaps if there are little hard pellets, or neutrons, or charges, it may be necessary to conceive them as moving through a continuous path. Even this seems to have been questioned by the theory that would have them jump from one orbit within the atom to another orbit without passing through the intervening distance. But if there are physical elements, and if such, to retain their identity, must move in a continuous path, there still seems to be no good reason for insisting that they exemplify the specific laws of mechanics.

In general, images can be more confusing than explicative. It is not the person who has the liveliest imagery who best analyzes and understands. Images are not ideas, as Berkeley supposed, and a dependence on them is unfortunate.

The philosophy of mechanism with its mechanical image emphasized physical phenomena and relegated human affairs to a subsidiary position. To replace the mechanical model, the Christian view of the world presents a "model" that is so unimaginable that its opponents are likely to call it inconceivable. The world of physics drops into the secondary position of stage scenery, and instead of picturing little hard pellets, the Christian view emphasizes a world of spirits or persons, or minds. The Apostle Paul said that in God we all live and move and have our being.[17] Even if the details of Malebranche's philosophy cannot be accepted, yet it must be insisted on that God is the "place" of spirits. Minds are not impenetrable pellets. Even human minds in some degree overlap or penetrate each other, and the Divine Mind that encloses or surrounds all others penetrates them completely. Another statement of Paul's has far reaching implications. He said, "Work out your own salvation in fear and trembling, for it is God that worketh in you, both to will and to do, of his good pleasure."[18] This statement asserts an interpenetration, at least of Christian minds, by the Divine Spirit such that not only the actions but even the will of the man is controlled by the good pleasure of God. And if this passage does not, other passages extend this control to heathen minds also, though it may not result in their salvation. There is a very significant statement in Exodus 34:24. The laws of Jehovah required that all the males of Israel should go up to appear before Jehovah three times a year. This requirement would naturally suggest to the Israelites the possibility of foreign aggression at the time of these religious observances. How could the country be defended? As if to answer this objection the Lord says he will so control the minds of the heathen that they shall not desire to attack at those times.[19]

There is some affinity between this view of the world and contemporary personalism in that the basic categories are

17. Acts 17:28.
18. Philippians 2:12-13.
19. For specific instance of mental control see also, II Sam. 17:14, I Kings 18:37, II Chron. 10:15.

mental and that personality and history are emphasized above the corporeal and mechanical; but the differences transcend the superficial similarity. The Christian view differs from the various forms of personalism in refusing to equate the physical world with the eternal consciousness of God,[20] but more especially it differs in its concept of the Person who "includes" all others and of his relation to them. Christianity speaks of an Almighty Creator. The other persons are brought into being by fiat; they are completely and in every respect dependent on God, but God is completely and in every respect independent of them. For Christianity God is not an ideal toward which the universe is approaching; he is not the axiogenetic or axiosoteric aspect of the universal process; he does not come to completion, to consciousness, or to perfection in history; he faces no conditions which his will does not control. God is above all the Omnipotent Creator and Absolute Sovereign.

Conclusion

Pursuance of this line of thought would take us rapidly away from the principles of epistemology and plunge us into all the varied detail of the encyclopedia of theology; but the extent and the compelling interest of such a series of studies would postpone indefinitely a conclusion that is now due.

This chapter has tried to show by an application of the law of contradiction — a law that is not merely formal but is itself an integral part of the system of truth — that truth exists and that knowledge is possible. Knowledge means the possession of truth. It is not necessary to work out a philosophical system and to demonstrate truths before having them. On the contrary, even in geometry, one usually has come into the possession of a truth before one attempts to demonstrate it; in fact this will be seen always to be true if we do not

---

20. Aside from the implication of the eternity of the world, could the visible universe with its primary and secondary qualities, or its proper and common sensibles, be the consciousness of God unless God had sense organs?

restrict our vision to a narrow field. Demonstration and the arrangement of truths into a logical system is undeniably a desideratum; it is precisely the progress in such systematization that distinguishes the philosophical student from the intellectually dull; but philosophers are not the only people who can know the truth. Disjointed truths possessed are still truths possessed and are therefore knowledge. The man who has the truth that God exists, though his reasons for so believing are philosophically scandalous, is better off — he knows more truth — than the man who with the most erudite of arguments attempts to justify the false statement that God does not exist. And since the philosopher himself, in possession of many truths, never escapes all disorder, since his systematization is never complete, there is only a difference of degree between him and the common herd. If it be said that the latter have only faith and not "knowledge," because their beliefs are not thoroughly integrated, the reply is that all knowledge is faith. Those opponents of theism who contrast knowledge and faith to the disparagement of the latter, and who like Carlson and Clifford deny Christians the right to believe, underestimate the limitations of their own integration. The important contrast is not between faith and knowledge, but between truth and error.

This chapter, in fact the volume as a whole, has also tried to show that Christian theism is self-consistent and that several other philosophies are inconsistent, skeptical, and therefore erroneous. With the presuppositions of Marx, Russell, or Spengler, history becomes meaningless; a humanistic utilitarianism and the Kantian autonomy of the will are equally incapable of justifying moral distinctions; and some forms of religious philosophy are inconsistent mixtures of naturalistic and theistic elements. As a contrast to these views it has been argued that Christianity is self-consistent, that it gives meaning to life and morality, and that it supports the existence of truth and the possibility of knowledge. Thus theism and atheism have been examined in considerable detail. It remains for each person to make his choice.

Perhaps the Harvard Report is correct when it predicts that society will never again choose Christianity as its unifying principle. But there is no other type of philosophy that has a unifying principle to offer. And a continued repudiation of Christian principles promises a future which, even more than the present, will be characterized by social instability, wars and rumors of war, brutality, and despair.